THE DARK SIDE OF SOCIAL MEDIA

The Dark Side of Social Media takes a consumer psychology perspective to online consumer behavior in the context of social media, focusing on concerns for consumers, organizations, and brands. Using the concepts of digital drama and digital over-engagement, established as well as emerging scholars in marketing, advertising, and communications present research on some unintended consequences of social media including body shaming, online fraud, cyberbullying, online brand protests, social media addiction, privacy, and revenge pornography. It is a must-read for scholars, practitioners, and students interested in consumer psychology, consumer behavior, social media, advertising, marketing, sociology, science and technology management, public relations, and communication.

Angeline Close Scheinbaum is Associate Professor at The University of Texas at Austin at the Stan Richards School of Advertising & Public Relations. She is a scholar of consumer behavior/consumer psychology, event sponsorship, and integrated brand promotions. Angeline is co-author on a leading textbook, *Advertising & Integrated Brand Promotions,* as well as edited scholarly books *Consumer Behavior Knowledge for Effective Sports and Event Marketing* (with Lynn Kahle) and *Online Consumer Behavior.*

THE DARK SIDE OF SOCIAL MEDIA

A Consumer Psychology Perspective

Edited by Angeline Close Scheinbaum

Routledge
Taylor & Francis Group

NEW YORK AND LONDON

First published 2018
by Routledge
711 Third Avenue, New York, NY 10017

and by Routledge
2 Park Square, Milton Park, Abingdon, Oxon, OX14 4RN

Routledge is an imprint of the Taylor & Francis Group, an informa business.

Library of Congress Cataloging-in-Publication Data

Scheinbaum, Angeline Close, editor.
Title: The dark side of social media: a consumer psychology perspective /
edited by Angeline Close Scheinbaum.
Description: 1 Edition. | New York: Routledge, 2018. | Includes
bibliographical references and indexes.
Identifiers: LCCN 2017018134| ISBN 9781138052550
(hardback : alk. paper) | ISBN 9781138052567 (pbk. : alk. paper) |
ISBN 9781315167718 (ebook)
Subjects: LCSH: Consumers–Psychology. | Advertising. | Social media. |
Computer crimes. | Consumer behavior.
Classification: LCC HF5415.32 .D37 2018 | DDC 658.8/343–dc23
LC record available at https://lccn.loc.gov/2017018134

ISBN: 978-1-138-05255-0 (hbk)
ISBN: 978-1-138-05256-7 (pbk)
ISBN: 978-1-315-16771-8 (ebk)

Typeset in Bembo
by Cenveo Publisher Services

CONTENTS

ABOUT THE EDITOR

Angeline Close Scheinbaum is Associate Professor at The University of Texas at Austin at the *Stan Richards School of Advertising & Public Relations*. She studied at the University of Georgia's *Terry College of Business* (Ph.D., 2006, Business Administration–Marketing) and *Grady College of Journalism & Mass Communication* (M.M.C, 2002, A.B.J, 2000). She has taught 15 different courses and enjoys mentoring graduate students. Her research stream is grounded in explaining and predicting linkages among consumer attitude, affect, cognition, behavioral intent, and consumer behavior. This chain has been developed in traditional mass communication contexts; yet, the experiential/live/face-to-face nature, along with the duality of event sponsorship, deserves distinct models. For this reason, the context is often sponsored events.

The theories she tends to develop come mainly from psychology—affect transfer, resistance, cognitive schema, social identity, image transfer, congruency, and balance theory. Dr. Close Scheinbaum has published over 20 peer-reviewed publications in leading journals such as *Journal of Academy of Marketing Science, Journal of Business Research, Journal of Advertising,* and *Journal of Advertising Research*. She has presented this research in over 30 conference proceedings. Dr. Close Scheinbaum co-authored "Advertising & Integrated Brand Promotion" and edited the scholarly books: "Consumer Behavior Knowledge for Effective Sports and Event Marketing" and "Online Consumer Behavior". She has served in national leadership roles with the American Marketing Association and The Academy of Marketing Science.

CONTRIBUTORS

Pia A. Albinsson Ph.D., is Associate Professor of Marketing and currently holds the John W. Guffey Jr. Professorship in the Walker College of Business at Appalachian State University where she has been teaching since 2009. Her research interests include consumer activism, sustainability, collaborative consumption and advertising effectiveness. Her research has been published in numerous journals such as: *Consumption, Markets, and Culture*; *Psychology and Marketing*; *European Journal of Marketing*; *Journal of Macromarketing*; *Journal of Public Policy and Marketing*; *Journal of Consumer Behaviour*; *Journal of Marketing Theory and Practice*; *Journal of Hospitality Marketing and Management*; *International Journal of Wine Business Research*; and *International Journal of Retailing and Distribution*.

Purificación Alcaide-Pulido is Researcher in the Communication and Education Department at Universidad Loyola Andalucía. She has undergraduate degrees in Advertising and Public Relations, University of Seville, Spain and in Marketing, ETEA, Córdoba, Spain. She earned her Master's in Methods of Research in Business and Economic Sciences, ETEA, Cordona, Spain, and is currently completing her Ph.D. at Universidad Loyola Andalucia. Her research focuses on neural networks, branding, and applications of social media tools and social networking sites in higher education institutions. She has presented her research at international marketing conferences.

Adriana M. Bóveda-Lambie is an assistant professor and researcher at the Ricciardi College of Business, Bridgewater State University. She holds a Ph.D. in business administration from the University of Rhode Island. Dr. Bóveda-Lambie's research examines social media/digital marketing, marketing and new technologies, and Hispanic marketing. Her work has appeared in *Marketing Letters* and the *Journal of*

Business Research. Dr. Bóveda-Lambie has presented her work at world-class marketing conferences including MarketingEdge Research Summit (DMA), American Marketing Association's summer and winter annual conferences, Association for Consumer Research North American conferences, Academy of Marketing Science, and Society for Marketing Advances. She won the SMA best paper in track in 2015.

Sarita Ray Chaudhury, Ph.D., is Assistant Professor of marketing at Humboldt State University. Sarita's research involves understanding cultural meanings in consumer behavior, e-marketing and pedagogy. She has published her research at numerous conferences and in journals such as: *Advances for Consumer Research*; *Journal of Macromarketing*; and *International Journal of Wine Business Research*.

Ryan E. Cruz is a third-year doctoral candidate in marketing at New Mexico State University. His research examines brand identity, brand communication, and consumer engagement across social media platforms. Specifically, he is interested in the role of brand and consumer identity signaling and its effect on consumer behavior and information processing.

Alexandra M. Doorey is a brand manager at The Richards Group in Dallas, Texas and holds a M.A. in Advertising from the University of Texas at Austin. She received bachelor degrees in Public Relations, B.S. and Plan II Honors, B.A. from UT at Austin. Her research focuses on investigating consumer behavior and strategic marketing management with a particular emphasis in exploring digital media, marketing, and privacy. Research topics include mobile marketing and the social and psychological antecedents of user engagement, data-driven advertising personalization, consumer information privacy concerns, data regulation, and e-commerce. Most recently, her research has appeared in *Computers in Human Behavior* and marketing and communication conferences, including the American Marketing Association.

Jenna Drenten, Ph.D., is Assistant Professor of Marketing in the Quinlan School of Business at Loyola University Chicago. Jenna's primary stream of research lies at the intersection of consumer culture and identity development, particularly focusing on social media and adolescent consumers. This includes related concepts such as adolescent consumption rituals and rites of passage, benefits and consequences of self-presentation through technology, and adolescent risk-taking behaviors. Jenna's research has appeared in: *Journal of Macromarketing*; *Journal of Business Research*; and *Journal of Research for Consumers*, among others.

Matthew S. Eastin, Ph.D., is Associate Professor at The University of Texas at Austin. Dr. Eastin's research investigates the diversity of the social cognitive model and its application across different media contexts. Here, his research theoretically centers on why, how, and with what effect audiences engage media. Addressing societal issues related to the digital divide, unregulated media consumption, media violence, and most recently, consumer privacy concerns, this research agenda extends to the media, information science, advertising and communication literatures, to name a few.

Lauren Gurrieri, Ph.D, is Senior Lecturer in Marketing at RMIT University in Australia. Her research focuses on the socio-cultural aspects of consumption and issues at the nexus of marketing and society. She has a particular interest in gender, consumption, and the marketplace. Her work has been published in leading business journals, such as: *Journal of Business Research*; *European Journal of Marketing*; and *Journal of Macromarketing*.

Jonathan A. Henson is a doctoral student in the Department of Communication Studies at the University of Texas at Austin. His research interests are centered on topics of rhetoric and public memory, specifically issues at the intersection of memorialization and public address.

Heather Honea, Ph.D., is Associate Professor at the San Diego State University College of Business Administration and a research fellow at the Centre for Integrated Marketing Communications. Dr. Honea's background in psychology and economics frame her different research areas in interactive consumption and integrated marketing experiences. Across these domains she explores the differential roles of rational versus non-rational (emotional) determinants of preference, perceptions, and consumption. Dr. Honea also models the impact of green and decentralized technologies on business, society, and consumer behavior. She lectures on how these technologies can be leveraged to generate economic, environmental, and social returns that increase the public and private bottom line. Her research allows her to bring a unique perspective to the digital marketing process. In addition to teaching courses at San Diego State University, she provides industry lectures and assists companies and non-profits with the coordination of their digital research and marketing strategies. Dr. Honea's research is published in top business and marketing journals.

John Hulland is the Emily H. and Charles M. Tanner Jr. Chair in Sales Management Professor, and Professor of Marketing at the Terry College of Business, University of Georgia (UGA). His research interests include understanding how social interactions—particularly in online communities—influence attitudes and behaviors, including both product choices and subsequent word-of-mouth. John's work has been published in a wide variety of leading journals, including: *Journal of Consumer Research*; *Marketing Science*; *Journal of Marketing Research*; and *Journal of Marketing*. Prior to joining UGA in 2011, John taught at the University of Pittsburgh for ten years (2001–2011), and before that at the University of Western Ontario in

Canada for even longer. He received his Ph.D. from MIT, his MBA from Queen's University, Kingston, Ontario, and his undergraduate degree in chemistry from the University of Guelph.

Axenya Kachen is a fourth-year undergraduate student at the University of California, Berkeley, double majoring in integrative biology and gender and women's studies (GWS). She has extensive research experience in various fields including biology, electrical engineering and computer science (EECS), and gender studies, and she completed an NSF funded research project in cybersecurity at an EECS lab at UC Berkeley. Kachen works as an intern at the Gender Equity Resource Center at UC Berkeley and directed Eve Ensler's play The Vagina Monologues in 2016. Kachen is an undergraduate student instructor for the anatomy course on campus (Integrative Biology 131L). She is currently working on her senior thesis in GWS, which she plans to publish in 2017. Kachen is hoping to attend medical school upon graduating from her undergrad degree.

Gerard E. Kelly III is a Ph.D. student in marketing at the University of Memphis. Prior to entering the Ph.D. program, Jerry held various marketing, sales, management, and consulting roles in mostly technology-related industries. He earned his M.B.A. from Binghamton University – State University of New York. Jerry's research interests lie in the effects of technology on the business-to-business sales process, particularly among Millennials and Gen Z.

Anjala Krishen has a B.S. in electrical engineering from Rice University, and an M.S. Marketing, MBA, and Ph.D. from Virginia Tech. She held a variety of management positions during a 13-year career before choosing to pursue a doctorate. She is currently Associate Professor of Marketing and International Business in the Lee Business School at the University of Nevada, Las Vegas. Her interdisciplinary research includes areas within decision-making, including heuristics and choice set design, e-marketing and social networking, and database marketing. As of 2016, she has over 40 published peer-reviewed journal papers and received numerous awards including the UNLV Foundation Distinguished Teaching award (2015) and the Barrick Scholar Award (2016).

Kaci G. Lambeth will graduate with a B.S. in Advertising from the Stan Richards School of Advertising & Public Relations at the University of Texas at Austin in 2017. She completed the McCombs Business Foundations Program with Highest Distinction, was named a college scholar, and has been included in the university honors list. She specializes in media strategy, and has experience working with clients in both Austin and New York. Growing up a digital native has made her interested in researching the impact that media and advertising have on culture and individuals. This interest led to her involvement with this project and continues to shape her perspective on the industry.

Amanda Mabry-Flynn is Assistant Professor in the Charles H. Sandage Department of Advertising at the University of Illinois at Urbana-Champaign. Her research focuses on exploring the role social and cultural norms play in advertising and marketing with a focus on public health social marketing campaigns. Specifically, she explores how normative influence relates to gender stereotypes, cultural conceptions of masculinity and femininity, and the prevalence of sexual violence.

Ashesh Mukherjee joined McGill University after completing his Ph.D. in marketing at The University of Texas at Austin. Dr. Mukherjee teaches consumer behavior, marketing management, and marketing research at the undergraduate, masters, and doctoral levels at McGill. He has also taught at universities in Brazil, Spain, Denmark, and India. Dr. Mukherjee's research focuses on marketing communications, word-of-mouth, online behavior, and pro-social behavior. In his research on marketing communications, Dr. Mukherjee has studied topics such as the use of humor in advertising, the use of scarcity in advertising, and the advertising of high technology products. In his research on word-of-mouth, Dr. Mukherjee has studied the impact of product advisors – such as movie critics and wine critics – on consumer decision making. In his research on online behavior, Dr. Mukherjee has studied consumer behavior in peer-to-peer markets such as Airbnb and Uber. In his research on pro-social behavior, Dr. Mukherjee examines methods to increase charitable donations and environmental conscious behaviors among consumers. His research has been published in leading marketing journals, such as: *Journal of Consumer Research*; *Journal of Consumer Psychology*; *Journal of Advertising*; *Psychology & Marketing*; and *Marketing Letters*, and he has presented his work at academic conferences such as the Association for Consumer Research and Society for Consumer Psychology.

Stacy Neier Beran is Senior Lecturer, in the Quinlan School of Business, Loyola University Chicago. She holds two B.S. degrees from the University of Missouri. She received her MBA and Ph.D. from Loyola University Chicago. Stacy began teaching in the Department of Marketing for Quinlan School of Business in 2008. Her professional background includes roles in marketing research and consumer insights for Gap Inc. and Euromonitor International. She teaches marketing research, consumer behavior, fundamentals of marketing, retailing and research practicum. Her research focuses on the scholarship of learning and she has published in journals such as *Journal of Marketing Education* and *Qualitative Market Research: An International Journal*.

Iryna Pentina is Associate Professor of Marketing at the University of Toledo. Her research interests are in the areas of internet marketing and retailing, social media marketing, and online consumer behavior. She has authored over 80 scientific publications and taught classes in over 15 marketing subjects. She founded and served as faculty director of the University of Toledo Interactive Marketing Initiative, and coordinated UT Annual Internet Marketing Conferences in 2009–2014. Dr. Pentina was a Fulbright Research Scholar for the 2013–2014 and 2014–2015 academic years. During her career in academia, she has served as journal guest editor, conference track and session chair, and reviewer for various journals. In 2015, she was named Elsevier Outstanding Reviewer for the *Journal of Interactive Marketing*.

B. Yasanthi Perera, Ph.D., is Assistant Professor of Business Ethics at Brock University. Her research focuses on social responsibility. In particular, she examines individuals' consumption and disposition patterns, and their participation in social media-driven activist efforts that are directed towards businesses. At the organizational level, she examines businesses' sustainability efforts, and various facets of for-profit social enterprises such as blended value creation and their management of social and financial aims. Her work has been published in numerous outlets including *Journal of Consumer Behaviour*, and *Journal of Marketing Theory and Practice*.

Paula C. Peter is a consumer behaviorist and an associate professor of marketing in the Department of Marketing, College of Business Administration at the San Diego State University. Originally from Switzerland, Paula Peter received her Ph.D. from Virginia Tech where she was also selected as the recipient of the 2007 Pamplin College Outstanding Graduate Student Award. Prof. Peter helps her students and profit/non-profit clients gain greater appreciation for consumer insights in order to guide marketing strategy, offline as well as online, and maximize return on investment. The foundation of her experience is marketing research. She has a passion for conducting research at the intersection of consumer psychology/behavior, marketing, and consumer well-being. Her research interests include the role of emotions and emotional intelligence in consumer decision-making, social marketing, cause marketing, and social media marketing with special emphasis on strategies in order to help consumers help themselves. Her research is published in: *Journal of Public Policy and Marketing; Journal of Business Research; Journal of Consumer Affairs; Marketing Theory; Journal of Research for Consumers; Journal of Applied Social Psychology;* and *Advances in Consumer Research* among others. Dr. Peter is an active member of the *Transformative Consumer Research* (TCR) movement.

Leyland F Pitt, MCom, MBA, Ph.D., is Professor of Marketing and the Dennis F. Culver EMBA Alumni Chair of Business at the Beedie School of Business at Simon Fraser University, Vancouver, Canada. He holds adjunct professorships in marketing at the Royal Institute of Technology, Stockholm, Sweden, and at the Vienna University of Economics and Business, Austria. He has also taught on executive and MBA programs at major international business schools such as the Graham School of Continuing Studies at the University of Chicago, the Graduate School of Business of Columbia University, Rotterdam School of Management, and London Business School. The author of more than 300 articles in peer-reviewed journals, his work has been accepted for publication by such journals as: *Journal of Advertising Research*; *Journal of Advertising*; *Information Systems Research*; *Journal of the Academy of Marketing Science*; *Sloan Management Review*; *Business Horizons*; *California Management Review*; *Communications of the ACM*; and *MIS Quarterly* (which he also served as Associate Editor), and in 2000 he was the recipient of the Tamer Cavusgil Award of the American Marketing Association for the best article in Journal of International Marketing. Professor Pitt has won many awards for teaching excellence, including Best Lecturer on the MBA Program, Henley Management College, UK; the Dean's Teaching Honor Roll, Beedie School of Business, Simon Fraser University, Canada; best professor and MBA Teacher of the Year, Copenhagen Business School, Denmark; and Best Professor of Program, Joint Executive MBA, University of Vienna, Austria and Carlson School of Management, University of Minnesota, USA. In 2002, Leyland Pitt was awarded the Outstanding Marketing Teacher of the Academy of Marketing Science, and in 2010 he was the recipient of the American Marketing Association's Solomon-Marshall-Stewart Pearson-Prentice Hall Innovative Marketing Teacher Award. He was elected a Distinguished Fellow of the Academy of Marketing Science in 2012. In 2006 he was awarded the TD Canada Trust award for outstanding teachers, and listed as one of Canada's top MBA professors in the magazine, Canadian Business, in 2005. Leyland Pitt has also presented in-house management development programs in major organization worldwide, including British Airways, Unilever, HSBC, Ernst and Young, Dixons, Volkswagen, SABMiller, the Australian Customs Service, Kone, Siemens and the Royal Metropolitan Police.

Claudia Rademaker is Assistant Professor in the Fashion Marketing and Entrepreneurship (FAME) at Stockholm Business School, Stockholm University. She is also affiliated with the Stockholm School of Economics and is a visiting researcher at Amsterdam School of Communication Research (ASCoR), University of Amsterdam. Claudia holds a Ph.D. in business administration from Stockholm School of Economics. Her doctoral thesis was conducted at the Center for Media and Economic Psychology. Claudia's research focuses primarily on corporate sustainability and conscious consumerism. Some of her recent work includes studies of corporate knowledge about and consumers' social connotations of brands regarding corporate marketing action. Her research has been published in: *Journal of Cleaner Production*; the *Media Convergence Handbook*; and other publications.

Nancy Ridgway is Professor of Marketing at the Robins School of Business at the University of Richmond. She received her undergraduate degree, M.B.A. and Ph.D. from the University of Texas at Austin. After teaching at Louisiana State University and the University of Colorado at Boulder, she joined the faculty at the University of Richmond in 2001. Her work is in the area of consumer behavior. Specifically, she studies unusual consumers such as those who use products in innovative ways, those who enjoy shopping, compulsive buyers and collectors and consumer hoarders. She has published articles in: *Journal of Consumer Research*; *Journal of Marketing Research*; *Journal of the Academy of Marketing Science*; and *Journal of Retailing*, among many others. She is a member of the American Marketing Association and the Association for Consumer Research. She has also edited a *Legends* volume on Kent Monroe and contributed chapters to five books.

Marla B. Royne, Stafford, is Great Oaks Foundation Professor and Department Chair of Marketing and Supply Chain Management in the Fogelman College of Business at the University of Memphis. She also holds affiliate faculty status with the School of Public Health and is a senior research fellow with the Le Bonheur Center for Healthcare Economics at the U of M. She is a past editor of *Journal of Advertising*. She holds a Ph.D. in marketing from the University of Georgia. Her current research focuses on social issues including health related topics and the environment. Her work has been published in numerous journals including: *Journal of Advertising*; *Journal of Advertising Research*; *Journal of Retailing*; *American Journal of Public Health*; *Journal of the American Academy of Child and Adolescent Psychiatry*; *Journal of School Health*; *Computers in Human Behavior*; and other publications.

Keith Marion Smith is Assistant Professor of Marketing at the D'Amore-McKim School of Business, Northeastern University. He conducts marketing research to understand the impact of digital products, social media, and online environments on key outcomes of importance to managers and marketers, including purchase, consumption, consumer helping, and product co-creation, among others. Keith leverages over ten years of industry experience in information technology and digital marketing to collect and analyze large-scale social media datasets that capture real customer behavior in online settings. Keith earned his Ph.D. in marketing from the University of Georgia, his MBA from Belmont University, and his MA in psychology from Vanderbilt University, establishing a foundation of academic research experience that informs a social science theory driven approach to large-scale dataset research. His work has been published in leading journals including: *Journal of Marketing Research*; *Journal of the Academy of Marketing Science*; *Journal of Marketing Theory and Practice*; and *Memory and Cognition*.

Scott R. Stroud is Associate Professor of Communication Studies at the University of Texas at Austin. His research focuses on topics at the intersection of philosophy and rhetoric, especially in regard to pragmatism, ethics, and comparative rhetoric. He has been a visiting fellow at the Center for the Study of Democratic Politics at Princeton University. His work has appeared in numerous journals in the fields of communication and philosophy, and he is the author of *John Dewey and the Artful Life* (Pennsylvania State University Press, 2011) and *Kant and the Promise of Rhetoric* (Pennsylvania State University Press, 2014).

Monideepa Tarafdar is Professor of Information Systems at Lancaster University's Management School, UK. She was a visiting scholar at MIT's Center for Information Systems Research in Fall 2016. Her primary areas of research are the impacts of information technology on individuals, organizations, and supply chains. She has published in, among others: *Information Systems Research*; *Journal of MIS*; *Journal of Operations Management*; *Sloan Management Review*; *Journal of Strategic Information Systems*; *Journal of Information Technology*; *Decision Sciences Journal*; *International Journal of Production Research*; *International Journal of Production Economics*; *Information and Management*; and *Computers and Human Behavior*.

David G. Taylor is Associate Professor of Marketing in the Jack Welch College of Business at Sacred Heart University in Fairfield, CT. His research focuses on digital marketing, social media and consumer-brand relationships, and has been published in academic journals such as: *Journal of Business Research*; *Journal of Advertising Research*; *Journal of Research in Interactive Marketing, Electronic Commerce*; and many others. His research has been presented at leading national and international conferences. In addition, Dr. Taylor is former director of Sacred Heart's master's program in digital marketing, and he has served on the editorial boards of several academic journals, as well as serving as a reviewer and guest editor. Dr. Taylor earned his Ph.D. in marketing from the University of North Texas.

Scott A. Thompson earned his Ph.D. in marketing from Arizona State University. Dr. Thompson possesses an extensive background in information technology and research methodology and leverages these skills to conduct marketing research that involves the programmatic collection and analysis of large-scale, multi-year datasets of customer behavior within online environments. His research focuses on managerially impactful issues including brand communities' influence on new production adoption, online consumer-to-consumer helping, the influence of word-of-mouth on the evaluation of products and promotions, and the management of brand relationships in social media environments. His research has been published in leading marketing journals including: *Journal of Marketing*; *Journal of Marketing Research*; *Journal of the Academy of Marketing Science*; *Marketing Letters*; *Journal of Interactive Marketing*; and *Journal of Marketing Theory and Practice*.

Gary B. Wilcox, Ph.D., is the John A. Beck Centennial Professor in Communication at the Stan Richards School of Advertising & Public Relations at the University of Texas at Austin. His opinions and work have been featured in such national media as *The New York Times, Los Angeles Times, U.S. News and World Report* and *AdWeek* among others. His most recent interests include unstructured data analysis, social media analytic models, and advertising's effects on various products and brands. His publications include one book, several book chapters, and articles that have appeared in: *International Journal of Advertising; Journal of*

Advertising Research; Journal of Advertising; Journal of Digital and Social Media Marketing; and *Journal of Food Products Marketing,* among others.

Linda Tuncay Zayer, Ph.D. is Associate Professor at the Quinlan School of Business, Loyola University Chicago. She holds an undergraduate business degree from Indiana University, MBA from University of Notre Dame, and Ph.D. from University of Illinois at Urbana-Champaign. She has published in journals such as: *Journal of Consumer Research; Journal of Retailing; Journal of Advertising;* and *Journal of Public Policy & Marketing;* among others and co-edited a book, *Gender, Culture and Consumer Behavior* (Routledge, 2017). Her primary research interest includes gender and consumer behavior.

FOREWORD

The Bright Side of Social Media

Given its ubiquity, we might think that social media has been with us forever. In fact, Facebook was only launched in 2004, Twitter in 2006, and Instagram in 2010. Within this short period of time, however, social media has assumed an outsized role in our lives. This book focuses on the downsides of social media of which there are many; but to be fair and balanced, we also need to keep the bright side of social media in mind. Like money or fame, social media is not good or bad in and of itself—it depends on how it is used. This brief preface will high-light some of the ways in which social media, when used correctly, can be an asset to individuals as well as society as a whole.

Think about your social life before social media. Perhaps you visited family, hung out with classmates, had drinks with colleagues, and went out for dates you met through friends or at work. From these examples, we can see that our social circle was limited by history and geography—our history of people we knew and the geography of where we happened to live, work, and learn. Not only that, our social circle tended to become smaller as we got older. We no longer had class-mates; we got busier at work; our friends moved away, got married and had children. Social media has freed us from these restrictions, and opened up a world of connections that we can now cultivate throughout our lives. We can stay in touch with friends and family living far away with hardly any effort, and thus maintain our social circle over a lifetime. We can find and reconnect with long-lost friends and distant family by simply typing their names in social search. We can expand our social circle by participating in online groups, chats, blogs, and bulletin boards. And, we can find love (or hookups) much more easily through social dating websites that connect interested couples in the same geographic area.

A more subtle benefit of social media is that it fosters a culture of openness, sharing and trust that brings people closer together. The more we share on social media, the more we learn about each others' lives, opinions, joys, and sadness, and the more we see our similarities as human beings. Social media is a platform for giving and receiving information, and both these activities help us grow as individuals. Giving helpful information to others on social media is good because it increases our visibility and builds our personal brand. Getting validation from others about the value of our opinions, such as getting likes or up-votes, increases our confidence in ourselves as subject matter experts. And the information we receive from social media in the form of news, updates, or trending topics is important because it helps us cut through the clutter of excess information on the internet. Our social network curates information for us, so we can go directly to what is likely to be most relevant and interesting to us.

Finally, social media is helpful to us not only as individuals, but also as members of society. We can set up social media groups to mobilize people around social or political issues, memorialize people we care about, and protest against policies we disagree with. Political movements such as the Arab Spring and the Color Revolutions would not have happened as quickly as they did without Twitter and Facebook, and this is why repressive regimes around the world try to control their citizens' use of social media. To sum up, the message of this preface is: social media is helpful in many ways, and we should seek to reap these benefits when we use social media in our own lives.

Ashesh Mukherjee

FOREWORD
The Dark Side of Social Media

The spouse of a presidential candidate "borrows", in her support speech, some of the exact words used by the spouse of the current president, also in a support speech just a few years before. Plagiarism undoubtedly, but did she really deserve the excoriation she received not only in mainstream media, but especially on social media such as Facebook and Twitter? A dentist on a hunting trip in Africa shoots a lion. The news hits social media in a flash. I don't like hunting, especially of wild lions, and don't think much of the dentist for doing it. But I question whether his actions were enough to warrant his having to close his business and move his family out of their home because of vigilante threats. Many of those involved in the 2011 Stanley Cup riots in Vancouver were named and shamed in social media. Some lost their jobs, probably deservedly, and were expelled from universities, probably deservedly, apart from facing court charges. Whether they merited death threats to themselves and families, however, is very questionable indeed. Social media (and I'll use the term as a collective noun) certainly has a dark side.

Social media has a lot to answer for. For example, the levels of narcissism, particularly among the young, seem to be significantly on the increase (Gray, 2014), while there are indications that average levels of depression in the general population have also risen dramatically over the past ten years. Social media might easily explain that we're becoming more narcissistic, because social media such as Facebook give us a platform for being so. I post pictures of happy occasions with family and friends, my career successes, fine meals enjoyed and exotic places visited on vacation. I hardly ever boast or post about being laid low with flu, or of having yet another paper rejected, or of serious disagreements with friends and family. Seemingly my only reason for depression would be that my so-called "friends" on Facebook don't "like" my stuff nearly enough. But of course my wonderful life just might be depressing my social media friends—after all, they reason, they don't have as idyllic a family, enjoy such rude good health, succeed nearly as often, or travel and dine in the same style. Viewed in this way, social media might be simultaneously responsible for the increases in narcissism and depression.

There's more to it. Thanks to the power of social media, my sister, who lives on another continent, can see the latest postings of my daughters, her nieces, on Facebook, and she and I can chat on Facebook Messenger at least once a week at a cost of close to zero. And yet one only has to dine out to view couples in a restaurant so engrossed in the social media on their smartphones that they say not a single word to each other for the duration of an entire meal. So, is the simple point that social media only has a dark side? The answer isn't that simple. Social media is a technology. And like all technologies, social media is indifferent to the human condition. It isn't simply, "bad" or "good". Its effects on us, like all technologies, are paradoxical. They are both good and bad, light and dark.

Our cars are good: they enable us to get from A to B speedily, in comfort and in style. Our cars are bad: they are sometimes dangerous, get us caught in traffic and pollute the environment. Our computers are good: they allow us to work far more productively, and do things we could never do before. Our computers are bad: we spend countless unproductive hours on them; they crash and give us back pain. The effects of all technologies are paradoxical as Mick and Fournier (1998, p.125) highlighted in their seminal work: "Some observers have argued that technology itself is paradoxical. For example, Winner (1994) claims that the same technology that creates radiant feelings of intelligence and efficacy can also precipitate feelings of stupidity and ineptitude. Goodman (1988) notes how appliances purchased for saving time regularly end up wasting time."

Yet most of us love technology, and social media is no exception. We love it because we feel that it gives us freedom, choice and control, and this, we believe, allows us to build and control our own realities. However, as Spider-man said, with greater power comes greater responsibility, and with greater freedom comes greater responsibility for our choices. These responsibilities are not only those of the individual, who certainly needs to think more carefully about what they do and say in an environment in which the world becomes your audience. They might love you perhaps for that cute video, but will just as easily vilify you for a thoughtless or careless remark.

The responsibilities are also the obligations of policy-and lawmakers, who need to adapt legislation to an environment in which the laws concerning bullying, slander, libel and threat take on an entirely new meaning. And they are certainly the responsibilities of marketers who can no longer simply find out what customers want and give it to them. They will need to understand that technology is just as likely an active force and that technologies possess trajectories (Berthon, Hulbert and Pitt, 2005), and that they evolve or change over time. Developments, choices, and changes at any one point in time not only facilitate, but also delimit the future path of a technology.

There is certainly much darkness among most of the chapters in this book. There is bullying and there are victims, there is overconsumption, and there are narcissists who only display their desired selves. There is even revenge porn! However there is light as well. Even the dark chapters offer solutions to dealing with social media's negative consequences, and there is much to learn from the more positive chapters on consumer privacy, information overload and higher education. So let us remember, in this age of technological paradox that has been hyper accelerated by the advent of social media: What happens in Vegas might stay in Vegas…but if it's been on Facebook or Twitter, it stays on Google forever (with acknowledgements to Jure Klepic).

Leyland Pitt

References

Berthon, P.R., Hulbert, J.M., and Pitt, L.F. (2005). Consuming Technology: Why Marketers Sometimes Get It Wrong, *California Management Review*, 88, 1, 110-128.

Goodman, E. (1988). Time Bandits in the Machine Age, *Chicago Tribune*, Tempo section (January 10), 2.

Gray, P. (2014). Why is Narcissism Increasing Among Young Americans? *Psychology Today*, January 16th, downloaded from: https://www.psychologytoday.com/blog/freedom-learn/201401/why-is-narcissism-increasing-among-young-american on September 21st 2016.

Mick, D.G., and Fournier, S. (1998). Paradoxes of Technology: Consumer Cognizance, Emotions and Coping Strategies, *Journal of Consumer Research*, 25, September, 123–143.

Winner, L. (1994). Three Paradoxes of the Information Age, in *Culture on the Brink: Ideologies of Technology*, ed. Gretchen Bender and Timothy Druckrey, Seattle: Bay, 191–197.

PART I

A Framework for the Dark Side of Social Media

1

A FRAMEWORK FOR THE DARK SIDE OF SOCIAL MEDIA

From Digital Drama to Digital Over-engagement

Angeline Close Scheinbaum

Let us foremost consider social media through a consumer psychology lens. In many ways social media does connect people—which overall is a very good thing. The point here is not to bash social media—which very well may be just the messenger for some dark topics. My view is not that social media is wrong nor bad for consumer psyche. *The point is that online consumer behavior via social media brings specific considerations of likely unintended consequences to both consumers and brands as a result of having this huge and largely visible interactive audience.* As such, the objective of this introductory chapter is to open a discussion of the topic and to provide a working framework for scholars who are interested in our continuing this important conversation.

Social media can do wonderful things for people and brands. From a corporate stance, social media has given massive exposure for brands and provides for psychographic and behavioral targeting with a relatively low advertising investment. There are many social and economic positive consequences for consumers and companies/organizations/brands. It helps connect old friends, helps inform, and gives a sense of human connection when one is alone. It has given exposure for emerging artists; for instance, one of the most successful recording artists in recent times is Justin Bieber, who is said to have been discovered via YouTube. In other examples of the bright side, people have met and married after meeting on social media and there have even been some accounts of people reconnecting with long lost family members.

Facebook Events, allows consumers to make a movement in a quick and transparent way. For instance, when we had an unfortunate tragedy on campus this year, our students quickly used Facebook Events to help organize and communicate a memorial. Then, Facebook Live can show an event or happening via live streaming video to the social media user's network. While this technology is amazing and does bring people together, there have been some unanticipated occurrences with live streaming of consumer content via social media. Most notably, Diamond Reynolds, the girlfriend of Philando Castile who was fatally shot by police in 2016, posted a Facebook Live video showing the social media world a glimpse of the effects of the tragedy on a community and their loved ones. Of course, an argument can be made that this exposure made possible by live video and social media can help bring awareness to some important social problems.

Still, we have not fully considered the effects of live streaming consumer content on social media or more broadly social media as a communication channel in general. While some are positive, other likely unintended effects can be problematic to consumers or brands. One example that is not yet touched on is that social media sites must consider what happens upon the death of a person and how their profile page and nostalgic memories are handled. In the case of the well-meaning nostalgic reminders of what the person did on this day in years past, sometimes these nostalgic reminders bring up sad reminders that a person is no longer with us.

For a related instance, especially in cases of tragedy, it has been hard for surviving family members who may want access to the account for many reasons that are emotional and logical. For this reason, Facebook has made a "legacy contact" setting that starkly reminds living Facebook users to set the legacy contact. In a harsh way, one day, my Facebook profile had a banner that literally said "Remembering (my name). We hope people who love (my name) will find comfort in the things others share to remember and celebrate her life." Talk about a reminder of mortality salience! After seeing this and feeling deeply disturbed, I found out that Facebook had a glitch and others also got a memorial message with their names on it on their page. Facebook then sent an apology saying that it was a mistake and the memorialization message was shown on the wrong profiles. This is just one example of how a human or artificial intelligence glitch in social media has some difficult unintended consequences to consumers. Some of these unintended effects may relate with two concepts suggested here—digital drama and digital over-engagement.

Digital Drama and Digital Over-engagement

Digital Drama

Social media has transformed the way we communicate with each other and brands. The intention is for social media to bring us together. Yet, it has the potential to highlight our differences and, in some cases, this brings digital drama. Digital drama, defined here, refers to occurrence of and reactions to negative online consumer behaviors such as sexting, cyberbullying, fear of missing out, abuse, and related online happenings. Digital drama can occur with other forms of technology.

It is not a new phenomenon, although digital drama is a new age term. Digital drama has occurred with emails, list-serves (namely replying all accidentally) and texts (especially group texts). Most notably, digital drama occurs via social media due to the large exposure and scope of who can see the online content—until the digital drama has become so bad that the original poster chooses to delete (or is forced to delete) the hurtful content. It is possible that social media is merely a platform for digital drama that would occur anyway via text messages or other communication technology. Again, social media is interactive and has a broad exposure; it may simply expose some of the issues that were occurring anyway.

Digital Over-engagement

Consumers may be engaging too much with digital platforms—including but not limited to social media. As a working definition, digital engagement is an online behavior resulting from a consumer's thoughts, emotional connection, and intrinsic motivation to interact and cooperate with a brand or its community members in a digital, mobile, or social media setting (Scheinbaum, 2016). This proposed working definition of digital over-engagement includes community and motivational aspects (Algesheimer et al., 2005), the multidimensional component (Brodie et al., 2011), as well as the mainstay of the behavioral component as suggested by Bolton (2010). Perhaps the reason for the lack of a consistent and clear agreement of what constitutes digital engagement is because engagement occurs on various levels and it can be conceptualized from the company's or consumer's perspectives (Scheinbaum, 2016).

Opportunities to digitally engage consumers present new risks with newer media platforms that are intertwined with social media and gaming. For instance, consider some aspects of potential over-engagement with augmented reality games that are widely disseminated and updated via social media. Digital over-engagement with a social media-related game, such as Pokémon Go, has been unfortunately associated with unintended consequences in the offline world. Playing an augmented reality game and or posting aspects of the game on social media may be a context for accidents. Augmented reality can take consumer attention away from the traditional, on-ground reality. Unfortunately, the Pokémon Go game has been purportedly associated with crimes, car accidents, untimely deaths, and even catching spouses in infidelity (Scheinbaum, 2016). Digital over-engagement may blur into social media-related obsessions—even social media-related addictions. A consumer can be tempted to keep up with various social media platforms. If a consumer is engaging too much (i.e., too many platforms or too much time doing things on social media), it could be unhealthy or even be an early indicator of a social media addiction.

Politics: A Context Ripe for Digital Drama and Digital Over-engagement

One of the contexts that has heightened an environment for potential digital drama and digital over-engagement is the recent election for the President of the United States.

The 2016 United States Presidential election between Donald Trump and Hilary Clinton was the first US Presidential election that truly was covered on social media by both consumers and other groups such as advertisers and the media. Interestingly, Trump accused the media of rigging the election and extensively used social media (namely Twitter) to communicate that stance. The tweets were pretty attention-worthy; I suspect much of the reason why is in shock value. In advertising, "shockvertising" is a tactic where the advertiser shocks the consumer as an attention-getting mechanism. Social media gave a large platform that was interactive—unlike some media of the past such as television, print, direct mail, outdoor, or radio.

As such, social media gave a large platform that was international as well as interactive. Another consequence of social media is that our country's presidential election seemed to have an especially international presence. Note that social media users who cannot even vote because they are not a citizen or they are under the age of 18 years still heavily weighed in via social media. While they cannot vote, they were still influencers whose digital footprint does not go away. Social media users from across the globe were posting opinions on the candidates and their personal characteristics. To a lesser extent perhaps, the candidates and consumers commented on tough issues via social media.

Historically, media has changed politics. Some presidents had "fireside chats" with Americans via the radio. When television came along, all of a sudden we could see more of what the politicians looked like. In some ways, the candidate's physical appearance became more noted. Now, with social media covering almost every aspect of major elections, the candidates' physical appearance is a topic of discussion more than ever. A candidate's looks should be discussed much less on social media than their stance on the important issues. Recall these specific descriptions of candidates from the 2016 race to the presidency including "little Marco" and "small hands Donald". Memes such as the one that was popular around Halloween, #Trumpkin (a pumpkin that looks like Donald Trump) were spread around social media.

Would the elections have been different if not for social media? Did the social media platforms heighten the upsetting digital drama felt and seen by many people—especially given a controversial election? Politics was in our face constantly during the political advertising season. Such may be an impetus for digital over-engagement. The distinction here from television is that the content on social media is largely consumer to consumer, whereas on television, much of the political content came from members of the traditional media or ads by PACS.

Regardless, most political content did not use to come from consumers/peers. With the two considerations of digital drama and digital over-exposure in mind, we may consider a working framework for the dark side of social media.

Working Framework for the Dark Side of Social Media

See Figure 1.1 for the conceptual framework of the dark side of social media as proposed here.

Here, I propose a framework for the dark side of social media for scholars to build on. This research book takes a consumer psychology perspective to consumer's online consumer behavior—specifically in the context of social media. In contrast to most research in the social media context, this book focuses on some of the darker issues facing both consumers and brands/companies in the social media era.

Figure 1.1 shows Part I (the overall framework) as it shapes some very unfortunate and disturbing areas of digital drama (Part II) such as revenge porn (Chapter 2), cyberbullying (Chapter 3), body image/body shaming (Chapter 4),

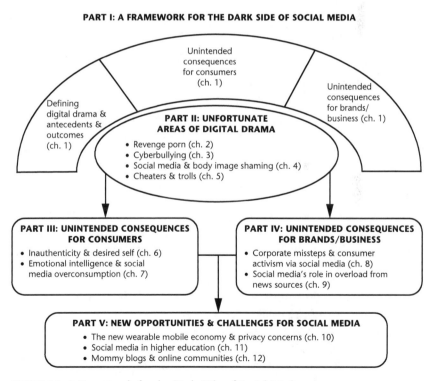

FIGURE 1.1 A Framework for the Dark Side of Social Media.

and cheaters and trolls on social media (Chapter 5). These areas of digital drama bring some (largely unintended) consequences to consumers (Part III) and brands/business (Part IV). For instance, consumers tend to feel a drive to display an inauthentic self on their social media pages and digital engagements on social media (Chapter 6). Such could be explained by image and the self-schema, while other aspects can be explained by social comparison theory—or constant comparisons with others. Social media makes self-comparisons very easy to do.

Social media may also be lessening consumers' emotional intelligence (Chapter 7). Or, at least social media provides a visible platform to expose some consumers' questionable emotional intelligence via the nature of the comments and photos they choose to post. Through a developmental psychology lens, young people now are digital natives. Their emotional intelligence is still developing, and social media behaviors for those younger consumers is a topic worth thinking about deeply.

There are also some consequences for brands and businesses. For instance, in this era, when there is a notable corporate misstep or mistake, consumers are in control with social media. Consumers can easily call the company out on the mistake in a more public and interactive way. Social media has become a major public relations tool and using it intelligently for corporate crisis communications is important. Social media brings a platform for consumer activism (Chapter 8). Brands and businesses may also not have accounted for the foreseeable massive shift in the way that news is delivered. Businesses, brands, and media organizations must think deeply about any dark side of the new way of news delivery via social media (Chapter 9). One of the reasons this is important is because the news now has an interactive and social element to it in real time that we really have not seen before. Artificial intelligence algorithms, for instance, tell us what is trending in the news at any given moment. The news feeds seem to be ranked in order of how many other entities are digitally engaged with the news story. This is a big change for journalism, the news business, advertisers, and marketers.

To conclude, consider some new directions and more unique contexts or settings for social media use. For one, a new wearable economy may be on our horizon (Chapter 10). The new wearables, such as an Apple watch that can connect to social media, can bring about some privacy issues associated with cross-devices. Other new directions are some unique contexts for using social media—such as for professors or working mothers. In higher education especially (Chapter 11), social media has become commonplace as a course topic. However, the way that professors and students elect to use social media in the modern classroom differs. One reason may be because of the potential (unintended) consequences that social media has in higher education—such as an avenue for cyber cheating on private Facebook pages that the professor is not invited to.

As a final unique context that may end on a bright side note is in online communities for specific groups that can help each other during certain life stages. In Chapter 12, we can see consumer sentiments as shared on mommy blogs that expose both positive and negative aspects of the psychology of working parents. While the dark side is that some of the struggles exist, the bright side to end on is that online communities such as those seen via social and digital media bring consumers together and can provide a platform for consumers reaching out and helping other consumers.

Discussion

It is plausible however that the dark side attitudes and behaviors seen in the working framework were always present. Perhaps social media is just the messenger. Bullying has been going on for many years for instance; now it is likely to be more visible. In a similar vein, social media has exposed some behaviors that likely were happening before the advent of social media—but we did not have such a platform and constant exposure. Television and radio are known for the ability to reach a wide audience; they are not that interactive though. Social media by nature is social; it is interactive. The comments and likes and pokes and other behaviors that show digital engagement can almost publically expose wrongs or miscommunications. For instance, a consumer puts up an inappropriate video that is offensive and within seconds others can comment or question the content. In some cases, the consumer becomes compelled to delete the content. On Twitter, this is the "Tweet and Delete"—which is a fascinating online consumer behavior in itself.

We as scholars and citizens of our society need to reflect upon and consider any unintended consequences of social media. There is a dark side of social media. Consider the following (unintended) consequences to some aspects of social media present in this framework: body shaming, online fraud, cyberbullying, online brand protests, social media addiction, and revenge porn. These are just a few of the topics.

Collectively, it is important to recognize that there is a dark side to social media in addition to its many positive virtues for both consumers and brands. This dark side is less discussed in scholarly research despite the broad impact and media interest in the topic. I hope that, with this writing, other scholars will join us in rigorous scholarly work on these topics and the theoretical mechanisms that underlie use of and consequences to social media use—both the good and the bad.

References

Algesheimer, R., Dholakia, U.M. & Herrmann, A. (2005). The social influence of brand community: Evidence from European car clubs. *Journal of Marketing,* 69, 3, 19–34.

Bolton, R.N. (2011) Customer engagement: Opportunities and challenges for organizations. *Journal of Service Research,* 14, 3, 272–274.

Brodie, R. J., et al. (2011). Customer engagement: conceptual domain, fundamental propositions, and implications for research. *Journal of Service Research,* doi. 1094670511411703.

Scheinbaum, A.C. (2016), Digital engagement: opportunities and risks for sponsors. *Journal of Advertising Research,* 56(4), 341-345.

PART II

Unfortunate Areas of Digital Drama

As Part I gave us an overview of a framework of some dark side of social media perspectives, Part II focuses on a few specific, unfortunate areas of what I call "digital drama". Recall from the introduction, that digital drama can be in texts, emails, and social media alike. The commonality is that the drama (unwanted issues and emotional reactions and occurrences) can be heightened because of the non-face-to-face communication component, which can bring misunderstandings. Or, to be blunt, some people are plain mean on social media and they act as if there are fewer or no consequences to their immature or pathological behavior because they are technically interacting with a screen and not another human being.

There should be no tolerance for some of these social behaviors—especially sharing of "revenge porn" (Chapter 2), cyberbullying (Chapter 3), and body shaming or propagating unhealthy body images, especially for girls or adolescents who are quite vulnerable (Chapter 4). This overall dark section concludes by explaining the importance of the concept of psychological ownership, and a contribution is a conceptual model showing the motives, causes, and consequences (many unintended) of psychological ownership via social media. While Chapter 5 does not provide an exhaustive investigation of psychological ownership theory in the social media context, it does demonstrate how unique insights can be drawn from the theory. The contribution is a conceptual model showing the motives, causes, and consequences of psychological ownership via social media.

2

SOCIAL MEDIA, ONLINE SHARING, AND THE ETHICAL COMPLEXITY OF CONSENT IN REVENGE PORN

Scott R. Stroud and Jonathan A. Henson

Social media excels at allowing users to instantly share their thoughts and feelings, often without much reflection about the wisdom or value of such communications. It also pairs exceptionally well with the realm of digital content, which holds forth a promise of easily and accurately disseminating identical copies of an original. One can share or post an exact image or video for others, in addition to simply creating verbal content of one's own. The confluence of expressive powers and audio-visual content duplication has created a pernicious new online threat—the posting of "revenge porn," or the distribution of nude or sexualized images of others with the intent to harm them in some way. It is also called "nonconsensual pornography," since it is said to lack the subject's consent for this content to be used in this fashion (Franks, 2015). Following much of the popular discourse, we will call this phenomenon "revenge porn," even though some uses of this content are not solely for the purposes of revenge. Whatever one labels it, revenge porn is a new online behavior that hurts careers, stunts educational plans, and in some cases leads to suicide (Ronneburger, 2009; Citron & Franks, 2014). By some estimates, there are over 3,000 revenge porn sites on the web, many using social media platforms such as Tumblr or Twitter to post or link to harmful content ("Revenge Porn," 2014). Even dedicated revenge porn websites mimic mainstream social media sites and their valuing of interactivity by employing their own comment sections and rating features (Stroud, 2014).

There has been a movement in state legislatures across the U.S. to criminalize the posting of online revenge pornography. There is even an organization devoted to "cyber civil rights," the Cyber Civil Rights Initiative, whose legislative advocacy to date has focused on one putative civil right—protecting online subjects from the posting of shared nude images. There is much thought and passion being directed at the target of "revenge porn." Yet when we think of "revenge porn" as a category or concept, we cannot help but think of a standard scenario. A couple is in an intimate relationship, during which they share nude or sexual photographs (content can involve videos, but for simplicity's sake, we will speak from here on of photographic content). These images were taken or shared because the partners trusted each other. After an acrimonious breakup, one ex-partner decides to use these images in an online campaign of shaming and harming the other partner. The embarrassing images are posted online, shared with employers and family members, and are even used to evoke threats and stalking behaviors from online (and unknown) others. This story is evident in the statement of Anisha Vora when she speaks of her experiences with revenge porn, and in favor of federal revenge porn legislation: "After being a victim of nonconsensual pornography, I was always paranoid and had a fear for what could happen. After my ex-boyfriend posted intimate photographs of myself on numerous websites, resulting in them expanding to over 3,000 links, I knew my family and I were no longer safe. With strangers approaching me in public and online, and even attacking me in my own home, I decided to fight back" (Congresswoman Speier, 2016). One sees the standard story: Ms. Vora trusted her partner, and he eventually set out on a deliberate path of harming her after they broke up. The ease of sharing content and feelings via social media only enhanced the ex-boyfriend's ability to do this. This story type has quickly been appropriated into a larger narrative of violations of privacy and consent. For instance, Mary Anne Franks simplifies these matters into the language of consent: "Consent always matters, whether for the sexual activity is physical or virtual, and there is simply no excuse for disregarding it" (Franks, 2016). Further simplification based upon this awful archetypal story of a disgruntled (typically male) lover turning on a prior partner occurs in the First Amendment debates over revenge porn legislation. One can see this when legal scholar Erwin Chemerinsky bluntly concludes that "The First Amendment does not protect a right to invade a person's privacy by publicizing, without consent, nude photographs or videos of sexual activity" (Franks, 2016).

While others have highlighted the more nuanced First Amendment problems posed by laws criminalizing revenge porn (e.g., Greenfield, 2016, July 16), we want to focus our attention in the present chapter on the challenges posed by the act of conceptualizing revenge porn. The straightforward and strong claims of consent, privacy violation, and relational harm illustrated previously all rely on "revenge porn" meaning one thing. That thing is usually taken to be the form exemplified by the relational story illustrated above. But consent in the online world of social media and sharing ecosystems is not that simple. A lot of sharing of content and commenting occurs in social media and online, but it is unclear what the consent status of most of this content is. One could google a term, say, "sexy elbows," find an image and share it. Perhaps one can identify whose elbow it was from a distinctive tattoo. What exactly does one know about consent in this case? What does the image itself tell you about consent, since the image alone is what you found online and replicated or reposted in other online forums? The ethical concerns over consent, privacy, and revenge porn are much more vexed than partisan advocates make them seem. This chapter will attempt to muddy the waters in an effort to enable a stronger response to the truly harmful cases of nonconsensual or revenge pornography. Clearly, we wish no one would use such content—whether it has been given, hacked, or found—to harm others they judge worthy of harm. Yet part of the challenge of legislating or morally evaluating online activities is being precise in what you condemn and punish. Thus, our argument will proceed as follows. First, we will review the eventful but short history of revenge porn in the online world. Then we will do something that is clearly needed in the debates that assume "revenge porn" denotes one simple activity—we will offer a detailed typology of the different types of online posting behavior that could be classed as or related to "revenge porn." One will quickly see that not all revenge porn is explicitly and purely nonconsensual porn, and not all nonconsensual porn has the features or harms of revenge porn. Third, we will briefly examine some leading accounts of privacy and its relation to consent. This will ground our final section, where we examine how different types of revenge porn posting behaviors may or may not entail an ethical violation of privacy and consent.

The Rise of Revenge Pornography

The sordid roots of internet-based revenge porn can be traced to the creation of a website in 2010 by Hunter Moore called *IsAnyoneUp*. The 26-year-old Moore created a website as a way to more easily share nude pictures of a girlfriend with his friends. Over the first week, however, the site was visited by over 14,000 visitors. As the site grew in popularity, Moore established rules for photo submission that required the victim's "full name, profession, social-media profile, and city of residence" (Morris, 2012, October 11). This requirement, ostensibly to allow Moore to verify the ages of the people in the photos, had a more perfidious effect; the inclusion of the information with the pictorial posting made the illicit photos appear in any search engine results for the person's name (Hill, 2011, July 6). This inclusion of personal information with the photos brought with it an increase in the outrage against Moore and his site. When individuals featured on the site begged Moore to remove their images, their pleas were met with mocking answers such as "LOL," and a subsequent posting of their removal plea to the website (Dodero, 2012, April 4). His obstinacy in the face of these requests could be attributed to the strong stream of revenue it provided him. According to some sources, Moore earned between $8,000-$13,000 every month from his advertising revenues (Hill, 2012, April 5). By Moore's accounts, it reached as high as $30,000 a month (Morris, 2012, October 11). However, despite this financial boon, pressure opposing his site grew and Moore eventually sold it to *BullyVille*, an anti-bullying organization interested in shutting it down, in April of 2012 (Dodero, 2012, April 19). Although the removal of *IsAnyoneUp* represented a win for the opponents of revenge porn, the popularity of the site and its content had already spawned several similar operations.

Moore's revenge porn legacy continued with sites like *Pinkmeth* which follows its predecessor's form by posting nude photos above links to the Facebook, LinkedIn, and MySpace profiles of the victim. Similarly, regionally-focused sites like *Texxxan* host nude images that have been submitted by users. Rather than explicitly post the images with links to the victims' identifying information, sites like *Texxxan* provide a comment section wherein visitors can post the names, social network profiles, and other identifying information (Kuruvilla, 2013, February 8). These websites and the damage they cause their victims have made the concept of revenge porn a serious topic in recent legislation.

Though existing laws can help put pressure on those running the websites, the content of the sites is more difficult to censor. Vigorous use of tort laws and some criminal laws have made it possible to shut down these types of websites; however, due to the permanency of the internet, many of these previously posted photos can be collected and re-posted when the site re-emerges with a different web address (Roy, 2012, December 4). While Moore made his money from advertising revenue, Kevin Bollaert, webmaster of *YouGotPosted*, made money through "take-down" fees. When any of the victims approached and asked to be removed from the site, Bollaert would charge them up to $350 to remove the images. However, Bollaert was tried and convicted of 27 felony counts of identity theft and extortion in April of 2015 (Zabala & Stickney, 2016, July 14). While there is clearly legal precedence to prosecute those who host revenge porn sites, many argue that that the act of posting the sexual images should be illegal rather than merely the means through which the site makes its money.

Attention to the creation of legal measures directly targeting the posting of revenge porn content has increased in recent years. Law professors Mary Anne Franks and Danielle Keats Citron published an article in the *Wake Forest Law Review* in which they argued that "states, along with the federal government, should craft narrow statutes that prohibit the publication of nonconsensual pornography" (Citron & Franks, 2014). The authors define revenge porn, or as they note, nonconsensual pornography, as "the distribution of sexually graphic images of individuals without consent ... as well as images originally obtained with consent, usually within the context of a private or confidential relationship (e.g., images consensually given to an intimate partner who later distributes them without consent, popularly referred to as 'revenge porn'" (Citron & Franks, 2014). Citron and Franks argue that the damage caused by revenge porn posting on its victims warrants its explicit criminalization. The damage caused is not necessarily physical (although it can be linked to physical abuse or threats), but emotional and professional as well. According to Citron and Franks, the presence of a photograph with names and social networking information on a revenge porn site can encourage strangers to confront the victim in the real world. Similarly, in a study they cited, the victims of revenge porn can develop anxiety and depression as a result of the fear that the people who post sexually explicit and violent comments and emails might follow through in person. Additionally, the professional costs to victims of revenge porn can be tremendous. According to Citron and Franks, the prevalence of revenge porn sites in search engine results of the victims' names could preclude them from professional opportunities (Citron & Franks, 2014).

In an effort to penalize this practice, Franks developed a "Guide for Legislators" in which she laid out the reasons for developing a revenge porn law as well as guidelines for what the law should cover. While there is a lot of import placed on the narrowness of the law (i.e. making sure that the people to be targeted are those who knowingly used the revenge porn images and delineating what types of explicit images should be covered), a major aspect of Franks' guidelines for an effective law focused on limiting the importance of the motive of the act. For example, while some revenge porn is, in fact, motivated by a desire for revenge, Franks suggests that the law should encompass the instances where it is guided by a desire for economic gain or even if the images were intended to stay within a private group of friends. Citing laws on voyeurism, theft, and sexual abuse, Franks argues that "whether a perpetrator intends to distress a victim is beside the point: the relevant question is whether he or she intentionally engaged in nonconsensual conduct" (Franks, 2015). Franks' guide helped 21 states develop their own revenge porn laws; however, Franks suggests that "when you're at 21 states with revenge porn laws, what happens is you have 21 definitions" and a federal bill would help develop a "concrete, clear definition of what nonconsensual pornography is" (O'Hara, 2016, July 14). With Franks' guidance, on July 14, 2016, Representative Jackie Speier introduced the first attempt at a federal law criminalizing nonconsensual pornography, the Intimate Privacy Protection Act (IPPA).

The IPPA seeks to provide a clear demarcation of the rights to privacy and consent of sexually explicit images. The main text of the bill states its purpose: "to provide that it is unlawful to knowingly distribute a private, visual depiction of a person's intimate parts or of a person engaging in sexually explicit conduct, with reckless disregard for the person's lack of consent to the distribution, and for other purposes" (O'Hara, 2016, July 14). Notably, the language of the bill does not seek to criminalize any specific motive for the act, but rather the *nonconsensual* violation of the person's privacy. While many are optimistic about the impact the law would have on the revenge porn sites and the restitution it might bring to the victims, others are wary of the implications the federal law would have for future issues of freedom of speech. Emma Llansó from the Center for Democracy & Technology suggests that the language of the proposed bill "is broad and lacking in some of the key protections that would be necessary to ensure that a law like this wouldn't have an unintended effective of chilling constitutionally protected speech" (Clark-Flory, 2016, July 14). The main concern of most of the bill's detractors is that the broadness of the bill might allow a prosecutor to use the IPPA to try to censor a reporter or media outlet that circulates images that fit within the law. Additionally, according to law professor John Humbach, any attempt to control speech acts (including images) based on the content of the speech would be in direct violation of the First Amendment. Humbach argues that "the Court could only protect private-information interests at the direct expense of an *express* constitutional right" (Humbach, 2015). The issues raised by the new federal bill suggest a need for a clearer understanding of how people produce and engage with revenge porn images. Through a more nuanced understanding of the types of behaviors lumped into categories such as "revenge porn" or "nonconsensual porn," issues of consent and privacy can be more adequately explored.

What Exactly is Revenge or Nonconsensual Pornography?

All of the passionate rhetoric and calls for legislative action assume that we know exactly what we mean when we issue calls against "revenge porn" or "nonconsensual porn." We want to argue that there is actually a plethora of behaviors potentially existing in the category of revenge porn, and not all of them entail the same harms, culpability, or, as we will discuss, the same issues of consent and privacy. First, let us see how some leading advocates of criminalizing revenge porn—also discussed as nonconsensual pornography—define the term. Citron & Franks (2014: p. 1) stipulate that: "Nonconsensual pornography involves the distribution of sexually graphic images of individuals without their consent. This includes images originally obtained without consent (e.g., hidden recordings or recordings of sexual assaults) as well as images originally obtained with consent, usually within the context of a private or confidential relationship (e.g., images consensually given to an intimate partner who later distributes them without consent, popularly referred to as 'revenge porn')." This definition parses into two categories, images obtained through secret recordings or voyeurism and those obtained with consent (but not consent to publish outside of the relationship, presumably). There is no mention here of any diversity among *posting* behaviors online or on social media; it is simply assumed that the image content carries a consent-status, and that harm comes from distributing images with a negative consent status. In another attempt at a definition, Franks (2015, August 17) states that "Nonconsensual pornography refers to sexually explicit images disclosed without consent and for no legitimate purpose. The term encompasses material obtained by hidden cameras, consensually exchanged within a confidential relationship, stolen photos, and recordings of sexual assaults." Here the same idea is proffered—imagistic content that is simply "disclosed" that comes from knowing or unknowing subjects depicted within the content. A new aspect is added, however, that defines nonconsensual pornography as images that uphold two criteria—they lack consent (presumably to distribute to others) *and* they serve "no legitimate purpose." Of course, the latter clause is usually how people will describe the objections and actions of their opponents, so it must be further defined if there is to be a clear test of non-consensual but "legitimate" disclosures and non-consensual but "illegitimate" disclosures.

Both of these definitions of revenge porn might serve us well if we are fixated on the horrible case of one former relational partner attempting to harm another partner through the disclosure of sexual images online. They do not serve us well, however, when we start to ask specific questions about the different ways that this content can be *posted*, or how it can remain *identifiable* or linked to that real-life subject. In other words, these cursory delineations of the category of revenge porn do not do justice to the various ways that the simple-sounding act of "disclosure" can happen online, and they do not seriously interrogate what it means for an image to have negative consequences through its connection with that identifiable person. These are, however, vital points, since the whole crux of controlling a phenomenon like revenge porn rests on having an understanding of what exactly one is trying to control with laws and moral approbation. Building on the actual and potential differences in revenge porn noted in previous studies (e.g., Stroud, 2014), let us divide the category of revenge porn (or nonconsensual porn) into four variable dimensions: (1) the *source* of the content posted; (2) the *consent-status* of the material posted; (3) the *intent* of the agent doing the posting; and (4) *identifying features* resident in the imagistic content. These can be found in Table 2.1. We will then describe each one of these aspects in further detail to arrive at a clear specification of the range of potential revenge or nonconsensual pornography practices in the online world.

The first dimension of revenge porn posting behavior involves where it came from prior to a given act of posting. This can be labeled as the *source* dimension. Did it come from the poster's actions, such as the use of their camera? Or was it sent to them from someone else—a relational partner or other conversant—who created that content? Thus, the source dimension can be divided into *poster*-created and *other*-created content. Some of this other-created content could be from a relational partner, or it could be from online conversational partners that send one nude images, as appeared to be the case in some of the major revenge porn sites (Peterson, 2013, February 18). One could also stumble across such content online, with no attributable source evident, of course. Call this material simply *online* content, since its story of authorship is unclear or hidden. This is what one might find if, per the second case mentioned in the introduction to this chapter, one googled a random term in an image search. Who exactly knows where the resulting images came from?

TABLE 2.1 Types of Revenge/Nonconsensual Porn Posting Behaviors

Content Source	Consent Status	Poster Intent	Identifying Content
Self	Granted	Praise subject	Known identifiers
Other	Not granted	Harm subject	Unknown identifiers
Online	Uncertain	Other intentions	No possible identifiers

The second dimension of revenge porn posting involves what we will call the *consent status* of the images. We will discuss consent more in the following sections, as this is a vital point about the ethics of posting such material. For now, however, it will help any analysis of the issue to be clear about the range of consent statuses that such material can possess. There is a tendency in how partisans talk about revenge porn images as coming *with* consent or *without* consent to be shared outside of the original instance of sharing. This is misleading in its simplification of the issue. First of all, the image is simply the image. One cannot look at an image and see the consent granted to its use. Thus, consent status is something behind and beyond the specific image, and it lay in the people involved in the transaction. An image can therefore be exchanged with *consent granted* for further distribution by the giving partner, or it can be exchanged *without consent being granted* for further distribution. Furthermore, the consent status of a given image could be *uncertain*. This is likely to be the case when an image is found online, or when the parties do not openly talk about the limits of future distribution. We will return to these issues in the following sections.

The third dimension that varies in revenge porn posting behaviors is the *intention* of the posting agent. Why do they post this material? In many cases, it is to harm or shame a former relational partner (Stroud, 2014). Another possibility is that someone posts material to *praise* the subject, either in their actions, character, or more likely, physical appearance. This appears to be a common practice, at least early on, in the history of revenge porn sites; Hunter Moore, if we are to trust his early media pronouncements, indicated that around 50% of his site's submissions were from individuals seeking their own quick internet fame (Hill, 2012). Regardless of the accuracy or veracity of Moore's claims, we do see conceptual room for the intention to praise the posted subject—especially when we move into content simply found on the internet (*online* sources) and shared. There can be *other* intentions, of course, some connected with posting for entertainment value or posting connected to financial gains (as seemed to be the motive in many revenge porn sites).

The most pernicious effects of revenge porn, clearly acknowledged in cases such as the one cited in the introduction to this chapter, do not come simply from the image existing or being seen by others. The worst harms—threats, stalking, targeted harassment, family embarrassment, and financial or job loss—all turn on damaging content being connected to an identifiable individual. Thus, we can discern another dimension of revenge porn posting: the presence and type of *identifying content* resident in the image or along with the image. There are millions of sexual or nude images online at any given moment, but when a known person is identified as connected to *that* image, and when an audience exists for that image, harm can occur. Usually this is through contacting real-life people connected to that individual and sharing the embarrassing image. Many posters want this outcome, so they post some amount of identifying material along with the image. This can include a range of information about the subject: first name, first name with last initial, full name, address, town, email address, employer's address or contact information, family member information, and even their social security number. It is important to stress that various sites and webmasters post various amounts of this information; some are rather minimal in what identifying information they post (Stroud, 2014). These bits of information can be called *known identifiers*, since they are attached to the image and connect the depicted person to an identifiable individual who putatively does not want the world to see them nude. As previous research has made clear, sometimes the crowd-sourced aspects of the internet communities surrounding the posting of revenge porn content supply the identifying information. In the usual story, the spurned relational partner posts the content and identifies the subject; in the wild west of the internet, however, often content is posted and the amorphous, unknown crowd then comments upon it, supplying more and more detail about the subject (Stroud, 2014). This is often due to others recognizing the individual in the picture, either through their face, objects in the background (e.g., a diploma on the wall, name tag, etc.), or other identifying marks (distinctive tattoos, a recognizable dorm room, etc.). Often these marks become useful through the crowd-sourced, mass agency of online users combining their powers of identification and inference. Thus, someone could post an image with no known identifying content, but still leave room for future identification through others noticing heretofore *unknown identifiers* resident in the image. As facial "tagging" and recognition software advances, one could argue that many pictures could contain such unrealized clues to the subject's real-life identity. Conceivably, one could post a photo with *no possible identifiers* in it; perhaps this would be the case in a close up shot of a body part with no identifying marks or background objects visible. Such non-identifying shots could be used for the purposes of revenge porn by posting them next to a non-nude image of some identifiable person, thereby making the visual argument that that person was the same person that was nude in the second, non-identifiable picture featuring nudity. This contingency, like many of the permutations mentioned previously are all ignored in most passionate discussion of revenge porn in favor of the standard "relationship gone bad" story discussed in the introduction. Yet one thing is clear: revenge porn is not one behavior, but instead a cluster of activities that vary in certain dimensions. What impact will the realization of its complexity have on our discussion of its ethical harms?

Privacy, Consent, and Control

The former discussion of the various ways that revenge or nonconsensual porn posting could occur is necessary to make sure that we acknowledge the complexity of this damaging phenomena. It will also aid us in talking about what kinds of postings lead to what kinds of harm or ethical violations. Since advocates tend to monolithically portray "revenge porn" as a breach of privacy and consent, it will help if we examine some relevant theories of privacy and then examine what permutations from this typology involve such breaches of trust. Privacy is a difficult concept, one with a clear basis in tort law but no clear statement in the constitution. It is, more importantly for our discussion, clearly an ethical concept—most would recognize the moral value in respecting some notion of privacy for individuals. When discussing definitions of privacy, it is necessary to parse out potentially occluding aspects of the concept. The most crucial of these is the distinction between normative theories of privacy and descriptive theories of privacy. Briefly stated, normative theories deal with privacy as a moral claim that one has on others to prevent them from doing certain things, whereas descriptive theories deal with privacy as a condition that one has or does not have. A well developed theory of privacy would be able to satisfy cases of both normative and descriptive privacy concerns.

Many authors, both philosophers and lawyers, have offered theories of privacy that take into account these aspects to varying degrees of satisfaction. Herman Tavani categorized previous theories of privacy into four main categories of perspective: non-intrusion, seclusion, control, and limitation. The first two of these categories represent what he calls "accessibility privacy," that is, privacy is viewed as the state of "being let alone" or "being alone" respectively (Tavani, 2007). While both of these views of privacy were, at one time, aimed at the preeminent concerns of the day (such as photographic intrusion into one's private home), with recent technological advances such as the internet these privacy concerns have shifted toward informational privacy. Theories aimed at an understanding of informational privacy concerns are largely grouped into the categories of control and limitation and, as such, will be given more of a focus in this discussion.

The control theory of privacy is mainly concerned with the ability of one to be able to withhold or divulge information about oneself. That is, "one has privacy if and only if one has control over information about oneself" (Tavani, 2007, p. 7). Unlike previous theories of privacy, the control theory is not predicated on one being removed from all interactions wherein one might divulge private information. According to Charles Fried, "[privacy] is not simply an absence of information about us in the minds of others, rather it is the control over information we have about ourselves" (Fried, 1990, p. 54). The control theory of privacy suggests that true privacy is the maintenance of one's own information rather than someone else controlling it. While certainly agreeable from a general perspective, this theory begins to reveal some weaknesses when examined more closely. For example, Tavani suggests that the control theory leaves unclear two main aspects of a comprehensive theory of privacy, namely: "(a) *which kinds of personal information* one can expect to have control over, and (b) *how much control* one can expect to have over one's personal information" (Tavani, 2007, p. 7). These questions suggest an issue with both the normative and descriptive aspects of the control theory. When one is in public, there is, in a sense, a loss of control over the divulging of personal information; a passerby can glean your physical characteristics as well as hazard a fair guess at your socio-economic status and gender. From a control theory perspective, these could be considered violations of privacy.

The second category of information privacy theories, the limitation account, suggests that "one has privacy when access to information about oneself is limited or restricted in certain contexts" (Tavani, 2007, p. 9). This view of privacy differs from control in that it is not focused on one purposefully withholding or divulging private information, but rather on the "limitation of others' access" to certain private information (Gavison, 1980). Although this theory of privacy provides an important characteristic of contingency to the concept of privacy, the focus solely on limiting others' access implies that withholding one's information from others is the only way to maintain privacy. As Tavani argues, "in the account of privacy offered in the limitation theory, privacy can easily be confused with secrecy" (Tavani, 2007, p. 9). While these two theories of privacy provide an important foundation for the understanding of informational privacy, taken separately, they are inadequate for a comprehensive exploration of the concept. As such, Tavani proffers a synthetic model of privacy that combines aspects of the two in order to create a theory that more effectively conceptualizes privacy.

The model Tavani expands upon is the Restricted Access/Limited Control (RACL) theory of privacy. The RACL theory of privacy, initially developed by James Moor, suggests that one has privacy "in a situation with regard to others if and only if in that situation the individual or group is ... protected from intrusion, interference, and information access by others" (Moor, 1997, p. 30). A key word in the definition for both Moor and Tavani is "situation." According to Moor, the term was used "deliberately because it is broad enough to cover many kinds of privacy: private *locations*, ... private *relationships*, ... and private *activities*" (Moor, 1997, p. 30). The broadness of the term allows for the privacy to be consistent both descriptively and normatively. Though from this perspective of the carving up of situational privacy, RACL may seem as merely an expanded form of the limitation theory, both Tavani and Moor suggest that limitation is not enough; people need to have some control over their private information. Rather than being the basis for the theory of privacy, control serves as the way that the privacy itself is managed (Tavani, 2007).

Proposing a similar theory of privacy, philosopher Adam Moore suggests that one way that control functions is through a giving up of control. Moore argues that "when one gives up control and yields access in an intimate relationship ... one is giving up privacy within a limited domain" and this giving up control is still a function of privacy (Moore, 2008, p. 415). This relinquishing of control, however, is not the end of the issue; the issue of relinquishing control is not a binary operation, but rather like Tavani and Moor, is dependent on the context. For example, "the secret shared between lovers is private in one sense and not in another—this secret is private in the sense of being held in confidence between two individuals and not known by others; it is not private in the sense of being known by a second person" (Moore, 2008, p. 416). The private information does not turn from private to public by virtue of being whispered to a partner, but rather is the controlled divulgence of still-private information. Additionally, Moore suggests that a "use-dimension" is necessary for the understanding of his theory of control. He argues that "even if someone has justifiably accessed sensitive personal information about another, it does not follow that any use of this information is permitted" (Moore, 2008, p. 418). For Moore, being allowed access to the private information of another does not make that private information yours to disclose.

In Tavani and Moor's RACL explicitly and Moore's control theory implicitly, one way that privacy is managed through control is through the concept of *consent*. Consent, as a means of privacy management, allows "what without it would be an invasion of privacy" (Tavani & Moor, 2001, p. 8). For example, the inclusion of consent as a means of privacy management allows for someone to invite a stranger into his or her home or car without it being a normative violation of privacy. While it is an important aspect of the RACL's management of privacy, the invocation of the concept of consent also brings with it some theoretical issues.

Consent, historically, has been broken down into two discrete types: express consent and tacit consent. Express consent reflects the most explicit form of consent. When one signs a document or asserts one's agreement to do or not do something, that is express consent. Express consent and tacit consent both incur a form of obligation. When I consent to holding a meeting, I am expected to follow through on that obligation. According to David Archard, "those to whom I give the consent thereby acquire rights or legitimate expectations in respect of what it is I have agreed to do or allowed to be done" (Archard, 1998, p. 3). By giving consent, either express or tacit, a certain obligation is transferred that should shape the foreseen action possibilities of the other party.

Tacit consent, or implicit consent, is the unspoken or assumed consent of a person to a course of action or an idea. This is the more problematic notion of consent, since it is not always clear what is being consented to and in what fashion. For instance, the most notable philosophical figure associated with the concept of tacit consent is John Locke, who in his *Two Treatises of Government* argued that by virtue of reaping the benefits of civilized society, one has given their general consent to be held to the laws governing that society (Locke, 1988). Such an approach to when consent is given tacitly faces some obvious problems in the case of confronting injustices by legally authorized governmental agencies, for instance. The governing idea behind the general concept of tacit consent is that when one partakes in an activity, one is consenting to the "rules of the game," whatever those may be. Archard in his discussion of tacit consent argues that "tacit consent can be and is given in those instances where there is a clear agreed convention of which the person is aware and which permits the consent of that person to be inferred from her deliberately chosen action" (Archard, 1998, p. 9). That is to say, tacit consent can be seen as a form of consent only when the rules of the game are known by all participants. Thus, a sense of *publicity* is still vital to implicit consent—parties must know how and when consent is tacitly given, even when there is no formal specification of the action of consenting. If one party does not know the rules of implicit consent procedures, then it is unclear if the other can bind them to these rules in the same ways as in an explicitly worked out situation of consent.

The Complexities of Consent in Revenge Porn

Revenge porn implicates a powerful mix of harm, privacy interests, and issues of the control over one's own image. Since the second section of this chapter illustrated the conditional presence of harm with revenge porn—namely, not all postings are or must be made with known identifiers present—let us sidestep that consideration in this final section. Not all that we would want to classify as "non-consensual porn" has the harm of *identifiable* revenge porn. We will take advocates at their word that "consent always matters, whether the sexual activity is physical or virtual, and there is simply no excuse for disregarding it" (Franks, 2016). Consent to access the material and then do something with the realm of the private seems to be the most important matter, above and beyond the presence of actual identifying marks connected to a digital image; indeed, Franks (2014) likens revenge porn more to actual situations of nonconsensual contact or assault than a mere privacy violation: "Non-consensual pornography is more accurately conceptualized as a form of sexual abuse than as an invasion of privacy" (p. 10). This type of approach draws heavily from our notions of consent in sexual activity; lack of consent to a specifiable or predictable course of action between two parties is what renders such activity sexual assault. Notice the present-focused notion of this level of consent: both individuals are present, the consent negotiation is or should be in the present, and the damage to sidestepping consent would be immediate. The immediacy also renders the choices and consequence clear: this person consented or didn't consent to this sort of action. Pursuing the action in the face of non-consent is what makes the action sexual assault. The case is seemingly different with objects shared between agents. With images online, we are dealing with objects separable from dialogues of consent, and consequences are often remote and varied (think of the various levels of identifying content, intentions, and so forth explored in previous sections). Consent is no longer attached to an immediate situation, or to individual bodies; consent is not always clear or present in the online world of images and "produser" content supplied by various online agents at vastly different times (Bruns, 2007). Even explicit contracts behind a certain image's production or distribution are usually flagged with symbols or rights-verbiage, highlighting the fact that an image in itself does not betray hints of its consent status. In other words, consent is not a simple issue in revenge or nonconsensual porn, nor is it inherently connected with the content of most images. We will suggest that instead of postulating simple notions of consent as obvious in any given image, there is a continuum of consent that suggests itself in various contexts, although this is far from determinate in its conceptual scope. This final section will explore four cases to show where consent-speak clarifies matters about the type of violation that occurs with revenge porn posting, and where it becomes difficult to see a simple and consistent account of consent behind revenge porn per se.

Let us take the case of computer-aided acquisition of revenge porn content, and its subsequent posting online. These could be the cases of hackers breaking into one's cloud backup drive to acquire photos (as occurred in the recent hack of celebrity images), or the cases of revenge porn webmasters "catfishing" adults seeking amorous relations through online postings, as seemed to be the case with some websites (e.g., Peterson, 2013, February 18). The former example is easy to diagnose—it involved individuals using their control over private information (e.g., images) to safeguard them by placing them in a putatively secure location. They used their powers of choice to take some steps, though perhaps not all they could, to maintain their control over this information. One could take this as not granting consent to hackers; indeed, there was no interaction with these hackers in the first place in which consent talk could even arise. The second case—call it the *catfishing case*—is more difficult, since it causes us to envision this sort of scenario: two individuals meet through some sort of online posting or forum. They form some sort of online relationship, but one (according to our example) is pretending to be online something he or she is not in real life. The other individual sends that person nude images, perhaps in a flirting or hopeful manner, and the "catfish" then uses those images in a fashion that the former most likely did not anticipate nor would approve of if given the chance. Do we have a clear status of consent or non-consent here? Consent to what, and explicit refusal of consent to what? The original sender might only know of or imagine what they should have made clear as forbidden after it is too late. What magnifies the complexities here are that some of the webmaster-catfished examples appear to not have been long-term online relationships; they seemed to involve someone sending out photos without many relational guarantees about the other person (e.g., Peterson, 2013, February 18). Such a case seems to involve an individual using the control over their private information (viz., images of their body) to relinquish some control over such information—indeed, they barely know their online respondent, yet they have shared private and potentially sensitive material. Unless they have uttered something along the lines of "do not share this image with others," it is difficult to imagine that their new online partner is bound by any clear rules of tacit or explicit consent. The status of consent with this content is uncertain, although one might think that an empathetic agent would see that they would not want this information shared. But individuals are all different, and the fact that this person shared the image with someone who was basically a stranger makes matters murky in this case. It seems to be a case of using control over your private information to give up such control in a situation that inclines toward further risk.

Let us imagine a second example, labeled the *false consent case*. One of the per-plexing gifts of the online world is that it allows for malleable identities, which are used in the pursuit of good or harm as determined by those donning them (Stroud, 2016; Stroud & Pye, 2013). Similar to cases of fake advertisements that led to sexual assaults (e.g., Browning, 2010; Correll, 2010), we can imagine a case involving an ex-partner or even a random stranger online pretending to be the subject in nude images that they are encouraging others to spread. Whereas the "real" subject of the photos may not agree to (or know about) the potential for distribution, other online agents hear an appeal to "please distribute my photos; I like it!" This seems like consent to use their control over their private informa-tion to relinquish future control over its use, and unless the other online agents have some reason to be skeptical of the poster's identity, this seems like the giving of consent. We can imagine some pseudo-subjects being very convincing in such a ruse, and surely we have as background information that there are all types of individuals and desires in every corner of the online world. Yet we would not wish for this type of distribution, as it involves some sort of deception. This deception is not evident to the other online agents, and hence shows us that consent and digital images are clearly separable in problematic ways. Pictures do not always come with a ready consent status, and some that do could be faked consent statuses.

A third case that falls within the realm of revenge or nonconsensual porn sketched above can be called the *online find case*. This is the case that is made pos-sible by the objective nature of the imagistic content: one could simply find a nude image online, containing or not containing identifiers of the subject's iden-tity, and repost it in another online venue. Let us assume the most difficult case: the reposting occurs *without* known identifiers being relayed in the reposting. This is not the classic case of revenge porn, but it may be an instance of noncon-sensual porn, since the depicted subject may not know of or consent to this form of distribution. The ethical question at stake, however, is this—does the indi-vidual doing the reposting do so without consent? This example shows the limi-tations to thinking of consent as an either/or question. This image is now removed from the person or interaction that led to its creation and initial distri-bution, and it is unclear what its consent status is from its objective features—one cannot tell what a depicted subject is thinking or consenting to just from the details of the picture. As Emma Llansó points out about revenge porn legislation focusing on consent, "The idea that people generally using the web will be able to anticipate the mindset of a person depicted in an image is just difficult if not impossible to achieve. … There are many explicit images available online and I think it's fair to say it's a difficult call which one of those were initially consensu-ally posted online" (Clark-Flory, 2016, July 14). The online find case is a case of uncertain consent status, and we would have trouble ethically condemning a re-poster (not engaging in a course of stalking or harassment, of course). Just as we do not find problematic the online sharing, linking to, and forwarding the vast majority of content on social media that does not state explicitly its status as shareable, we would not fault someone for sharing the "sexy elbow" image search results from the example in our introduction to this chapter. Yet a strong reading of consent as inherently and always *attached* to the content of online content would render that view incorrect. This case makes us see that consent is something between persons, but images online are often removed from personal meanings and agreements. The case of found online images that perhaps lacked consent in their origins may no longer contain any hints of lacking such a consent status at a removed future time, thus rendering their consent status as uncertain.

The final case, one that fits the typical case noted previously, can be labeled as the *relational revenge case*. This is the case that starts with imagistic content supplied by one's own actions (taking a picture of a relational partner) or through the actions of another (one's partner sending them an image). The relationship fails, and one partner posts these images without the explicit consent of the other party to do so. We must note that even though this is the archetypical case highlighted by advocates for the criminalization of revenge porn, it is by no means the only type of case related to or contained in the concept of "nonconsensual porn." In many of the relational revenge cases, known identifiers can be highlighted in the original posting to maximize harm to the partner whom the posting agent believes spurned them, but this is not essential to the use of this content or to our question here. The images by themselves could be shared without consent. Let us assume that the subject of the images freely sent these pictures to the other partner. What was the consent status of the images shared? They consented to the sharing of these images, but perhaps only with that partner—indeed, they purposely emailed or texted those images to just that person, and not to a wider range of viewers.

This is a vexing issue, as it appears to conflate two different concerns in privacy theory—access and use. Moore (2008) asserts that consent to access does not equate to consent over use:

> Privacy also includes a right over the use of bodies, locations, and personal information. If access is granted accidentally or otherwise, it does not follow that any subsequent use, manipulation, or sale of the good in question is justified. In this way, privacy is both a shield that affords control over access or inaccessibility and a kind of use and control right that yields justified authority over specific items—like a room or personal information. (p. 420)

No convincing argument is given for this very general claim, however. As it is, it seems to go too far. Suppose one has a large collection of "Precious Moments" statues in their home that may prove embarrassing if joked about in certain contexts. It is clearly a violation of one's control over personal space and information if an agent breaks into your house, observes or photographs this collection, and then proceeds to joke about it to others later. Yet it is far from clear that the same violation of privacy has occurred if you invite the agent into your house, where they observe your statue collection. Are they not allowed to talk about what they saw while inside your house at later times? This would be a strong ethical principle, something along the lines of consenting to one predictable line of action binds one to foreseeable limitations of actions in other, later contexts. Thus, it would seem to entail that my allowing you access to my home would not allow you to use any information gained in such a dinner event, say, in later conversations with others. That seems too strong, as any event in a potentially restricted area would then constrain all future speech directly or indirectly building on or using information gained from such events. As Humbach (2015) notes, this sort of principle rendered in criminal revenge porn laws would serve as a prior restraint on speech—consent to see something at time x strongly prevents one from talking about it at a later time in any fashion whatsoever.

Revenge porn criminalization advocates typically respond to such examples with the supposed counter-examples of protected private medical and financial (e.g., credit card information) data (see Citron & Franks, 2014); these are not exactly the same thing, since they bind specific individuals (doctors, merchants) through explicit contracts understood by each party. In the realm of the relational revenge case, it is unclear that such a contract has been enunciated, or that standards and actions are publically assumed enough to warrant a claim of implicit consent being given. If a partner has signed an explicit contract about future use of an image, our condemnation can clearly follow because it is clear that they and the sending partner were explicit about the consequences and actions that were about to happen and that never could happen. But relationships rarely operate at the level of clarity and explicitness as medical and financial relationships, and people assume, think, or demand a range of differing things. Perhaps we can ethically fault the future sharing if the partner verbally enunciated limitations on future actions, and the receiving partner agreed to such limitations, as this would imply their giving up control only in a specified limited way.

The contested conflux between *access* and *control* over use becomes murkier when we think of the principles that are being emphasized with a straightforward ethical denunciation in the case of shared images being used in later courses of revenge. We clearly would not want to rule it a vicious action if one gets a gift from some agent, and then later complains about the cheapness of this gift to a third party and remarks on the flawed character of the original gift giver. There seems to be no clear principle that implies continued control over *future* use in such a way by a gift giver, even if the gift giver thought far enough ahead to think of such a critical use as a possible consequence to their act of gift giving. On the other hand, the intimate images in question are most likely—but not always—shared with some idea that if they were public, they may immediately provoke embarrassment or harm, hence the typically targeted sharing. But such a reticence may apply to other information shared in relationships, secrets that we would not want to say bind agents forever in all possible ways. In discussing how revenge porn statutes are content-based restrictions on speech, Rachel Budde (2015) brings up similar issues—the actual and proposed laws do not assume a consent-based binding on the future sharing of pictures of a relational subject smoking an illicit drug, for instance. Sharing such a picture of illicit drug use could be damaging, but it is not clear that simply sharing it within a close friendship entails that both parties know and acknowledge a future control over its use. Perhaps one friend will immediately change their view of the friendship, and speak of the cause, supplying this photo as some sort of proof of their claims of their ex-partner being an addict. Perhaps the image or its depicted action will become relevant to conversation later, when the friends have drifted apart and one no longer cares about the former's trust or private hobbies or activities. Where is the ethical dividing line that separates assumed consent—meant as strict control over future use of some information or image—from situations free from control and that allow using past experience of some relationship in future situations that one judges as calling for such interventions? Explicit or implicit-but-clear situations of contract and consent to specific courses of action might address this problem, but simply claiming that relationships by themselves ethically bind participants over damaging information is too hasty a judgment. Consent may matter in relationships, but only when it reaches the public clarity between the parties over exactly what is and is not allowed, now and in a specified period in the future.

Conclusion

This chapter has shown the complex nature of the phenomena denoted by terms such as "revenge porn" or "nonconsensual pornography." Not all cases of revenge porn are clearly nonconsensual porn, nor are all cases of nonconsensual porn characterized by the harm we think of when we think of revenge porn. These terms do not point at one case, nor at one type of behavior or set of consequences. Some of this behavior is clearly awful, and has significant harms to the subjects of pictures posted on the internet along with identifying information. But as we have illustrated, not all cases of revenge porn involve known identifiers being posted, nor do all cases of posting or reposting photos without clear consent involve explicit violations of consent. There is a vast quantity of content that comes with uncertain consent status, or even misleading consent indicators in the case of online pseudo-identities. Even in the clearest and most typical case revenge porn criminalization advocates point toward—the case of relational revenge—issues of consent are far from clear. Consent assumes a binary decision in most of its applications, as well as a maintained level of control over a situation, but in many of these sharing instances, future uses and limitations are not spelled out nor are they all under the control of the image giver. In some cases, the right to have control allows you the power to give up that control and its accompanying protections. What we must avoid is the binary thinking that all of this rests on clear, either/or matters of consent we import from discussions of sexual assault; the removed nature of objectified content such as online images entails that many instances will have an unknown or undetermined consent status, whereas the question of a present and immediate physical advance will be settled with consent or no consent being given. Regardless of how the legislative maneuvers end up in regard to criminalizing revenge porn, we maintain the view that it is misleading to characterize this harmful phenomenon as always and everywhere a simple violation of privacy and consent. The online world is much too creative, cruel, and imaginative for any of its trends to be so uniform and one-dimensional.

References

Archard, D. (1998). *Sexual consent*. Oxford, Eng.; Colo.: Westview Press.

Browning, W. (2010, October 11). Wyoming Craigslist rape survivor rebuilds her life, plans for marriage. *Caspar Star-Tribune*. Retrieved from: http://trib.com/news/local/wyoming-craigslist-rape-survivor-rebuilds-her-life-plans-for-marriage/article_e4651a43-95ab-52b7-a62a-66b8dfc70571.html.

Bruns, A. (2007, June 14). Produsage: Towards a Broader Framework for User-Led Content Creation. Paper presented at Creativity & Cognition Conference, Washington, DC.

Budde, R. (2015). Taking the Sting out of Revenge Porn: Using Criminal Statutes to Safeguard Sexual Autonomy in the Digital Age, *Georgetown Journal of Gender & Law*, 16, 407–444.

Citron, D. K., & Franks, M. A. (2014). Criminalizing Revenge Porn. *Wake Forest Law Review*, 345(49), 1–38.

Clark-Flory, T. (2016, July 14). Bill that would make revenge porn federal crime to be introduced. *Vocativ*. Retrieved from http://www.vocativ.com/339362/federal-revenge-porn-bill/

Congresswoman Speier, Fellow Members of Congress Take on Nonconsensual Pornography, AKA Revenge Porn" (2016, July 14). Retrieved from https://speier.house.gov/media-center/press-releases/congresswoman-speier-fellow-members-congress-take-nonconsensua

Correll, D. (2010, January 11). Former boyfriend used Craigslist to arrange woman's rape, police say. *Los Angeles Times*. Retrieved from http://articles.latimes.com/2010/jan/11/nation/la-na-rape-craigslist11-2010jan11.

Dodero, C. (2012, April 4). Hunter Moore makes a living screwing you. *The Village Voice*. Retrieved from http://www.villagevoice.com/2012-04-04/news/revenge-porn-hunter-moore-is-anyone-up/

Dodero, C. (2012, April 19). Bullyville has taken over Hunter Moore's Is Anyone Up? *The Village Voice*. Retrieved from http://blogs.villagevoice.com/runninscared/2012/04/bullyville_isanyoneup.php

Franks, M. A. (2015). *Drafting an effective "revenge porn" law: A guide for legislators*. Retrieved from https://www.cybercivilrights.org/wp-content/uploads/2016/09/Guide-for-Legislators-9.16.pdf

Franks, M. A. (2016, July 18). Mary Anne Franks, Congresswoman Jackie Speier Introduces Federal Bill against NCP. Retrieved from http://www.cybercivilrights.org/fed-bill-intro/

Fried, C. (1990). Privacy: A Rational Context. In M. D. Ermann, M. B. Williams, & C. Gutiérrez Carranza (Eds.), *Computers, Ethics, and Society* (pp. 50–63). New York: Oxford University Press.

Gavison, R. (1980). Privacy and the Limits of the Law. *Yale Law Review*, *89*, 421–471.

Greenfield, Scott H. (2016, July 17). Beware The Loyal Opposition, ACLU Edition. Retrieved from https://blog.simplejustice.us/2016/07/17/beware-the-loyal-opposition-aclu-edition/

Hill, K. (2011, July 6). Revenge porn with a facebook twist. *Forbes*. Retrieved from http://www.forbes.com/sites/kashmirhill/2011/07/06/revenge-porn-with-a-facebook-twist/

Hill, K. (2012, April 5). Why we find Hunter Moore and his "identity porn" site, IsAnyoneUp, so fascinating. *Forbes*. Retrieved from http://www.forbes.com/sites/kashmirhill/2012/04/05hunter-moore-of-isanyoneup-wouldnt-mind-making-some-money-off-of-a-suicide

Humbach, J. A. (2015). The Constitution and Revenge Porn. *Pace Law Review, 35*(1), 215–260.

Kuruvilla, C. (2013, February 8). Revenge porn curators defend their x-rated websites. *New York Daily News*. Retrieved from http://www.nydailynews.com/news/national/minds-revenge-porn-curators-article-1.1259114

Locke, J. (1988). *Two Treatises of Government*. Cambridge, UK; New York: Cambridge University Press.

Moor, J. (1997). Towards a Theory of Privacy in the Information Age. *Computers and Society, 27*(3), 27–32.

Morris, A. (2012, October 11). Hunter Moore: The most hated man on the internet. *Rolling Stone*. Retrieved from http://www.rollingstone.com/culture/news/the-most-hated-man-on-the-internet-20121113

O'Hara, M. E. (2016, July 14). How a new federal ban on revenge porn could change the lives of survivors. *The Daily Dot*. Retrieved from http://www.dailydot.com/irl/federal-revenge-porn-bill-introduced/

Peterson, H. (2013, February 18) Revenge porn website operator accused of "catfishing" to trick woman into sending him nude photos so he can upload to site. *Daily Mail*. Retrieved from: http://www.dailymail.co.uk/new s/article-2280598/Revenge-porn-website-operator-accused-catfishing-trick-woman-sending-nude-photos-upload-site.html.

Revenge Porn: Misery Merchants, *The Economist,* July 5, 2014.

Ronneburger, (2009). Sex, Privacy, and Webpages: Creating a Legal Remedy for Victims of Porn 2.0, *Syracuse Science and Technology Law Reporter, 21, 1–35.*

Roy, J. (2012, December 4). The battle over revenge porn: Can Hunter Moore, the web's vilest entrepreneur, be stopped? *Betabeat*. Retrieved from http://www.betabeat.com/2012/12/the-battle-over-revenge-porn-can-hunter-moore-the-webs-vilest-entrepreneur-be-stopped

Stroud, S. R. (2014). The Dark Side of the Online Self: A Pragmatist Critique of the Growing Plague of Revenge Porn. *Journal of Mass Media Ethics, 29*(3), 168–183.

Stroud, S. R. (2016). "Be a Bully to Beat a Bully": Twitter Ethics, Online Identity, and the Culture of Quick Revenge. In A. Davisson & P. Booth (eds.), *Controversies in Digital Ethics* (pp. 264–278). London: Bloomsbury Press.

Stroud, S. R. & Pye, D. (2013). Kant on Unsocial Sociability and the Ethics of Social Blogging. In M. E. Drumwright (ed.) *New Agendas in Communication: Ethics in Communication Professions* (pp. 41–64). New York: Routledge.

Tavani, H. (2007). Philosophical Theories of Privacy: Implications for an Adequate Online Privacy Policy. *Metaphilosophy, 38*(1), 1–22.

Tavani, H., & Moor, J. (2001). Privacy Protection, Control of Information and Privacy-enhancing Technologies. *Computers and Society, 31*(1), 6–11.

Zabala, L., & Stickney, R. (2016, July 14). "Revenge Porn" defendant sentenced to 18 years. *NBC San Diego*. Retrieved from http://www.nbcsandiego.com/news/local/Kevin-Bollaert-Revenge-Porn-Sentencing-San-Diego-298603981.html

3

POWERFUL BULLIES AND SILENT VICTIMS IN CYBER SPACE

The Darkness of Social Media

*Marla B. Royne, Claudia Rademaker,
and Gerard E. Kelly III*

Barely a teenager at 13 years old, Amanda Todd (NoBullying.com, n.d.; http://
www.amandatoddlegacy.org/) was contacted by a stranger on social media.
Amanda responded to his communication, unaware he was a 35-year-old man.
Through his charm and flattering nature, this man easily gained Amanda's trust,
convincing her to pose topless online and in front of a camera. This man subsequently blackmailed Amanda by threatening to circulate the picture online unless
Amanda was willing to expose herself even more. The image soon went viral,
resulting in a major cyberbullying attack against Amanda. She spiraled quickly into
depression, and began abusing alcohol and drugs; she also started cutting herself.

Although Amanda's family subsequently moved numerous times to other
states, the stranger always found her. He even created a Facebook profile using
Amanda's topless picture as the profile image and contacted Amanda's newest
classmates causing a continuous onslaught of bullying, both online and in real life.
This harassment contributed to two unsuccessful suicide attempts. People even
posted abusive messages on Facebook about the failed suicide attempts. Amanda
eventually posted a video on YouTube, using flash cards to tell her story and
asserting her strength. But on October 10, 2012, one month after the release of
her video, Amanda attempted suicide one more time. Unfortunately, she was
successful. Even after her death, the online taunting continued, with comments
such as "you deserved this" posted on Facebook.

As an 18-year-old freshman at Rutgers University, Tyler Clementi had just
come to terms with being gay. His school roommate, 20-year-old Dharun Ravi,
was clearly intolerant of Tyler's sexuality. Dharun secretly streamed a live webcam
featuring Tyler engaged with a boyfriend in their dorm room while tweeting his
friends and encouraging them to watch the live stream. Now the subject of ridicule and embarrassment, Tyler committed suicide the next day by jumping off

the George Washington Bridge into the Hudson River (Foderaro, 2010; https://tylerclementi.org/tylers-story/).

These stories are just two of the countless examples of the most devastating effects of cyberbullying worldwide. In today's world of advanced technology, people can interact with others at almost any place at any time, spreading information (true or false) with virtually no geographical borders. This increasing accessibility can be viewed as positive and in line with democracy where freedom of speech is a crucial element. Moreover, there is little doubt the Internet is a useful and helpful social outlet for people, particularly for individuals who may be physically or emotionally distanced from others. Social media both enables and helps keep people socially connected, while online support groups can unite individuals with common physical or emotional issues. Anyone with Internet access can share common interests and lifestyles such as cooking, sports, human sexuality, or a wide range of hobbies. Unfortunately, however, as the stories of Amanda and Tyler demonstrate, a dark side of social media exists, and one that has the most extreme negative consequences—suicide. This dark side is the ability of individuals to bully others through electronic means—and often anonymously.

Powerful Bullies and Silent Victims

Bullying as a phenomenon has been studied ever since Heinemann (1972) first described the concept of bullying. Today, a solid body of literature exists on traditional face-to-face bullying. The newer cyberbullying phenomenon linked to the rapid and widespread expansion of high-speed Internet access that began in the 1990s, has not yet received the same attention. Studies on cyberbullying are fewer, and hence, there is an urgent need for further research (Casas et al., 2013). Traditional bullying can be described as "an essentially psychosocial problem involving the intentional, repetitive harming of another person and the creation of a power imbalance between the victim and the aggressor, with negative consequences for both parties." (Casas et al, 2013, p. 580). While traditional bullying typically involves a physical threat by a stronger person or group exerting power over someone who is actually (or is perceived as) weaker, online or cyberbullying is often anonymous and usually involves a social or psychological power imbalance (Vannucci et al., 2012).

Formal definitions of cyberbullying vary. The broadest definition refers to cyberbullying as "bullying that occurs via the Internet or text messaging" (Kowalski et al., 2016). Dating applications, chat rooms, social networking sites and apps, and even gaming sites are just a few of the many venues for cyberbullying. This type of bullying can include

> sending mean messages or threats to a person's email account or cell phone, spreading rumors online or through texts, posting hurtful or threatening messages on social networking sites or web pages, stealing a person's

account information to break into their account and send damaging messages, pretending to be someone else online to hurt another person, taking unflattering pictures of a person and spreading them through cell phones or the Internet, sexting, or circulating sexually suggestive pictures or messages about a person. (Chapin, 2016; National Crime Prevention Council, n.d.)

Any form of involvement in cyberbullying can have lasting physical and emotional consequences for adolescents (Modecki et al., 2014), including for both the victim and the bully (Bonanno and Hymel, 2013). Cyberbullies can be classmates, online acquaintances, and even anonymous users, but most often the cyberbullies know their victims (National Crime Prevention Council, n.d.).

Similar to traditional face-to-face bullying, cyberbullying potentially leads to suicidal behavior, substance use, violent behavior, and unsafe sexual behavior (Litwiller & Brausch, 2013; Wang et al., 2011; Kim & Leventhal, 2008). Considering that suicide is the third leading cause of death among young Americans between the ages of 10 and 24 years, and the fact that cyberbullying as well as traditional bullying can lead to suicidal and/or other destructive behavior, it is critical that a better understanding of the topic is gained so that successful prevention and protection efforts can be developed and implemented. This includes developing prevention and intervention programs against bullying as well as policies and legal changes that will better protect people against bullying.

The information and communication technology (ICT) revolution saw the Internet grow from 400 million users to an estimated 3.2 billion Internet users and 2.1 billion smartphone users in 2015 (Statista, 2016). Even if just a small fraction of one percent of those users engaged in bullying activity online, the results would be substantive and overwhelming. Yet the proportion of people who bully or are bullied online is significantly more than that, although reports of cyberbullying differ significantly. One report indicates that about one in five teenagers in the United States is a victim or perpetrator of cyberbullying (Statista, 2016). Another study shows that more than 50 percent of teenagers in the U.S. have experienced cyberbullying, but that the majority of those do not take any action, such as telling an adult; just 10–15 percent of cyberbullied teens tell their parents (Bullyingstatistics.org, 2016). Chapin (2016) found 30 percent of adolescents are cyberbullied and only 18 percent tell a parent or school representative. Chapin also suggests that middle school students are the most vulnerable to cyberbullying. Specifically, he notes that although adolescents exhibited optimistic bias, i.e. believing that the likelihood of being cyberbullied themselves is lower than their peers, 75 percent of middle school adolescents have experienced cyberbullying.

Interestingly, variation exists between genders. In 2011, 22 percent of high-school females and 18.2 percent of high-school males recounted being physically bullied, while 22.1 percent of high-school females and 10.8 percent of high-school males reported being electronically bullied (or cyberbullied)

(Statista, 2016). This report shows high-school females are bullied virtually equally, whether in person or online, yet high school males are more likely to be bullied in person than online. And while females are likely to be bullied by other females and males alike, males are most likely to be bullied by other males (Statista, 2016).

Cyberbullying has extended beyond children and teenagers to the college environment, the adult workforce, adult focused social and professional websites, and even into the world of politics. The 2016 U.S. presidential race marked the first time a candidate for the highest national office in the land was widely criticized for cyberbullying (Burns and Haberman, 2016). Moreover, cyberbullying has become a global phenomenon, with similar scenarios and outcomes found throughout North America, South America, Europe, Asia, the Middle East, Africa, and Australia (Chisholm and Day, 2013). In fact, Amanda Todd lived in Canada, and the 35-year old man eventually found responsible for the bullying behaviors, was from the Netherlands.

Who Are the Cyberbullies and Why Do They Bully?

Cyberbullying shares many of the same psychological processes and outcomes with traditional bullying. Based on social interactive learning theory, research shows that traditional and cyberbullying are the result of conflictual and harsh parenting styles and low parental monitoring (Low and Espelage, 2013). Bullying of either type involves a perpetrator who is perceived as stronger, preying on someone perceived as weaker, i.e. a power imbalance is present in all forms of bullying. Traditional bullying conjures up images of a physically larger or older boy beating up a smaller boy for his lunch money or nicer backpack, or a group of older girls taunting and harassing a younger girl or group. In a physical bullying situation, the threats are real, "in your face," and instantly apparent, and the damage is usually immediately observable and consequential. However, with cyberbullying, the "stronger" perpetrator is often a person with more and better access to technology and expertise in using it. In one study, almost 53 percent of cyberbullies considered themselves expert Internet users, compared to about 29 percent of non-cyberbullying perpetrators or victims (Ybarra and Mitchell, 2004). Common causes found for cyberbullying are issues related to romantic relationships (rejection, jealousy, breaking up), non-conformity and revenge. As such, common types of cyberbullying include telling lies about a person, threatening to harm a person, and revenge for perceived mistreatment (Chapin, 2016).

Cyberbullying threats started out in the early days of online communication in a more concealed manner. Email and chat rooms required users to go online, generally from a home desktop computer to interact with others. The effects of online bullying (pre-dating the term cyberbullying) were often delayed and not readily apparent to the bully. The later inventions of smart phones, apps, and push technology, however, enabled cyberbullies to post harassing messages that can reach the targeted victim, along with infinite audiences, instantaneously. However, the cyberbully cannot immediately see the damage that he or she has caused and the reward for engaging in cyberbullying is often delayed compared to traditional bullying (Vannucci et al., 2012). This suggests the cyberbully may derive satisfaction from the very act of bullying, and not the effects on the victim or bystanders as in face-to-face bullying (Kowalski et al., 2014). As such, the cyberbully has no indication of the consequences of his actions.

Commonly, cyberbullies also tend to engage in face-to-face bullying. But because of the ability to often remain anonymous online, a new group of bullies has emerged that engage solely in cyberbullying. One explanation is that in contrast to face-to-face bullying, anonymity on social media allows cyberbullies to ignore feelings of empathy with the victim. Such bullies are opting to use the power of social media to harm their victims anonymously (Kyriacou & Zuin, 2014).

Research has shown a significant overlap exists between being a perpetrator and a victim of traditional bullying and being a perpetrator and a victim of cyberbullying. However, projections of the degree of overlap vary widely; estimates range from 65 to 93 percent respectively (Hase et al., 2015). Moreover, there is much debate among experts in the field over which form of bullying—traditional or cyber—is more harmful to the victim. There is even disagreement in the research about whether the two types of bullying are indeed different categories, or if cyberbullying is just another manifestation of traditional bullying and should even be studied outside of that context (Olweus, 2012). Regardless of the definition, one thing is clear: the potential anonymity of cyberbullying allows opportunities for some people to bully who may never do so in a traditional, physical sense that often contributes to a lack of empathy by the bully. That is, because the bully cannot see the effects in person, he is unable to process the consequences that his actions produce. Hence, cyberbullies can have far more "protection" as a result.

Earlier research on cyberbullying was based on the assumption that it was, by its very nature, more distressing and more harmful than traditional bullying (Chisholm & Day, 2013). Conventional wisdom reasoned that because the cyberbully is often anonymous, the very fact that a victim is unable to directly confront the perpetrator and stop the bullying causes the insidious nature of cyberbullying to be more distressful than traditional bullying. Moreover, the content associated with cyberbullying spreads more rapidly than school yard comments, and once something is posted online—either a picture or words—it is virtually impossible for it to be totally erased. While the debate continues over the degree of harm, similar outcomes occur in both traditional and cyberbullying and these outcomes are not in dispute: depression, poor self-esteem, anxiety, suicidal ideation, and psychosomatic issues such as headaches and sleep problems (Olweus, 2012).

Fear of Missing Out (FOMO) and Social Media Use

Given the very real potential for cyberbullying and other dangerous behaviors, the question remains about why people use social media sites and apps so often. The use of social media networks has been found to have positive outcomes, such as social capital (Yoder and Stutzman, 2011). Viewing one's own profile on social media networks such as Facebook can lead to more self-awareness and enhanced self-esteem among adolescents (Gonzales and Hancock, 2010). Yet, individuals who have used Facebook for a longer period are found to suffer from lower self-esteem and believe others to be happier and/or have better lives. This group of adolescents also tends to agree less with the notion that life is fair. Adolescents who accept more friends on Facebook than they personally know also believe others have happier lives (Chou and Edge, 2012). While 84 percent of adolescents use Facebook on a daily basis, only 12.5 percent among those who are cyberbullied quit using Facebook (Chapin, 2016).

A literature base is emerging on social networking and its academic, social and psychological effects among adolescents. Adolescents lean toward email and instant messaging to coordinate group assignments, ask questions and share files. Students tend to use Facebook and other social media networks on a regular basis to communicate with fellow classmates (Chapin, 2016), and spend considerable time on social media searching for content not related to schoolwork. As a result, adolescents are increasingly engaging in multitasking while doing schoolwork, which leads to lower grade point averages (GPA) (Junco & Cotten, 2012). As such, there are contradictory views among adolescents on the benefits of using social media for educational purposes (Hrastinski & Aghaee, 2012).

Despite the negative consequences and emotions often associated with social media use, social media users tend to feel pressured to log in to their account frequently to keep updated and maintain relationship demands because of the fear of missing out (FOMO) (Fox and Moreland, 2014). FOMO is defined as "the fear that others have things that you don't, or are experiencing things that you wish you were" (Hetz et al., 2015) and as a "pervasive apprehension that others might be having rewarding experiences from which one is absent" (Przybylski et al., 2013). As such, individuals suffering from FOMO feel the urge to stay continuously connected and updated with what others are doing (Alt, 2015).

Many people, in particular, Baby Boomers (the generational cohort whose birth years are generally mid 1940s to mid 1960s) and older Gen Xers (whose birth years are generally early-to-mid 1960s to the late 1970s/early 1980s) question the attractiveness of being connected 24/7, and wonder why Millennials and Post-Millennials spend so much time online, even at the expense of real-time friendships and relationships. Millennials are the first generation to grow up with digital technology as an integral part of their lives; they are considered "digital natives" rather than "digital immigrants" (Prensky, 2001). In contrast, the older generations grew up with the telephone as their primary device for communicating over a distance. Millennials came of age using personal computers, laptops, cell phones, smart phones, and tablets as their devices of choice. Phone calls became emails, which then were overwhelmingly replaced by text messages and social media posts. In short, the need to interact with others is a key reason Millennials use social media (Palfrey & Gasser, 2008). Further, electronic communications are easier than face-to-face or telephone conversations, particularly for individuals who are more introverted or lacking in self-esteem.

Although more predominant with the younger generations, FOMO is a key motivator of perpetual online connection among other generations as well. This is generally based on the logic that nobody wants to be the last person to hear about an important social event. Psychologists theorize that FOMO is linked to satisfying needs, i.e. the need to communicate, the need to develop social competence, and the need to deepen social ties. FOMO has been found to be a key reason in explaining social media engagement; high FOMO leads to higher levels of social media usage (Przybylski et al., 2013). A 2015 survey of Australian youth, aged 13–17 years, found that teens spent an average of 2.7 hours per day on social media and that teens connecting more than five times per day are significantly more likely to experience aspects of FOMO (Australian Psychological Society, n.d.).

Because of the constant desire to be "in the know," people continue to use social media, despite recognizing its negative impacts on life. In January 2016, Facebook was estimated to have nearly 1.6 billion active users worldwide (Statista, 2016). Unfortunately, many people often use the Internet, and social media in particular, as a distraction from accomplishing tasks that must be completed. From checking Facebook or Instagram for the latest posts, to shopping online, time spent online is often just a work-avoidance mechanism for people of all ages. Researchers tracked the Internet usage of college students and found, by way of post-monitoring interviews, that continually checking social media sites provided a way to avoid studying, to procrastinate, or just to pass time. Some of the interviewees reported feeling a lack of control to stay offline. Moreover, some even wished for an app that would prevent the use of social media during study time (Wang et al., 2015). These feelings have been found to contribute to student anxiety and stress levels, and can either lead to or worsen depression. Much of this is driven by the fear of missing out (Przybylski et al., 2013).

Students are not alone in being distracted from their work by social networking websites and phone apps. More than half of the working adults in the UK admitted that online activities, such as checking and responding to emails or a social media alert notification, helped fuel procrastination and lower levels of productivity by providing them access to an immediate menu of instant distractions (Williams, 2014). Adults also experience stress from "keeping up with the Joneses," and feel the need to continually highlight and post items online that improve their self-image: the recent family vacation, a romantic night at an upscale restaurant, or their youngest child's report card (Dick, 2013). This comparison to others is known as social comparison orientation (SCO). In general, social comparative information can be helpful for a variety of purposes such as self-evaluation, self-enhancement, and self-improvement (Corcoran et al., 2011; Vogel et al., 2015)

However, studies also showed negative consequences of social comparison, particularly on social media, such as low self-esteem (Vogel et al., 2015), poor self-evaluations (Haferkamp and Kramer, 2011), depression (Feinstein et al., 2013) and negative affect balance (Vogel et al., 2015). Further, individuals high in SCO tend to exhibit heavier Facebook usage. Not surprisingly, research on the relationship between self-esteem and communication behaviors found 36 percent of consumers believe social media influences the products and brands they buy. Those who believe so to a greater extent also experience significantly more stress in their lives compared to those who believe so to a lesser extent (Dick, 2013).

Forms of Cyberbullying and the Legal Environment

Although there seems to be a clear juridical system for the different forms of bullying in real life, there is no such system for similar forms of bullying online. In fact, there seems to be a fine line between what is illegal and what is merely mean because it often depends on the motivation/intention or situation. Perhaps the lack of clear definitions of the different forms of cyberbullying is one of the reasons why the majority of those being cyberbullied do not report to their parents or schools. Consequently, many lawyers and other legal experts are not always certain about what rules are valid regarding cyberbullying. One major hindrance for developing clear penalties against cyberbullying may lie in the fact that national borders do not limit cyberbullying. Thus, solutions should be developed such that it can be applied across borders. For example, in Sweden, although cyberbullying cases are reported to the police almost daily, very few cases actually make it to court and only few offenders are being convicted. (SOU, 2016).

Cyberbullying can take on various forms. The most common ones are insults, libel, threats and harassment (Chapin, 2016). Insults occur when a person deliberately makes mean remarks about somebody, ultimately personally attacking and hurting that person. In general, the law is stringent when such remarks are of racist, religious and/or sexual character. Libel exists when a written statement that is damaging to a person's reputation is published.

A threat is a violation of somebody's right to feel safe. On social media, threats can come in different ways, but protection from threats is often difficult to obtain. Moreover, only when somebody's life or health is threatened directly is legal protection even possible. Harassment exists when somebody sends a barrage of messages to an individual who does not want to be contacted. When a person repeatedly asks someone to send sexually explicit pictures it is considered sexual harassment. It is considered child exploitation when an adult asks someone under 15 years of age to pose naked or in underwear in front of a (web) camera.

A new form of cyberbullying, called "roasting," was first exposed in the U.K. in 2015. The term "roasting" has an innocuous origin; it began as a good-natured, comedic, and often self-efficacious mocking tribute to a person. In its cyberbullying form, however, it is mean-spirited and incessant, perpetrated by girls "ganging up" on boys until they crack and lash back. The sinister aspect of roasting is that it is done under the auspices of humor among friends; however, anti-bullying experts see it as yet another form of cyberbullying (Newsweek, 2016).

Cyberbullying will generally take at least one of these forms, and some of the harshest examples of cyberbullying will likely include more than one of them. The following story of Megan Meier is a prime example where several types of cyberbullying were implemented with heartbreaking and tragic results.

On Sunday, October 15, 2006, 13-year-old Megan Meier hanged herself in her bedroom closet, in her family's suburban home in O'Fallon, Missouri. Five weeks prior to her death, a 16-year-old boy named Josh Evans asked to become friends with Megan on MySpace, a social networking website. Megan had long struggled with weight and self-esteem issues and welcomed the attention from Josh, who told her she was pretty. After a few weeks of friendly conversation Josh's tone of communication suddenly turned cruel; he began saying mean things to Megan because of rumors that had circulated. Josh even told her "Everybody in O'Fallon knows how you are. You are a bad person and everybody hates you. Have a shitty rest of your life. The world would be a better place without you." (Megan Meier Foundation, 2016). Some of Megan's other classmates joined Josh in the insulting and harassing behaviors. Negative things about Megan were posted on bulletin boards, repetitively and publicly such as "Megan Meier is a slut," and "Megan Meier is fat." Megan never understood why this happened, and these attacks pushed Megan over the edge; she subsequently committed suicide.

Even more disconcerting is that it was discovered that Josh never even existed. He was an online persona created by a former friend to Megan and this former friend's mother. Also involved was the mother's 18-year-old employee. Local law enforcement never arrested any of the three perpetrators of the fake Josh Evans profile because no existing statutes were violated. A single federal charge of a misdemeanor violation of the Computer Fraud and Abuse Act was vacated by a federal district court on appeal (Wired, 2009). In response to this incident, local officials in Dardenne Prairie, MO enacted an ordinance a year later that prohibits any harassment utilizing an electronic medium. The State of Missouri followed with an even stronger statute in 2008 that, at the time, was among the strongest in the nation; crimes for violation of the statute by an adult against a child (17 years old or younger) escalated from misdemeanors to felonies.

Today, in the U.S. all 50 states and the District of Columbia have laws prohibiting bullying. Forty-eight states and the District of Columbia have laws prohibiting electronic harassment or bullying by use of electronic means, although only 23 of these laws specify cyberbullying (Hinduja and Patchin, 2016). In contrast, there are no federal statutes outlawing bullying, cyberbullying, or any form of electronic harassment. HR1966, the "Megan Meier Cyberbullying Prevention Act," was introduced by Rep. Linda Sanchez, D-California, on April 2, 2009 to address these issues on the federal level. However, the bill stalled in the Judiciary Committee and was never brought to a vote by the full U.S. House of Representatives. The U.S. is not alone in lacking national laws against cyberbullying. Only Canada and the United Kingdom have what are considered the strongest cyberbullying laws in the world, while the Philippines and Australia have "medium-level" laws (uKnowKids.com, 2014).

In European countries such as Sweden, current debates revolve around urging the government to implement immediate laws for preventing and punishing cyberbullying. In particular, laws against spreading pictures or information regarding a person's sexual orientation and health conditions should be implemented. One proposal is to implement new penalties against so-called revenge porn (e.g., spreading nude pictures of one's ex-partner after a break-up). Another is to propose legal penalties for those offenders who create so-called hate pages and post threats, and even for those posting hateful comments and/or insults. Further, the petition also urges compensation for the victim of bullying because according to the current legislation, compensation is not possible for defamation crimes. These debates/petitions are in line with Antemar (2016) who argues that hateful comments should be punished as personal harassment, and people should be held responsible for the content they post. Unlike traditional bullying, a cyberbullying victim cannot simply move to escape the torment because the Internet is everywhere. Hence, while the legal landscape surrounding cyberbullying is moving forward, it is not yet where it needs to be.

Prevention and Intervention Programs

Today, organizations, companies and schools are working in various ways with cyberbullying issues. Examples include implementing ID logins before a person can publish comments online, closing comment-fields altogether, limiting student access to social media during the school day, and moderating certain pages on sites such as Facebook so that threatening comments can be removed. However, it is still difficult to discern which strategy for fighting cyberbullying is the most effective, both for the short and long term (Internetfonden, 2013).

Facebook introduced its "Bullying Prevention Hub" in 2013, although critics had been pushing Facebook to do more for several years before that (NPR, 2013). The hub, created through a partnership with the Yale Center for Emotional Intelligence, serves as a resource center for teens, parents, and educators for dealing with bullying behavior and its consequences (Facebook, n.d.). Resources for teens include helpful information on what to do if they or their friends are bullied, and what to do if they are called a bully. Educator resources include how to take action against a bully, how to assist the victim of bullying, and—arguably most important—how to prevent bullying in the first place.

Undeniably, bullying in any form is a complex phenomenon incorporating personality, individual backgrounds and contextual factors (Law et al., 2012). Empathy is found to be one of the personality traits influencing the prevention of involvement in bullying in the aggressor (Casas et al., 2013).

School climate plays an important role in the prevention and intervention of bullying, including cyberbullying (Casas et al., 2013), and hence the development of appropriate programs. Such programs are particularly important for the implementation and/or revision of disciplinary rules, values and expectations for support in case of a bullying incident (Cohen et al., 2009). Moreover, studies have found that bullying prevention and reduction programs can significantly decrease levels of victimization and bullying (Ttofi and Farrington, 2011; Williams and Guerra, 2007) including cyberbullying (Casas et al., 2013). Studies also emphasize that such programs need to be continuously evaluated with regard to their design and implementation (Del Rey et al., 2012; Casas et al., 2013), as well as their effectiveness.

As we have noted in this chapter, the law plays a crucial part in addressing cyberbullying. While a detailed discussion of these laws is outside the scope of this chapter, (cyber)bullying laws cannot exist in a vacuum. "Legal responses and mandates can be at their best only facilitating the harder non-legal work that schools must undertake" (Sacco et al., 2012). As indicated, empathy and perceived school climate are valid predictors for (cyber)bullying prevention/intervention and have been found to reduce (cyber)bullying and, as such, can have positive effects on overall school climate (Casas et al., 2013). Considering the non-reporting problem of cyberbullying incidents, such programs could aid and stimulate students to report cyberbullying cases. Thus, in the quest to battle cyberbullying among adolescents, a clear legal cyberbullying landscape goes hand in hand with a healthy school climate. In short, creating a healthy school climate is fundamental for creating a kinder, braver and safer world for today's and future generations.

Discussion and Conclusions

The Internet is a vast network of information and communication, filled with possibilities for individuals and groups to express their thoughts and ideas, contributing to a broad knowledge base and creating an engaging environment for debate where everybody can learn from one another. But this openness in cyberspace also comes with negative intentions and consequences, including cyberbullying, due in large part to the explosive growth of high-speed Internet and cheap smart phones. The cyberbullying problem is growing and we have only begun to grasp the magnitude of negative effects of this phenomenon on the younger generation.

This chapter reinforces that not only is urgent legislation needed to protect people and in particular adolescents, but also more education and carefully-developed actions against cyberbullying. For example, organizations wishing to use social media should consider the particular reasons they want to use these channels and select media outlets carefully to ensure they are staffed appropriately to quickly and effectively handle cyberbullying issues taking place on their own websites.

A necessity to address the many problems caused by cyberbullying is to solve the issue of non-reporting by cyberbullying victims. As noted, only a minority of victims reports the incident(s), and cyberbullying is the least frequent form of bullying reported. This chapter discussed some possible reasons for this non-reporting by cyberbullying victims, and emphasizes the urgent need for educating people and society at large about the severity of the various forms of cyberbullying. However, at the core is the need for more specific, stringent legal regulations to battle the devastating effects of cyberbullying. Today, the legal landscape on cyberbullying remains somewhat fragmented, unclearly formulated, giving much room for various interpretations. As such, today's legal environment makes it fairly easy for the bully to dodge punishment or disciplinary actions related to the bullying act.

Yet, merely having a stringent legal system is not enough. Prevention and intervention programs contribute to a better quality of school climate, which is critical to provide school personnel with guidelines on the issue that can be implemented both to prevent and deal with cyberbullying. Parents must play an important role in these programs as well. Parents should also help their own children manage their digital reputation, which includes monitoring of their children's social network profiles.

Generally, a bully lacks empathy toward the victim. The impersonal and seemingly anonymous online environment that can explain cyberbullying emphasizes this. Real-life signals that would normally trigger empathy are simply not present in an online environment. On the other hand, a bully who takes on-ground bullying into the online arena has already ignored the signals of empathy toward the victim(s) in a real-life environment and would most likely do so online. Therefore, communication etiquette, proper social media behavior, and the effects of bullying should be integrated into every school's curriculum, complementing parents' efforts at home.

Finally, cyberbullying is and should be seen as a global societal problem and this chapter has simply provided a glimpse of the complexity and severity of this dark phenomenon. There are many resources available for the prevention of cyberbullying and suicide. Significant efforts must be made to ensure that bullies, victims and bystanders become more aware of these available resources and share them via the Internet just as easily as cyberbullies share scathing and hurtful words across the vast network.

Cyberbullying and Suicide Prevention Resources

- ConnectSafely: http://www.connectsafely.org/wp-content/uploads/sc_cyberbullying.pdf
- Cyberbullying Research Center: http://cyberbullying.org/
- Facebook Bullying Prevention Hub: https://www.facebook.com/safety/bullying/
- It Gets Better Project: http://www.itgetsbetter.org/
- Megan Meier Foundation: http://www.meganmeierfoundation.org/
- National Crime Prevention Council: http://www.ncpc.org/topics/bullying
- National Suicide Prevention Lifeline: http://www.suicidepreventionlifeline.org/
- Stopbullying.gov: www.stopbullying.gov
- The Trevor Project: http://www.thetrevorproject.org/

References

Alt, D. (2015). College students' academic motivation, media engagement and fear of missing out. *Computers in Human Behavior*, 49, 111–119.

Antemar, G. (2016). How can hatred online be stopped with new laws? DN Debatt. Retrieved May 17, 2016, from http://www.dn.se/debatt/sa-kan-hatet-pa-natet-stoppas-med-nya-lagar/

Australian Psychological Society. (n.d.). Fear of missing out survey results 2015. Retrieved February 15, 2016, from www.psychology.org.au/psychologyweek/survey/results-FoMO/

Bonanno, R. A., & Hymel, S. (2013). Cyber bullying and internalizing difficulties: above and beyond the impact of traditional forms of bullying. *Journal of Youth Adolescence*, 42, 685–697.

Bullyingstatistics.org (2016). Cyberbullying statistics. Retrieved August 2, 2106, from http://www.bullyingstatistics.org/content/cyber-bullying-statistics.html

Burns, A., & Haberman, M. (2016). To fight critics, Donald Trump aims to instill fear in 140-charated doses. *The New York Times*. Retrieved March 13, 2016, from http://www.nytimes.com/2016/02/27/us/politics/donald-trump.html

Casas, J. A., Del Rey, R., & Ortega-Ruiz, R. (2013). Bullying and cyberbullying: convergent and divergent predictor variables. *Computers in Human Behavior*, 29, 580–587.

Chapin, J. (2016). Adolescents and cyber bullying: the precaution adoption process model. *Education and Information Technologies*, 21(4), 719–728.

Chisholm, J. F., & Day, S. K. (2013). Current trends in cyberbullying. *Journal of Social Distress and the Homeless*, 22(1), 35–57.

Chou, H. T., & Edge, N. (2012). They are happier and having better lives than I am: The impact of using facebook on perceptions of others' lives. *Cyberpsychology, Behavior and Social Networking*, 15(2), 117–121.

Cohen, J., McCabe, L., Michelli, N. M., & Pickeral, T. (2009). School climate: Research, policy, practice and teacher education. *Teachers College Record*, 111(1), 180–213.

Corcoran, K., Crusius, J., & Mussweiler, T. (2011). Social comparison: Motives, standards, and mechanisms. In D. Chadeem (Ed.) *Theories in Social Psychology*, 119-139. Oxford, UK: Wiley Blackwell.

Del Rey, R., Elipe, P., & Ortega-Ruiz, R. (2012). Bullying and cyberbullying: Overlapping and predictive value of the co-occurrence. *Psicothema*, 24(4), 608–613.

Dick, J. (2013). Why do social networks increase stress? Retrieved March 13, 2016, from *The Huffington Post*: http://www.huffingtonpost.com/john-dick/social-networks and-stress_b_3534170.html

Facebook (n.d.). Put a stop to bullying. Retrieved August 3, 2016, from: https://www.facebook.com/safety/bullying/

Feinstein, B.A., Hershenberg, R., Bhatia, V., Latack, J.A., Meuwly, N., & Davila, J. (2013). Negative social comparison on Facebook and depressive symptoms: Rumination as a mechanism. *Psychology of Popular Media Culture*, 2(3), p.161.

Foderaro, L.W. (2010, September 30). Private Moment Made Public, Then a Fatal Jump. The New York Times. Retrieved February 13, 2016, from https://query.nytimes.com/gst/fullpage.html?res=9B07E6D91638F933A0575AC0A9669D8B63.

Fox J., & Moreland, J. J. (2014). The dark side of social networking sites: An exploration of the relational and psychological stressors associated with Facebook use and affordances. *Computers in Human Behavior*, 45, 168–176.

Gonzales, A. L., & Hancock, J. T. (2010). Mirror, mirror on my facebook wall: effects of exposure to facebook on self-esteem. *Cyberpsychology, Behavior and Social Networking*, 14(2), 79–83.

Haferkamp, N., & Krämer, N. C. (2011). Social comparison 2.0: Examining the effects of online profiles on social-networking sites. *Cyberpsychology, Behavior, and Social Networking*, 14(5), 309–314.

Hase, C. N., Goldberg, S. B., Smith, D., Stuck, A., & Campain, J. (2015). Impacts of traditional bullying and cyberbullying on the mental health of middle school and high school students. *Psychology in the Schools*, 52(6), 607–617.

Heinemann, P. P. (1972). *Antibullying group selected among children and adults.* Stockholm: Nature and Culture.

Hetz, P. R., Dawson, C. L. & Cullen, T. A. (2015). Social media use and the fear of missing out (FoMO) while studying abroad, *Journal of Research on Technology in Education*, 47(4), 259–272.

Hinduja, S., & Patchin, J. W. (2016, March 7). State Cyberbullying Laws: A brief review of state cyberbullying laws and policies. Retrieved from Cyberbullying Research Center: http://cyberbullying.org/Bullying-and-Cyberbullying-Laws.pdf

Hrastinski, S., & Aghaee, N. (2012). How are campus students using social media to support their studies? An exploratorive interview study. *Education and Information Technology*, 17(4), 451–464.

Internetfonden (2013). Countering näthat. Retrieved June 2, 2016: https://www.Internetfonden.se/att-motverka-nathat/

Junco, R., & Cotten, S. (2012). No a 4 U: the relationship between multitasking and academic performance. *Computers and Education*, 59(2), 505–514.

Kim, Y. S. & Leventhal., B. (2008). Bullying and suicide. A review. *International Journal of Adolescent Medicine and Health*, 20(2), 133.

Kowalski, R. M., Giumetti, G. W., Schroeder, A. N., & Lattanner, M. R. (2014). Bullying in the digital age: A critical review and meta-analysis of cyberbullying research among youth. *Psychological Bulletin*, 140(4), 1073–1137.

Kowalski, R. M., Morgan, C. A., Drake-Lavelle, K., & Allison, B. (2016). Cyberbullying among college students with disabilities. *Computers in Human Behavior*, 57(2016), 416–427.

Kyriacou, C. & Zuin, A. (2014). Characterising the cyberbullying of teachers by pupils. *The Psychology of Education Review*, 29(2), 26–30.

Law, D. M., Shapka, J. D., Hymel. S., Olson, B. F., & Waterhouse, T. (2012). The changing face of bullying: An empirical comparison between traditional and Internet bullying and victimization. *Computers in Human Behavior*, 28(1), 226–232.

Litwiller, B. J., & Brausch, A. M. (2013). Cyber bullying and physical bullying in adolescent suicide: the role of violent behavior and substance use. *Journal of Youth and Adolescence*, 42(5), 675–684.

Low, S., & Espelage, D. (2013). Differentiating cyberbullying perpetration from non-physical bullying: Commonalities across race, individual, and family predictors. *Psychology of Violence*, 3(1), 39–52.

Megan Meier Foundation. Be the Change. Stop Bullying & Cyberbullying. Retrieved July 11, 2016: http://www.meganmeierfoundation.org/megans-story.html

Modecki, K. L., Minchin, J., Harbaugh, A. G., Guerra, N. G. & Runions, K. C. (2014). Bullying prevalence across contexts: A meta-analysis measuring cyber and traditional bullying. *Journal of Adolescent Health*, 56, 602–611.

National Crime Prevention Council. What is Cyberbullying? Retrieved August 3, 2016, from http://www.ncpc.org/topics/cyberbullying/what-is-cyberbullying

Newsweek (2016). Teenage Girls are 'Roasting' Young Boys in U.K. Cyberbullying Craze. Retrieved August 5, 2016, from: http://www.newsweek.com/teenage-girls-are-roasting-young-boys-new-cyberbullying-craze-483741

NoBullying.com (n.d.). The Unforgettable Amanda Todd Story. Retrieved February 23, 2016, from https://nobullying.com/amanda-todd-story/

NPR (2013). Facebook takes on cyberbullies as more teens leave site. Retrieved August 3, 2016, from: http://www.npr.org/sections/alltechconsidered/2013/11/07/243710885/facebook-takes-on-cyberbullies-as-more-teens-leave-facebook

Olweus, D. (2012). Cyberbullying: An overrated phenomenon? *European Journal of Developmental Psychology*, 9(5), 520–538.

Palfrey, J., & Gasser, U. (2008). *Born Digital: Understanding the First Generation of Digital Natives*. New York: Basic Books.

Prensky, M. (2001, September/October). Digital natives, digital immigrants part 1. *On the Horizon*, 9 (5), 1–6.

Przybylski, A. K., Murayama, K., DeHaan, C. R. & Gladwell, V. (2013). Motivational, emotional, and behavioral correlates of fear of missing out. *Computers in Human Behavior*, 29, 1841–1848.

Sacco, D. T., Silbaugh, K., Corredor, F., Casey, J. & Doherty, D. (2012). *An Overview of State Anti-bullying Legislation and Other Related Laws*. The Kinder & Braver World Project: Research Series. Harvard University.

SOU—Statens Offentliga Utredningar (2016). Integritet och straffskydd. SOU 2016:7. Retrieved August 16, 2016, from: http://www.regeringen.se/contentassets/207048837827439b9d1 dce919d0dd6f9/integritetoch-straffskydd-sou-20167

Statista, Inc. (2016). Leading social networks worldwide as of January 2016, ranked by number of active users (in millions). Retrieved April 1, 2016, from http://www.statista.com/statistics/272014/global-social-networks-ranked-by-number-of users/

Ttofi, M. M., & Farrington, D. P. (2011). Effectiveness of school-based programs to reduce bullying: A systematic and meta-analytic review. *Journal of Experimental Criminology*, 7(1), 27–56.

U.S. Department of Health and Human Services—Centers for Disease Control and Prevention. (2012, June 8). *Youth Risk Behavior Surveillance - United States, 2011.* Morbidity and Mortality Weekly Report, 61. Retrieved February 6, 2016, from http://www.cdc.gov/mmwr/pdf/ss/ss6104.pdf

uKnowKids.com. (2014, October 16). Cyberbullying laws around the globe: Where is legislation strongest? Retrieved June 12, 2016, from: uKnowKids.com: http://resources.uknowkids.com/blog/cyberbullying-laws-around-the-globe-where-is-legislation-strongest

Vannucci, M., Nocentini, A., Mazzoni, G., & Menesini, E. (2012). Recalling unpresented hostile words: False memories predictors of traditional and cyberbullying. *European Journal of Developmental Psychology*, 9(2), 182–194.

Vogel, E. A., Rose, J. P., Okdie, B. M., Eckles, K., & Franz, B. (2015). Who compares and despairs? The effect of social comparison orientation on social media use and its outcomes. *Personality and Individual Differences*, 86(November), 249–256.

Wang, Y., Niiya, M., Mark, G., Reich, S. M., & Warschauer, M. (2015). Coming of age (digitally): An ecological view of social media use among college students. Proceedings of the 18th ACM Conference on Computer Supported Cooperative Work & Social Computing (pp. 571–582). New York: ACM.

Wang, J., Nansel., T. R., & Iannotti, R. J. (2011). Cyber bullying and traditional bullying: Differential association with depression. *Journal of Adolescent Health*, 48(4), 415.

Williams, K. R., & Guerra, N. G. (2007). Prevalence and predictors of Internet bullying. *Journal of Adolescent Health*, 41(6), S14–S21.

Williams, R. (2014, February 23). Internet 'fuels procrastination and lowers productivity'. *The Telegraph*. Retrieved March 11, 2016, from http://www.telegraph.co.uk/technology/Internet/10654987/Internet-fuels-procrastination-and-lowers-productivity.html

Wired (2009). Judge Acquits Lori Drew in cyberbullying case, overrules jury. Accessed August 6, 2016, from: https://www.wired.com/2009/07/drew_court/

Ybarra, M. L., & Mitchell, K. J. (2004). Online aggressor/targets, aggressors, and targets: A comparison of associated youth characteristics. *Journal of Child Psychology and Psychiatry*, 45(7), 1308–1316.

Yoder C., & Stutzman, F. (2011) Identifying social capital in the Facebook interface. In Proceedings of the SIGCHI Conference on Human Factors in Computing Systems 2011 May 7 (pp. 585–588). ACM.

4

CROSSING THE #BIKINIBRIDGE

Exploring the Role of Social Media in Propagating Body Image Trends

Jenna Drenten and Lauren Gurrieri

> 4Chan manipulated social media and fooled all of us into thinking [the bikini bridge] was actually the next unhealthy obsession of teen girls. [...] we're so conditioned to think we need to be thin that we actually believed this was true.
>
> *Cassey Ho, founder of Blogilates.com (2014)*

Social media websites such as Tumblr, Instagram, Pinterest, and Twitter provide visual and verbal representations of idealized body images and motivational phrases, creating an online culture of "thinspiration," or thin inspiration (Balter-Reitz & Keller, 2005). The potentially negative role of marketing and media in shaping body image ideals is nothing new (D'Alessandro & Chitty, 2011; Grabe, Ward, & Hyde, 2008; Thompson & Hirschman, 1995). Previous research suggests the prevalence of thin models in advertising can negatively affect body image perceptions and evaluations of one's own attractiveness (Martin & Gentry, 1997; Myers & Biocca, 1992). In today's digitally driven marketplace, social media are increasingly supplementing or replacing traditional media in terms of how consumers learn and interact (Hanna, Rohm, & Crittenden, 2011). Although extant research on body image and traditional marketing media is extremely valuable, it fails to account for the rapidly changing digital media landscape. Thus, the purpose of this chapter is to explore how body image trends evolve in the social media marketplace and to examine the power of social media in shaping body image ideals. Specifically, we examine the emergence, propagation, and reappropriation of the #bikinibridge phenomenon, which began as an Internet hoax and quickly developed into an online body image trend. First, we outline our theoretical foundation at the intersection of body image and social media. Next, we outline our methodology, employing a netnographic approach to understanding the evolution of one body image trend online: the bikini bridge. Findings suggest body image trends, even those that are unsubstantiated, can go viral quickly through social media. Based on our analysis of the bikini bridge phenomenon, we identify four factors which helped it to emerge as an online body image trend: 1) simplicity (i.e., the singularization of skinny), 2) believability (i.e., the reality of the body image "hoax"), 3) cooptation (i.e., adoption by pre-existing communities), 4) controversy (i.e., conflicting narratives among users).

Body Image and the Internet

Traditional advertising media have been deemed one of the biggest influencers of how women view their bodies (Grabe et al., 2008). A well established body of research explores the role of culture and traditional media in shaping consumers' body image perceptions (e.g. D'Allesandro & Chitty, 2011; Groesz et al., 2001; Levine & Smolak, 1996; Thompson & Hirschman, 1995). A meta-analysis of studies published between 1975 and 2007 examining the link between media use and women's body image and related concerns conducted by Grabe et al. (2008) demonstrates that media use is negatively related to women's body image, including bodily dissatisfaction, increased investment in appearance and increased endorsement of disordered eating behaviors. The increasingly thin ideal communicated via movies, magazines and television programs is pervasive and normatively reinforces the value of this ideal in spite of it being unattainable to most. It communicates to all that a woman's worth is demonstrated through her body, an object of desire which in turn becomes a burdensome lifelong project (Brumberg, 1997). Consequently, exposure to and internalization of the thin ideal has been linked to a variety of physical and health problems for women, including disordered eating, low self-esteem and depression (Neumark-Sztianer et al., 2006; Paxton et al., 2006).

Although extant research on body image and traditional media is extremely valuable, the media landscape is rapidly changing. Not only do magazines, television programs, and movies provide outlets of influence, but today's generation is exposed to a whole new beast: social media. Social media driven by active consumer engagement and user-generated content are increasingly displacing traditional media in terms of how consumers learn, interact, and even consume products, services, and lifestyles (Hanna et al., 2011). Shankar and Malthouse (2007) suggest that "the Internet has empowered consumers to interact with companies on their terms, and enabled them to communicate with other consumers" (p. 3). Increasingly, consumers turn to the Internet for weight loss advice and discover social support for their efforts (Hwang et al., 2010). However, such weight loss communities are not always healthy. Recent years have seen an emergence of pro-anorexia online communities that serve to perpetuate and support the eating disorder (Burke, 2009). An online culture of "thinspiration" has emerged from such websites (Balter-Reitz & Keller 2005), in which users share online images or montages of slim to emaciated bodies, often as motivation for weight loss.

Recent studies have highlighted that, like traditional media, social media perpetuates body idealization for women (Slater et al., 2011; Tiggemann & Slater, 2013; Holland & Tiggemann, 2016). Research has demonstrated that time spent on social media is associated with increased body surveillance, body shame, internalization of the thin ideal, heightened body dissatisfaction, decreased sexual assertiveness and appearance-based comparisons (Fardouly & Vartanian, 2015; Manago et al., 2015; Tiggemann & Miller 2010; Tiggemann & Slater 2013; Vandenbosch & Eggermont, 2012). In particular, engagement in photo-based sharing activities is significantly related to body image and eating concerns (Meier & Gray, 2014) and the increasingly visual impression management that is conducted online by consumers reinforces traditional gender stereotypes and reproduces dominant cultural ideologies of attractiveness (Bailey et al., 2013; Kapidzic & Herring, 2011; Strano, 2008; Whitty, 2008).

While there is an increasing body of literature on individual disposition and vulnerability to the effects of social media on body image (Perloff, 2014; Valkenburg & Peter, 2013), other researchers argue that a broader range of approaches are needed, such as better accounts of embodiment (Williams & Ricciardelli, 2014). Researchers also point to the vast differences between social media and traditional media and the need for theory to account for this accordingly (Andsager, 2014; Turner, 2014). Importantly, Manago et al. (2015) identify that investigations of the relationship between social media and body image must not focus on social media use in isolation but rather the "investment in a cultural milieu where social interactions mediated by images on a screen promote a disembodied experience of the self" (p.3). One underexplored area in this regard is how body ideals communicated in and through social media gain traction and attain "trend" status.

Message Diffusion in a Digital Era

Social media websites such as Tumblr, Instagram, Pinterest, and Twitter provide visual and verbal representations of idealized body images and motivational phrases. In particular, Twitter facilitates real-time propagation of information to a large group of users, making it an ideal environment for the emergence and dissemination of trends (Castillo et al., 2011). Previous consumer research has explored the factors characteristic of online viral messages (Berger, 2016; Berger & Milkman, 2012; Gensler et al., 2013). That is, what makes something shareworthy online? How does one trend catch on in a sea of digital information overload? Berger and Milkman (2012) find content that elicits strong negative or positive affective responses (e.g., awe, anger), is more likely to go viral. In a study of how political messages spread on Twitter, Bastos et al. (2013) found that messages can spread quickly through the intense activity of individuals with relatively few connections. This is in contrast to traditional gatekeeping approaches (e.g., traditional newspapers), in which highly connected individuals and highly trusted media outlets serve as a bottleneck for delivering messages. On social media, hashtagging and trending topic algorithms contribute to the visibility of online messages.

Hashtagging is a common feature across modern social media (e.g., Tumblr, Twitter, Instagram). Hashtags have traditionally been employed to help consumers sort, find, and organize content; however, more recently, hashtagging has transitioned from a functional tool to a cultural genre. Daer et al. (2014) suggest that hashtagging serves as a metacommunicative process in which consumers tag photographs with words and phrases reflective of their own inner thoughts and feelings about the photograph itself. For example, a posted selfie may include a semantic tag (e.g., #selfie) in addition to a metacommunicative tag (e.g., #selfiesareawkward). These tagged "metacomments" demonstrate how consumers have repurposed online hashtagging from a utilitarian search tool to a method of identity performance (Daer et al., 2015). Similarly, body part hashtags (e.g., #thighgap, #bikinibridge, #hotdoglegs, #thighbrow) palpably capture the market-driven emergence of body image trends by giving them cultural brand names, or "that part of a brand which can be vocalized" (Kotler, 1991, p. 442). Body-related hashtags are a "disturbing outgrowth of the thinspiration and body dysmorphia issues that proliferate on Tumblr, Pinterest, and Instagram. In particular, the position, lighting, and summery backgrounds seen in these images make for great 'inner thigh gap' shot — inner thigh gap, or ITG, is one of the popular tags used alongside thinspiration on the Internet — an absurd beauty standard that defines a space between one's thighs as an indicator of ideal thinness and sex appeal" (Greenfield, 2013). Hashtags provide context for the content with which they are posted and offer consumers a searchable resource for discovering and sharing online trends. Contributing to the stream of literature on marketing and body image ideals, the purpose of this chapter is to better understand how body image trends evolve in the social media realm and to examine the power of user-generated content in shaping body image trends.

Method

Our research adopts a case study approach to exploring the role of social media in shaping body image trends. We selected the evolution of the *bikini bridge* as a unique case for understanding the diffusion of body image ideals through social media. A bikini bridge occurs when "bikini bottoms are suspended between the two hip bones, causing a space between the bikini and the lower abdomen" (Urban Dictionary, 2009). The term *bikini bridge* dates back to at least 2009. In 2014, the bikini bridge became popularized through strategic and organized social media efforts, initiated by members of the social network 4chan.org. 4chan has over 7 million users. Content on its popular online imageboard, /b/, is notorious for pushing boundaries in order to "hack the attention economy" (Bernstein et al., 2011; boyd, 2010). 4chan/b/ is responsible for notorious and often harmful pranks. For example, in 2014, 4chan users created and publicized an advertisement for a fake iOS8 feature called Apple Wave, which convinced consumers that iPhone devices could be charged wirelessly by microwaving the hardware. Apple warned Twitter followers not to microwave their iPhones, but it was too late. Pictures of melted and flaming iPhones began to appear online. In this same vein of Internet trolling, 4chan members aimed to create a new body image ideal through social media. On January 5, 2014, 4chan users launched Operation Bikini Bridge, a campaign to garner buzz for the bikini bridge (see Figure 4.1, which is reprinted with permission from 4chan.org.). As part of Operation Bikini Bridge, 4chan users were encouraged to create bikini-bridge-themed social media accounts on Twitter, spread bikini bridge propaganda (see Figure 4.2), and target consumers who have body conscious predispositions. The bikini bridge was revealed as an Internet hoax within days of its launch; however, many online users and media outlets had already succumbed to the prank. The purpose of this chapter is to uncover insights on how body image ideals emerge through social media, specifically analyzing the development of Operation Bikini Bridge as an exemplary case.

Following previous online case research in marketing (e.g., Cova & Pace, 2006), our study utilizes a netnographic approach to exploring the bikini bridge phenomenon. Netnography operates in an interpretivist paradigm, allowing the researchers to understand a cultural phenomenon through in-depth examination of associated meanings and contexts (Kozinets, 2002). Data consist of tweets associated with the "bikini bridge" hashtag (#bikinibridge) on Twitter. Twitter restricts posted messages to 140 characters in length, and users can link to photos

FIGURE 4.1 Operation Bikini Bridge, Reprinted with Permission from 4chan.org.

FIGURE 4.2 Illustrated Recreation of Bikini Bridge Propaganda

or external hyperlinks. Tweets were downloaded from Twitter using hashtag harvesting software (i.e., Twitter Archiving Google Spreadsheet, or TAGS), which collects public tweets associated with a given hashtag (#bikinibridge) in addition to supplemental data (e.g., username, date posted, location). TAGS software is an automated system that works within Twitter's API guidelines. Previous research suggests the search API may fail to capture a robust representation of fringe activity within the social network (González-Bailón et al., 2014); however, for the purpose of our research, we are more interested in the central social media conversation spurred by Operation Bikini Bridge. We created one data archive per day, for eight consecutive days, beginning with the January 5, 2014 when Operation Bikini Bridge was initiated on 4chan.org. This unique dataset tracks the rise of the bikini bridge trend in real-time. A sample of tweets was automatically downloaded each day. This amounted in a total of 10,310 tweets from 3,627 users between January 5, 2014 and January 12, 2014. Table 4.1 provides an overview of the daily data collected. The top contributor made 163 tweets using the #bikinibridge hashtag; however, most users tweeted three times or less. An additional unique feature of the data is the conversational nature of the tweets. Conversations between users were captured as they unfolded. The tweets were coded for common themes and allocated into categories. We utilized the aggregated tweets to characterize the bikini bridge trend in terms of the temporal evolution of the tweets and the pulse of the sentiment observable in the tweets. Data analysis was deemed complete when no new themes emerged (Wolcott, 2012).

TABLE 4.1 Twitter Data

Date	Number of #BikiniBridge Tweets in Sample
January 5th	610
January 6th	1,463
January 7th	1,448
January 8th	1,477
January 9th	1,493
January 10th	1,448
January 11th	898
January 12th	1,473
Total Tweets in Sample	10,310

Findings

Our study aims to understand how body image ideals are presented, propagated, and perpetuated in the marketplace through social media. Here, we identify four factors which contributed to the notoriety of the bikini bridge trend through social media: 1) simplicity (i.e., the singularization of skinny), 2) believability (i.e., the reality of the body image "hoax"), 3) cooptation (i.e., adoption by pre-existing communities), and 4) controversy (i.e., conflicting narratives among users). We provide exemplary tweets to support each theme. Twitter handles have been replaced with psuedonyms.

Simplicity: The Singularization of Skinny

The spread of the bikini bridge trend was due in part to its simplicity. In marketing, brand names can reflect a product's quality, use, and value (Rao & Monroe, 1989; Richardson et al., 1994). Similarly, the bikini bridge term acted as a simple name for a body part for which females should strive. The sheer simple act of naming the "bikini bridge" body part resonated with consumers. Twitter users acknowledged that girls have always sought to have a slender frame, a flat stomach, or prominent hipbones. However, these generalized goals did not have the same level of simplicity as the term: *bikini bridge*.

Riley suggests the body image ideal of the bikini bridge, pre-existed the *bikini bridge* term itself. The term bikini bridge contributes to singularizing the idea of skinny and provides a specific goal for which female consumers can strive. The use of hashtagged body image trends indicates an obsession with small physical aspirations, in which the ideal body image is determined by a singularlized physical feature (e.g., bikini bridge). Social media exacerbates the body image trend toward singularizing the skinny ideal body image and encouraging women to fixate their body consciousness on one individual body part. Given the

I'm calling it the 'bikini bridge'

FIGURE 4.3 The Illustration Above is a Recreation of the #BikiniBridge Social Media Content Posted with this Tweet:

> Riley (1/7/2014, 9:34 PM): Y is having a #bikinibridge suddenly 2014 news? Please, I was obsessed w/ bikini bridge before it even had a name.

importance of hashtags on social media, the bikini bridge trend initially gained traction online due in part to its hashtagability. The #bikinibridge trend is not the first hashtagged body part to create buzz. Some online users in the data referenced the thigh gap (#thighgap), a term referring to the separation between the inner thighs when standing with one's feet together. Thigh-gap-related online images have been popularized throughout the past few years on social media. In fact, websites like Tumblr and Instagram now provide an eating disorder warning on the screen when a user searches for the thigh gap hashtag.

> Kelly (1/11/2014, 6:34 PM): Thigh gap. Bikini bridge. Can we stop coming up with cutesie nicknames for women to starve themselves to achieve? #ED #thighgap #bikinibridge

Like Riley, Kelly's tweet highlights the important role names play in popularizing body image ideals on social media. The name *bikini bridge* provides online users with a quick and easy way to refer to the singularized body part it represents. Lee and Baack (2014) find brand names with greater sound fluency lead to higher brand recall. Likewise, the bikini bridge term refers to one single body part and uses alliteration to, as Kelly says, make it a "cutesie nickname." This shift toward the online singularization of skinny is in line with previous body objectification research (Vandenbosch & Eggermont, 2012). Simplistic, social media driven, body image ideals, such as the bikini bridge, move cultural messages away from generalized ideals of body perfection (e.g., "you should be skinny," "you should lose weight") and toward a singularized version of body perfection (e.g., "you should have a bikini bridge," "you should have a thigh gap").

Believability: The Reality of the Body Image "Hoax"

The data suggest initial acceptance of the bikini bridge resulted from its innate believability as a body image trend. Despite the fact that it was almost immediately outed as a hoax, the bikini bridge trend gained traction in the media and among social media users. Media outlets referred to the bikini bridge as "the next thigh gap." Similarly, social media users quickly accepted the bikini bridge as a body image trend in 2014, given the previous notoriety of the thigh gap trend in 2013. In this way, the thigh gap created a gateway for online body image trends like the bikini bridge to materialize. The following example tweets reveal the familiar thigh gap provided a reference point for the bikini bridge.

> *Pat (1/5/2014, 5:13 PM)*: Bikini bridges are in. Thigh Gaps are out. #bikinibridge
>
> *Keeley (1/6/2014, 5:31 PM)*: What the fuck is this #BikiniBridge shit? Thigh gap V2.0?
>
> *Danielle (1/12/2014, 10:24 AM)*: If 2013 was the year of the thigh gap, then 2014 is looking to be the year of the #bikinibridge I don't want to live on this planet anymore.

In the midst of Operation Bikini Bridge, Twitter users reacted to the bikini bridge as if it was a real goal – in large part because it seemed like something that *could* be real. As the previous tweets suggest, the thigh gap paved the way for a category of social media driven body image goals to emerge. Despite its impetus as an internet prank, the bikini bridge was, at its core, a believable body image goal. In an exemplary case, Cassey Ho, founder of the popular fitness blog, Blogilates (@blogilates), found herself among the masses of consumers duped into believing the bikini bridge trend was real. Cassey immediately condemned the bikini bridge trend and called for her online followers to do the same. The following day, Cassey discovered the bikini bridge trend was a prank initiated by 4chan and tweeted a link to her blog article about the issue (Ho, 2014).

> *Cassey (1/6/14, 7:00 AM)*: Wow. Apparently the #bikinibridge is the new inner thigh gap of 2014.

– *(1/6/14, 7:01 AM)*: #bikinibridge: phenomenon wherein bikini bottoms are suspended between the two hip bones, causing a space btwn the bikini & the lower abs.

– *(1/6/14, 7:04 AM)*: Be aware of this weird #bikinibridge obsession…a space between your abs and your bikini bottoms does not define your beauty ladies!

– *(1/7/14, 3:53 AM)*: *#BIKINIBRIDGE WAS A HOAX!!!! http:// t.co/skO2sRASDz*

Cassey's article, quoted in the beginning of this chapter, suggests the bikini bridge body image trend is initially believable because it draws on the innate cultural beliefs in society about how a female body should look. Her argument echoes many others in the data. 4chan users made the bikini bridge trend go viral, but they did not create the obsession in the first place. Notably, bikini pictures, such as those used in the Operation Bikini Bridge propaganda, were pre-existing on websites like Tumblr, Instagram, and Pinterest. Data suggest the bikini bridge trend was nurtured by an existing culture of comparison, objectification, and body image issues.

> *Chrissy (1/10/2014, 1:46 PM)*: You can't blame the Internet for a body image culture that already existed #bikinibridge http://t.co/ xWdnBGWuKh via @thedailybeast

> *Nick (1/9/2014, 12:54 AM)*: So #thighgap is real but #bikinibridge is a hoax? Starting to wonder if this internet thingy is really my best source of body image advice…

> *Melanie (1/10/2014, 9:44 PM)*: Heard of #BikiniBridge? Started as a prank, but it could have a greater, dangerous effect on body image.

> *Ellie (1/11/2014, 10:03 AM)*: #bikinibridge Trends like these only exist due to insecurity and it's fucked up that people would try to escalate it for their own kicks.

> *Laura (1/12/2014, 6:52 PM)*: Regardless if #bikinibridge is a real or planned viral trend, +body image responses are worth perusing. #bodyimage http://t.co/dUNkonV8Bi

For better or worse, the bikini bridge resonated with online consumers who operate in a culture obsessed with body image. The plausibility of the bikini bridge trend blurred the line between fact and fiction on social media. As social media users were quick to point out, it did not matter if the bikini bridge was "real" – the greater concern lay in that it was believable. In a culture in which young consumers turn to social media for information and social cues about their bodies (Perloff, 2014), the line between real and fake is increasingly blurred. A dark side of social media lies in its ability to make something fake (e.g., the bikini bridge) appear real. The images used in Operation Bikini Bridge propaganda were not created for the mission itself. Many of the images used were selfies young women posted while lying at a pool or beach. These images pre-existed the bikini bridge hashtag. The creators of Operation Bikini Bridge gave these images a collective life, centered on the common body image goal of achieving a bikini bridge. The bikini bridge joke reflects the prevailing unhealthy relationship some women have with their bodies. Social media, in this case, was used to perpetuate the societal expectations of the female body.

Cooptation: Adoption by Pre-existing Communities

The bikini bridge trend was initially propagated by 4chan users but was quickly accelerated by other online communities. Tweets on the first day of Operation Bikini Bridge (January 5th) were primarily generated by brand new Twitter accounts, presumably created for the sole purpose of promoting the #bikinibridge trend on Twitter through multiple tweets. One week later (January 12th), 63.2% of the #bikinibridge tweets were one-off tweets from a multitude of Twitter users. The bikini bridge body image ideal was quickly adopted by social media users outside of the 4chan community. As the creators of Operation Bikini Bridge suggest, in Figure 4.1, the #bikinibridge hashtag aimed to "target NYRers [New Years resolutioners], weight loss pages/groups(as a "goal"), etc." because "these people already hold a predisposition." Operation Bikini Bridge was dependent upon its cooptation by pre-existing online communities. Specifically, the data reveal two online communities that emerged as fundamental to the diffusion and ongoing espousal of the bikini bridge trend: pro-anorexia groups and online pornographers.

Health and fitness-oriented communities have become increasingly present on social media (Teodoro & Naaman, 2013; Vaterlaus et al., 2015). The January 2014 launch of Operation Bikini Bridge strategically paralleled existing marketing strategies of health and fitness brands (e.g., gyms, weight loss supplements), which tend to increase advertising around the beginning of the year when many women make weight loss goals and resolutions. On Twitter, the bikini bridge hashtag (#bikinibridge) was paired with hashtags (e.g., #GetChallengED, #thinspo) affiliated with the weight loss and, more commonly, pro-anorexia communities.

> *Arianna (1/12/2014, 12:35 AM):* The #bikinibridge might not have had a name until now, but the concept is not new to the #eatingdisorder world. #Recovered

> *Emily (1/11/2014, 9:54 PM):* Thin is in laddies! The newest craze to the #thinspo is the #bikinibridge which IMO is more realistically obtainable than #thighgap!

> *Bexley (1/12/2014, 10:19 PM):* I was feeling pretty sexy until I heard the term #BikiniBridge, didn't know what it was, and Google Imaged it. Now I hate myself. #Thinspo

Pro-anorexia communities use social media to share weight loss tips and promote eating disorders (Veer, 2010). The previous example tweets demonstrate how the bikini bridge hashtag was used as a form of "thinspiration," or thin inspiration. The pro-anorexia community on Twitter adopted the bikini bridge terminology, using it as a shared goal within the community and as an indicator of extreme weight loss success. Pro-anorexia social media users posted images of very thin girls paired with the bikini bridge hashtag. Many of these users' accounts were deleted as they were found to be in violation of Twitter's regulations and potentially harmful to online users. The following exemplary tweets demonstrate how the online pro-anorexia community co-opted the bikini bridge hashtag for its own purposes.

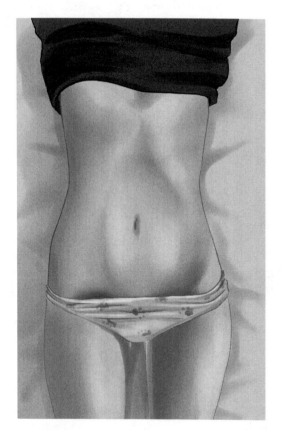

FIGURE 4.4 The Illustration Above is a Recreation of the #BikiniBridge Social Media Content Posted with this Tweet.

Ashley (1/12/2014, 8:05 PM): Perfectly concave #thinspo #bikinibridge #hipbones

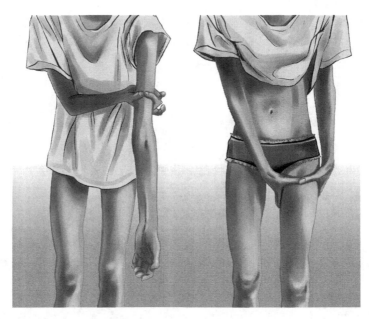

FIGURE 4.5 The Illustration Above is a Recreation of the #BikiniBridge Social Media Content Posted with this Tweet.

Selena (1/12/14, 2:28 PM): I wish… #thinspo #thighgap #bikinibridge #skinny

Taking the bikini bridge trend to an extreme, Twitter users in the existing pro-anorexia community urged one another to strive for a bikini bridge as a measure of anorexic achievement. The bikini bridge was acutely salient for members of online pro-anorexia groups, who were already predisposed to body consciousness, body dysmorphia, and unattainable body image ideals. Thus, pro-anorexia communities on social media co-opted the bikini bridge term.

A second online community playing a key role in the success and proliferation of the bikini bridge trend is online pornographers. Social networks like Tumblr and Twitter have become portals for posting, sharing, and viewing online pornography (Tiidenberg, 2015; Tziallas, 2016). The anonymity and freedom of social networks appeal to both professional and amateur pornographers. The bikini bridge was co-opted by these online pornographers as an overtly sexual term, coupled with highly sexualized bikini bridge images. The data include many nude or sexually suggestive photographs of women accompanying the bikini bridge hashtag. Sexually charged hashtags (e.g., #hotgirls, #sexyselfie) were often coupled with the posts. Within existing online communities of pornographers, the bikini bridge became an impetus for sexual objectification.

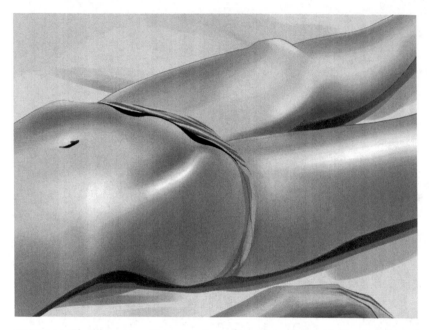

FIGURE 4.6 The Illustration Above is a Recreation of the #BikiniBridge Social Media Content Posted with this Tweet.

Macho Magazine (12 Jan 2014, 12:30 PM): Would you dare cross this #BikiniBridge? #SexySunday #HotPicAtNoon

The previous example tweets reveal the sexualized nature of the bikini bridge term on social media. Spreading bikini bridge images alongside sexually explicit hashtags and captions re-emphasized the idealized cultural perceptions of attractiveness in women. In Western culture, a bikini, in and of itself, is not sexually suggestive. Yet, when paired with sexually explicit commentary or images, the bikini bridge term became a facilitator for online pornography. In an effort to curtail online pornography, social networks, such as Tumblr, censor some searchable "NSFW," or not suitable for work, hashtags (#sex, #porn, #breasts, #panties; Romano, 2013). The bikini bridge hashtag was coopted by the online pornography community as a workaround for users to solicit and search for sexually charged content.

Andy (1/7/2014, 11:36 PM): Instead of arguing, post more pics of #bikinibridge #hotgirls

Chris (1/11/2014, 7:27 PM): RT @Sean: I'm sorry but there is something very sexy about the #bikinibridge // I'm not sorry at all. It's the naysayers who are sorry.

FIGURE 4.7 The Illustration Above is a Recreation of the #BikiniBridge Social Media Content Posted with this Tweet.

BikiniBridges (1/7/2014, 6:34 AM): Sometimes you dont need a bikini for a #bikinibridge! #Sexy

Many Twitter users, like Andy and Chris, responded favorably to highly sexualized images of the bikini bridge. Sexualized bikini bridge pictures and those who solicit them encourage women to present their bodies as parts of a whole, from the waist down. Previous research suggests advertising media uses dismemberment, or a focus on one part of the body (e.g., breasts, legs; Kilbourne, 2017). The hips-only focus of the bikini bridge demonstrates how dismemberment of women's bodies continues to operate in an online user-generated context. The bikini bridge started as a body image ideal; however, online pornographers co-opted the term to share and spread sexually suggestive content.

Controversy: Conflicting Narratives Among Users

Social media, particularly Twitter, thrives on controversy (Garimella et al., 2016). Social media platforms have been heralded as democratizing spaces in which all users have a voice and debate is encouraged. Our data suggest controversy surrounding the bikini bridge trend was a key factor in its proliferation. Much of the bikini bridge debate was purposefully generated by Internet trolls involved in the 4chan operation. 4chan members created conflicting Twitter handles for and against the bikini bridge, and social media users took the bait by joining the conversation. From a macro perspective, online debaters found themselves in two camps: pro-bikini bridge and anti-bikini bridge. Pro-bikini bridgers supported the bikini bridge trend through spreading bikini bridge propaganda and dismissing critics of the body image ideal.

> *Chris (1/11/2014 7:27 PM)*: #Bikinibridge: Body image experts are calling it another unhealthy trend, but then, they're all ugly & lonely.

> *Cary (1/8/2014, 11:55 PM)*: #bikinibridge movement is an effort to get women to be healthy. Not saying big isn't beautiful..... My two cents

> *Andrew (1/8/2014, 11:42 PM)*: My tweet praising the #bikinibridge was my most retweeted ★ever★. Remember haters, nobody held a gun to ladies' heads & made them eat cake

Anti-bikini bridgers criticized the bikini bridge trend by promoting body positivity and satirizing the body image ideal.

> *Eva (1/9/2014, 9:10 AM)*: this #bikinibridge thing is making me lose hope in humanity. the protrusion of you hip bones does not define your attractiveness.

> *Kellie (1/11/2014, 3:53 AM)*: Was going to post a selfie of my bikini bridge, but it just looks like a crepe lying against the edge of a frying pan… #bikinibridge

> *Alysia (1/12/2014, 10:54 PM)*: cuz I have a bridge AND a beer gut. Are we burning bikinis now? Can't think for self. Help.

Within each of these camps, social media users presented narratives to support their own beliefs. For instance, 4chan users purposefully presented the bikini bridge as a feminist ideal suggesting that women should be able to look however they want; however, online feminists quickly criticized the bikini bridge movement as one more societal trend telling women what it means to be attractive. The following debate between users demonstrates conflicting narratives.

> *BridgesAreBest (1/7/2014, 12:06 AM)*: @FeministGroup This is a movement for feminists, by feminists. Free your body. Its your choice. Embrace the #bikinibridge

> *FeministGroup (1/7/2014, 12:08 AM)*: No way! The #bikinibridge craze is the new thigh gap - telling young women their worth is based on their lack of body size. Not ok!

Beth (1/7/2014, 12:48 AM): Actually its the only feminist movement of the year. Every woman has the right to have the looks she loves #feminism #bikinibridge

Amanda (1/7/2014, 1:21 AM): I'm a person with an opinion. #bikinibridge is a patriarchal standard that fetishizes little girls.

Much of the outcry against the bikini bridge centered on body positivity, a movement which suggests women should feel comfortable, beautiful, and culturally accepted no matter what their bodies look like (Wood-Barcalow et al., 2010). In the case of the bikini bridge, Twitter users argued that women should not be held to a specific societal standard of beauty; however, others accused these users of ironically "thin-shaming," or making one feel guilty for being thin. Beggan and DeAngelis (2015) find individuals who are normally or naturally thin report receiving unwanted attention and otherness as a result of their bodies. Similarly, the conflicting narratives on social media spurred by the bikini bridge trend included fat-shaming and thin-shaming.

Mac (1/11/2014, 5:10 AM): hey fatties, stop whining and work out. Then maybe you can get a #bikinibridge by the time summer comes around.

Jenny (1/10/2014, 1:34 AM): Fuck the #bikinibridge. Fuck the #thighgap. Fuck the notion that the only form of pretty is skinny. "Beautiful" isn't synonymous with skinny

Individual perceptions of beauty depend on "a complex set of influences on preferences, including socio-cultural factors such as ideal body sizes ('beauty norms') and the stigmatization of overweight ('obesity penalty') or underweight" (Ali et al., 2013, p. 539). The bikini bridge spurred controversy about agency and stigmatization surrounding body image. Online participants felt compelled to voice their opinions in a public forum, such as Twitter. In this way, the controversy became less about the bikini bridge itself and more about cultural perceptions of beauty and the role of social media in shaping body image ideals.

Case Implications and Future Directions

The overarching goal of this research was to explore how body image trends are presented, propagated, and perpetuated through social media. The case of the bikini bridge hoax provides an initial understanding of how body image ideals can quickly become viral sensations through social media. The bikini bridge case is unique because it was purposefully prompted by a group of self-proclaimed Internet trolls seeking to prank unsuspecting consumers. Yet, the bikini bridge case offers a rare perspective on viral body image trends in the digital age. Our research suggests the bikini bridge trend gained social media notoriety due to four factors: 1) simplicity (i.e., the singularization of skinny), 2) believability (i.e., the reality of the body image "hoax"), 3) co-optation (i.e., adoption by pre-existing communities), 4) controversy (i.e., conflicting narratives among users). In terms of body image concerns and the future of social media, the first two factors are most disturbing.

First, our case suggests body image ideals are becoming increasingly singularized. Young women growing up in the digital age are receiving constant cues from their friends, peers, celebrities, and strangers through social media. While previous body image research tends to focus primarily on traditional media, the rise and diffusion of the bikini bridge trend on social media is alarming given previous research which suggests young girls, in particular, increasingly internalize body norms from online communities (Oksanen et al., 2016). Singularized body image ideals (e.g., #bikinibridge, #thighgap) simplify cultural perceptions of beauty and undercut healthy body image. Through trends like the bikini bridge, consumers are encouraged to value women's fragmented bodies. Online body image trends like the bikini bridge reward women for achieving a desirable single body part, rather than focusing on overall health and well-being.

Second, our case provides evidence toward an increasingly blurred line between perception and reality. Unlike traditional media (e.g., television, radio), consumers can easily create and disseminate their own content to a wide audience with little concern for regulation or standards. Thus, as evident in the bikini bridge case, social media users can create an entire body image phenomenon through a series of keystrokes. Advancements in social media have certainly afforded consumers the ability to gather information, make more informed decisions, and achieve their goals in a shorter period of time; however, the increased opportunities for social comparison and the wide distribution of potentially illegitimate information may prove to negatively impact body image across genders. Of critical note, social media users identify body image goals or ideals through naming them and giving them life. For instance, prior to the thigh gap or bikini bridge, societal norms intrinsically suggested women should be conscious of their legs and hips. Thus, hashtaggable body image ideals (e.g., #bikinibridge, #thighgap) lie latent in culture, waiting for social media to identify them as the next new body image craze. For instance, the bikini bridge phenomenon caught on quickly because it reflected women's underlying insecurities about their bodies. In a way, the Internet popularizes and perpetuates existing cultural body image ideals by giving them branded nicknames.

Many consumers find positive health and body image support through the Internet. Yet a dark side of social media lies in its ability to dictate body image ideals and expectations. The bikini bridge case study presented here marks a first step in understanding the complex role of social media in shaping modern body image ideals. Future research should build upon previous body image and non-traditional media studies to better understand the role of user-generated social media in shaping cultural perceptions and ideals of body image among both men and women (Perloff, 2014). Social networks provide platforms for consumers to instantly engage in multiple conversations and express divergent views. Future research should explore how consumers actively navigate social media conversations surrounding body image ideals. We must better understand consumers' lived experiences in negotiating body image through online media. How do social media experiences affect online perceptions of one's body, and vice versa? Young consumers are growing up in a digital age of filtered photos and doctored selfies. If the #bikinibridge and the #thighgap are evidence of future cultural norms, a glib outlook might expect young girls to hashtag their bra or clothing sizes as they mature. From a more optimistic perspective, future research might analyze how the democratic nature of social media can be used to combat potentially harmful body image expectations. For instance, social media users were quick to berate the popular retailer, Target, for photoshopping a thigh gap on several images of bikini models for its website (Stampler, 2014). Through social media, consumers can keep companies accountable for their representations of body standards. Future theoretical and substantive research should better understand the public policy and regulatory implications prompted by potentially harmful online body image ideals.

References

Ali, M. M., Rizzo, J.A., & Heiland, F. W. (2013). Big and beautiful? Evidence of racial differences in the perceived attractiveness of obese females. *Journal of Adolescence*, 36(3): 539–549.

Andsager, J. (2014). Research directions in social media and body image. *Sex Roles*, 71(11), 407–413.

Bailey, J., Steeves, V., Burkell, J. & Regan, P. (2013). Negotiating with gender stereotypes on social networking sites: From "bicycle face" to Facebook. *Journal of Communication Inquiry*, 37(2), 91–112.

Balter-Reitz, S. & Keller, S. (2005). Censoring thinspiration: The debate over pro-anorexic web sites. *Free Speech Yearbook*, 42(1), 79–90.

Bastos, M. T., Raimundo, R. L. G. & Travitzki, R. (2013). Gatekeeping Twitter: Message diffusion in political hashtags. *Media, Culture & Society*, 35(2), 260–270.

Beggan, J. K. & DeAngelis, M. (2015). "Oh, my God, I hate you:" The felt experience of being othered for being thin. *Symbolic Interaction*, 38(3), 371–392.

Berger, J. (2016). *Contagious: Why Things Catch On*. New York, NY: Simon & Schuster.

Berger, J. & Milkman, K. L. (2012). What makes online content viral? *Journal of Marketing Research*, 49(2), 192–205.

Bernstein, M. S., Monroy-Hernández, A., Harry, D., André, P., Panovich, K. & Vargas G. G. (2011). 4chan and/b: An analysis of anonymity and ephemerality in a large online community. In *Proceedings of the Fifth International AAAI Conference on Weblogs and Social Media*. Barcelona, Spain: 50–57.

Brumberg, J. J. (1997). *The Body Project: An Intimate History of American Girls*. New York, NY: Random House.

boyd, d. (2010, June 12). for the lolz: 4chan is hacking the attention economy. Retrieved from http://www.zephoria.org/thoughts/archives/2010/06/12/for-the-lolz-4chan-is-hacking-the-attention-economy.html.

Burke, E. (2009). Pro-anorexia and the internet: A tangled web of representation and (Dis) Embodiment. *Counselling, Psychotherapy, and Health*, 5(1), 60–81.

Castillo, C., Mendoza, M. & Poblete, B. (2011). Information Credibility on Twitter. In *Proceedings of the 20th International Conference on World Wide Web*, Hyderabad, India: 675–684.

Cova, B. & Pace, S. (2006). Brand community of convenience products: New forms of customer empowerment – the case "My Nutella The Community". *European Journal of Marketing*, 40(9/10), 1087–1105.

Daer, A. R., Hoffman, R. & Goodman, S. (2014). Rhetorical functions of hashtag forms across social media applications. In *Proceedings of the 32nd ACM International Conference on The Design of Communication*, Colorado Springs, CO: 1–3.

D'Alessandro, S. & Chitty, B. (2011). Real or relevant beauty? Body shape and endorser effects on brand attitude and body image. *Psychology & Marketing*, 28(8), 843–878.

Fardouly, J. & Vartanian, L. R. (2015). Negative comparisons about one's appearance mediate the relationship between Facebook usage and body image concerns. *Body Image*, 12(1), 82–88.

Garimella, K., Mathioudakis, M., de Francisci Morales, G. & Gionis, A. (2016). Exploring Controversy in Twitter. In *Proceedings of the 19th ACM Conference on Computer Supported Cooperative Work and Social Computing Companion*: 33–36.

Greenfield, R. (2013, August 19). Hot dog legs is a disturbing example of Tumblr's body image issues. *The Wire: News from The Atlantic*, retrieved from http://www.thewire.com/technology/2013/08/hot-dog-legs-disturbing-example-tumblrs-body-image-issues/68483/.

Gensler, S., Völckner, F., Liu-Thompkins, Y. & Wiertz, C. (2013). Managing brands in the social media environment. *Journal of Interactive Marketing*, 27(4), 242–256.

Gonzalez-Bailon, S., Wang, N., Rivero, A., Borge-Holthoefer, J. & Moreno, Y. (2014). Assessing the bias in samples of large online networks. *Social Networks*, 38(3), 16–27.

Grabe, S., Ward, L. M. & Hyde, J. S. (2008). The role of the media in body image concerns among women: A meta-analysis of experimental and correlational studies. *Psychological Bulletin*, 134(3), 460–476.

Groesz, L. M., Levine, M. P. & Murnen, S. K. (2002). The effect of experimental presentation of thin media images on body satisfaction: A meta-analytic review. *International Journal of Eating Disorders*, 31(1), 1–16.

Hanna, R., Rohm, A. & Crittenden, V. L. (2011). We're all connected: The power of the social media ecosystem. *Business Horizons*, 54(3), 265–273.

Ho, C. (2014, January 6). #BikiniBridge – pointing out our mental flaws. Blogilates.com, retrieved from http://www.blogilates.com/blog/2014/01/06/bikinibridge-pointing-out-our-mental-flaws/.

Holland, G. & Tiggemann, M. (2016). A systematic review of the impact of the use of social networking sites on body image and disordered eating outcomes. *Body Image*, 17(3), 100–110.

Hwang, K. O., Ottenbacher, A. J., Green, A. P., Cannon-Diehl, M. R., Richardson, O., Bernstam, E. V. & Thomas, E. J. (2010). Social support in an Internet weight loss community. *International Journal of Medical Informatics*, 79(1), 5–13.

Kapidzic, S. & Herring, S. C. (2011). Gender, communication, and self-presentation in teen chatrooms revisited: Have patterns changed? *Journal of Computer-Mediated Communication*, 17(1), 39–59.

Kilbourne, J. (2017). Beauty and the beast of advertising. In B. K. Scott, S. E. Cayleff, A. Donadey, & I. Lara (Eds.), *Women in Culture: An Intersectional Anthology for Gender and Women's Studies* (pp. 183-185), Malden, MA: John Wiley and Sons, Ltd.

Kotler, P. H. (1991). *Marketing Management: Analysis, Planning, and Control*, 8th ed. Englewood Cliffs, NJ: Prentice-Hall, Inc.

Kozinets, R. V. (2002). The field behind the screen: Using netnography for marketing research in online communities. *Journal of Marketing Research*, 39(1), 61–72.

Lee, S. & Baack, D. W. (2014). Meaning or sound? The effects of brand name fluency on brand recall and willingness to buy. *Journal of Promotion Management*, 20(5), 521–536.

Levine, M. P. & Smolak, L. (1996). Media as a context for the development of disordered eating. In L. Smolak, M. P. Levine & R. Striegel-Moore (Eds.), *The Developmental Psychopathology of Eating Disorders* (pp.235–257). Hillsdale, NJ: Erlbaum.

Manago, A., Ward, L., Lemm, K., Reed, L. & Seabrook, R. (2015). Facebook involvement, objectified body consciousness, body shame, and sexual assertiveness in college women and men. *Sex Roles*, 72(1), 1–14.

Martin, M. C. & Gentry, J. W. (1997). Stuck in the model trap: The effects of beautiful models in ads on female pre-adolescents and adolescents. *Journal of Advertising*, 26(2), 19–33.

Meier, E. P. & Gray, J. (2014). Facebook photo activity associated with body image disturbance in adolescent girls. *CyberPsychology, Behavior & Social Networking*, 17(4), 199–206.

Myers, P. N. & Biocca, F. A. (1992). The elastic body image: The effect of television advertising and programming on body image distortions in young women. *Journal of Communication*, 42(3), 108–133.

Neumark-Sztianer, D., Paxton, S., Hannan, P., Haines, J. & Story, M. (2006). Does body satisfaction matter? Five-year longitudinal associations between body satisfaction and health behaviors in adolescent females and males. *Journal of Adolescent Health*, 39(2), 244–251.

Oksanen, A., Garcia, D., Sirola, A., Näsi, M., Kaakinen, M., Keipi, T. & Räsänen, P. (2015). Pro-anorexia and anti-pro-anorexia videos on YouTube: Sentiment analysis of user responses. *Journal of Medical Internet Research*, 17(11) e256.

Paxton, S., Neumark-Sztianer, D. & Hannan, P. (2006). Body dissatisfaction prospectively predicts depressive mood and low self-esteem in adolescent girls and boys. *Journal of Clinical Child and Adolescent Psychology*, 35(4), 539–549.

Perloff, R. (2014). Social media effects on young women's body image concerns: Theoretical perspectives and an agenda for research. *Sex Roles*, 71(11), 363–377.

Rao, A. R. & Monroe, K. B. (1989). The effect of price, brand name, and store name on buyers' perceptions of product quality: An integrative review. *Journal of Marketing Research*, 26(3), 351–357.

Richardson, P. S., Dick, A. S. & Jain, A. K. (1994). Extrinsic and intrinsic cue effects on perceptions of store brand quality. *Journal of Marketing*, 58(4), 28–36.

Romano, A. (2013, July 18). 29 tags Tumblr banned from its mobile app (and 10 it didn't). *The Daily Dot*, retrieved from http://www.dailydot.com/business/banned-tumblr-tags-mobile/.

Shankar, V. & Malthouse, E. C. (2007). The growth of interactions and dialogs in interactive marketing. *Journal of Interactive Marketing*, 21(2), 2–4.

Slater, A., Tiggemann, M., Hawkins, K. & Werchon, D. (2011). Just one click: A content analysis of advertisements on teen web sites. *Journal of Adolescent Health*, 50(4), 339–345.

Strano, M. M. (2008). User descriptions and interpretations of self-presentation through Facebook profile images. *Cyberpsychology*, 2(2), retrieved from http://www.cyberpsychology.eu/view.php?cisloclanku=2008110402&article=1.

Stampler, L. (March 11, 2014). Can you spot Target's incredibly awkward Photoshop fail? *TIME.com*, retrieved from http://time.com/19938/target-photoshop-fail-thigh-gap/.

Teodoro, R. & Naaman, M. (2013). Fitter with Twitter: Understanding personal health and fitness activity in social media. In *Proceedings of Seventh International AAAI Conference on Weblogs and Social Media*, Cambridge, MA: 1–10.

Thompson, C. J. & Hirschman, E. C. (1995). Understanding the socialized body: A post-structuralist analysis of consumers' self-conceptions, body images, and self-care practices. *Journal of Consumer Research*, 22(2), 139–153.

Tiggemann, M. & Miller, J. (2010). The Internet and adolescent girls' weight satisfaction and drive for thinness. *Sex Roles*, 63(1), 79–90.

Tiggemann, M. & Slater, A. (2013). NetGirls: The Internet, Facebook, and body image concern in adolescent girls. *The International Journal of Eating Disorders*, 46(6), 630–633.

Tiidenberg, K. (2015). Boundaries and conflict in a NSFW community on Tumblr: The meanings and uses of selfies. *New Media & Society*, published online before print January 14, 2015, 1-16: doi:10.1177/1461444814567984.

Turner, J. (2014). Negotiating a media effects model: Addendums and adjustments to Perloff's framework for social media's impact on body image concerns. *Sex Roles*, 71(11), 393–406.

Tziallas, E. (2016). Pornophilia: porn gifs, fandom, circuitries. *Porn Studies*, published online before print April 20, 2016, 1–3: doi: 10.1080/23268743.2016.1148329.

Urban Dictionary (2009). Bikini bridge. Retreived from http://www.urbandictionary.com/define.php?term=bikini%20bridge.

Valkenburg, P. M. & Peter, J. (2013). The differential susceptibility to media effects model. *Journal of Communication*, 63(2), 221–243.

Vandenbosch, L. & Eggermont, S. (2012). Understanding sexual objectification: A comprehensive approach toward media exposure and girls' internalization of beauty ideals, self-objectification, and body surveillance. *Journal of Communication*, 62(5), 869–887.

Veer, E. (2010). Hiding in plain sight: 'Secret' anorexia nervosa communities on Youtube. In D. W. Dahl, G. V. Johar & S. M. J. van Osselaer (Eds.), *NA - Advances in Consumer Research* (Vol. 38). Duluth, MN: Association for Consumer Research, retrieved from http://www.acrwebsite.org/volumes/display.asp?id=15846.

Whitty, M. T. (2008). Revealing the 'real' me, searching for the 'actual' you: Presentations of self on an Internet dating site. *Computers in Human Behavior*, 24(4), 1707–1723.

Wolcott, H. F. (1999). *Ethnography: A way of seeing*. Lanham, MD: Rowman Altamira.

Wood-Barcalow, N. L., Tylka, T. L. & Augustus-Horvath, C. L. (2010). "But I like my body": Positive body image characteristics and a holistic model for young-adult women. *Body Image*, 7(2): 106–116.

Williams, R. J. & Ricciardelli, L. A. (2014). Social media and body image concerns: Further considerations and broader perspectives. *Sex Roles*, 71(11), 389–392.

Vaterlaus, J. M., Patten, E. V., Roche, C. & Young, J. A. (2015). #Gettinghealthy: The perceived influence of social media on young adult health behaviors. *Computers in Human Behavior*, 45(April), 151–157.

5

CHEATERS, TROLLS, AND NINJA LOOTERS

The Dark Side of Psychological Ownership

Keith Marion Smith, John Hulland,
and Scott A. Thompson

Marketing academics have typically studied possession or ownership through the theoretical lens of the endowment effect (Kahneman et al., 1990; Thaler, 1980), which persistently shows that consumers' valuations of objects increase once they have taken ownership. This effect has been investigated across a variety of settings and possession objects, and such factors as loss aversion and length of ownership have been found to influence consumer valuation (e.g., Brenner et al., 2007; Strahilevitz & Loewenstein, 1998). Feelings of ownership have been found to be so pervasive that merely touching or thinking carefully about a target object can increase its perceived value and influence consumer choice (e.g., Fuchs et al., 2010; Peck & Shu, 2009; Shu & Peck, 2011).

In general, these studies have focused predominantly on tangible products consumed without regard to the presence of other consumers, while neglecting intangible products as well as products and services more commonly consumed with a group of like-minded consumers (e.g., Kahneman et al., 1990). Yet these intangible, collectively owned products make up an increasingly large part of our consumption experiences. In particular, social media, which encompasses not just social networking sites (such as Facebook) but a wide range of platforms such as online communities and virtual game worlds, plays a key role in the lives of many contemporary consumers (e.g., Martinez-Lopez et al., 2016). The continuing proliferation in the number and types of social media platforms is rapidly expanding the opportunities for consumers to develop psychological ownership of intangible, collectively owned products and services, ranging from "my Followers" to "my Warcraft guild".

In an attempt to examine ownership in a social media context, and to better understand the potential negative outcomes that arises out of ownership, we first review psychological ownership theory, and demonstrate how it might be applied to the social media marketing context by drawing on related previous work (Hulland et al., 2015; Jussila et al., 2015). We then briefly discuss some of the unique implications of psychological ownership in social media contexts. Finally, using a netnographic approach (Kozinets, 2002) to draw on data collected from online social media forums we illustrate and discuss a number of potential negative outcomes that arise from psychological ownership, both for consumers and for firms that use social media. While we do not provide an exhaustive investigation of psychological ownership theory in the social media context, we demonstrate how unique insights can be drawn from the theory.

Psychological Ownership Theory

The concept of psychological ownership as a state of mind was originally studied in the management and organizational literatures to better understand individual workplace motivations, attitudes, and outcomes. Over the past fifteen years, use of this theoretical lens has facilitated a better understanding of a range of workplace and employee phenomena, both positive and negative in nature (Brown et al., 2005; Pierce & Jussila, 2011). More recently, the concept of psychological ownership has been applied to the marketing context in order to better understand the connections and relationships that customers develop with products and services (Jussila et al., 2015).

Psychological ownership can be defined in its broadest terms as the "state in which individuals feel as though the target of ownership (material or nonmaterial in nature) or a piece of it is 'theirs'" (Pierce et al., 2001, p. 299). This conception of ownership contrasts sharply with the economic perspective that adopts a legalistic view of ownership and ascribes a utilitarian value or benefit to the state of ownership. This view also differs from the more traditional marketing perspective of ownership as endowment (Kahneman et al., 1990; Thaler, 1980), which has persistently shown that consumers' valuations of objects increase once they have taken ownership.[1]

A more detailed examination of the concept developed by Pierce, Kostova, and Dirks (2001, 2003) reveals a set of key characteristics of psychological ownership. First is a sense of possession that extends beyond the brand/company connection developed in consumer brand relationships and company identification research (Bhattacharya & Sen, 2003). Psychological ownership manifests actual feelings of possession, such as "It is MINE!" (Jussila et al., 2015, p 122). Thus, psychological ownership is a state independent of the legal definition of ownership. Furthermore, the state of psychological ownership is both cognitive and affective, including components of thoughts, attitudes, and beliefs, but also emotions and feelings about the target of ownership. This sense of individual possession combined with the thoughts and feelings generated by the target of ownership in the consumer highlights the integration of the target of ownership with the self. Similar to the concept of the extended self that explores the incorporation of certain valued possessions into individual's self-identity (Belk, 1988, 2013), psychological ownership casts a large role for 'owned' targets in each consumer's conception of self. However, psychological ownership extends beyond just highly valued possessions to encompass mundane and even ephemeral objects.

Motivations to Develop Psychological Ownership

The sense of psychological ownership, whether it is of a tangible product (e.g., smart phone, car) or a more intangible service (e.g., sports team, social media account, virtual item) is easily identified, and most consumers readily admit to sometimes having thoughts and feelings of psychological ownership. However, what motivates or drives the need for individuals to engage in this combination of possessing thoughts and feelings around specific products? Jussila and Tuominen (2010) highlight four separate human needs that motivate individuals to develop a sense of psychological ownership: efficacy and effectance, self-identity, having a place, and stimulation. These needs are shown on the left hand side of Figure 5.1, which summarizes our conceptual discussion of psychological ownership theory.

Efficacy and effectance motivations are fundamentally rooted in a drive for consumer control. Individual control over one's environment and one's self-identity can be facilitated through control over relevant products and services. A sense of ownership may grow as mastery over the product/service develops and the individual feels better capable of exercising control.

The need for a preferred space that can be claimed by a consumer provides another motivation for psychological ownership. Consumers seek control over their environment in an attempt to claim a space that reflects their attitudes and preferences. As this space is claimed, feelings of ownership arise for the space and for those things associated with the space (Duncan, 1981). These spaces need not be tangible in nature and can include intangible 'spaces' such as electronic environments, virtual worlds, or shared communities. Thus, products and services

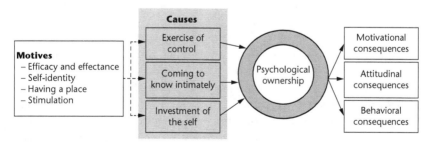

FIGURE 5.1 Conceptual Framework – Psychological Ownership in a Social Media Context

Adapted from Jussila et al. 2015

associated with these tangible and intangible spaces become prime targets for the development of psychological ownership.

Consumers have an intrinsic need to develop and make sense of their own self-identity, and to establish how they might interact with other consumers who share their attitudes and beliefs about the world. Products and services provide a unique role in facilitating this basic need. Ownership of products and services can provide consumers with clarity regarding the values and attitudes they find important. Through the process of interacting and connecting with fellow owners, consumers obtain information about common values and attitudes, and can determine to what degree they share those common values. Thus, psychological ownership of products and services provides a means through which consumers can both discover and reveal to others their own expectations and attitudes.

Finally, research suggests that individuals have a need for activation and stimulation that is often satisfied by the use of possessions (Duncan, 1981). As these products and services are utilized in everyday activity, a sense of increased psychological ownership develops around them. Furthermore, the objects used for stimulation today may change in the future, reflecting the shifting preferences and identities of consumers over time. These changes provide a potential framework to understand how consumers adopt and dispossess products and services, and how the need for stimulation may provide an immediate shift that takes longer to be fully adopted by the consumer's self and their environment.

Mechanisms of Psychological Ownership

While it is relatively straightforward to identify the underlying motivations that potentially drive the development of psychological ownership, determining exactly how those motivations are converted into the final state of psychological ownership is less clear. Some research has theoretically explored these processes (Jussila et al., 2015; Pierce & Jussila, 2011), but they continue to be somewhat vague and unclear, especially in the marketing context. Drawing from literature across psychology, social psychology, and sociology, three potential mechanisms have been identified by researchers (see second block in Figure 5.1): exercise of control, intimate knowledge, and investment of the self.

Exercise of control represents the first of these potential mechanisms. As consumers adopt and use products to satisfy core needs, their sense of psychological ownership develops as these products and services provide them with increasing control over their own identity and their environments. Some products and services are more conducive to fostering a sense of control for consumers; for example, Fuchs et al. (2010) show that when firms provide consumers with more control over product design, stronger feelings of psychological ownership emerge.

Second, the more consumers learn about an object (i.e., a product or service), the more they understand the congruities between the object and themselves and, in the process, their own self-identity and their environment. Those products/services that strongly facilitate crystallization of a consumer's self-identity and help to define the consumer's environment will be more likely to engender a strong sense of psychological ownership.

Finally, psychological ownership may develop through the investment of the self into products and services. While this concept has its inception in the early sociological literature of the Renaissance, its more recent integration in the marketing literature has been through the concept of value co-creation (e.g., Fuchs et al., 2010; Prahalad & Ramaswamy, 2000; Vargo & Lusch, 2004). As consumers engage in product and service consumption, they invest a part of themselves in the product or service, and thus co-create shared value with the firm and other consumers (Thompson & Loveland, 2015). Thus, the more a product or service is involved in value co-creation, the more likely consumers are to develop stronger feelings of psychological ownership.

Outcomes of Psychological Ownership

While the motivations, mechanisms, and boundary conditions governing the development of a state of psychological ownership are important for marketers to understand, the impacts of psychological ownership on potential outcomes are equally important, and are arguably of much greater interest to most firms. Three broad classes of outcomes have been identified by past psychological ownership research (e.g., Jussila et al., 2015; Pierce & Jussila, 2011), and these are shown at the right hand side of Figure 5.1: motivations, attitudes, and behaviors.

The first set of outcomes is motivationally based, reflecting the cyclical and self-reinforcing nature of psychological ownership. Key motivational outcomes include the very same needs that drive consumers to adopt a state of psychological ownership in the first place: efficacy and effectance, self-identity, having a place, and stimulation (Pierce & Jussila, 2011). When the needs are meet, this virtuous cycle creates a feedback loop whereby the objects for which consumers adopt states of psychological ownership are identified as part of the self, and therefore consumers are motivated to develop an even stronger sense of psychological ownership around those objects. However, when the original needs are not met, the consumer will suffer reduced feelings of ownership and—in the extreme—discontinue use of a product or service.

Traditionally, empirical research looking at the outcomes of psychological ownership has identified attitudinal consequences such as satisfaction, commitment, and self-esteem (Pierce & Jussila, 2011). While most of this work has studied these attitudes in an organizational or employee context, similar attitudes have been theorized to impact marketing outcomes (Jussila et al., 2015). Satisfaction and commitment have been studied across a wide range of marketing contexts, including products, brands, and firms, among others. It follows logically that psychological ownership may influence these key attitudinal marketing outcomes, as well as related constructs such as loyalty and willingness to pay.

Finally, behavioral outcomes represent the observable manifestations of motivational and attitudinal states, and are the outcomes typically of most interest to firms. In the management literature, a wealth of different behavioral outcomes have been noted, including organizational citizenship behavior, personalization, and job search behavior, among others. From a marketing perspective, word-of-mouth behavior, community participation, and customer-to-customer helping can all draw corollaries to citizenship behavior. Similarly, job search behavior decreases when employees develop a sense of psychological ownership towards their job or firm; it can be compared to loyalty, which may be increased as a result of stronger feelings of psychological ownership relating to a product or brand (Jussila et al., 2015). Finally, personalization, which is manifested in organizations by employees modifying their space to reflect their own identity, can be compared to the extensive co-creation cultures within some product categories, wherein customers modify products or services both to meet their own unique needs, and to more closely align with their own identities.

Collective Psychological Ownership

Thus far, we have discussed psychological ownership as an individual-level phenomenon. However, Pierce, and Jussila (2010) propose that this sense of ownership can also exist at the group level, defining collective psychological ownership as "the collectively held sense (feeling) that [a] target of ownership (or a piece of that target) is collectively 'ours'" (p. 812). They argue that individual perceptions of psychological ownership transition to the group level in three stages (which can occur nearly simultaneously or over an extended period of time): 1) the individual comes to view an object as "mine"; 2) the individual recognizes that other individuals are also psychologically tied to the object; and then 3) a shift in personal reference takes place from the individual (i.e., the object is "mine") to the group (i.e., the object is "ours").

While space here is too limited to describe the collective ownership model in detail, several aspects seem particularly worthy of emphasis in the marketing context. First, Pierce and Jussila (2010) suggest that a target object with the potential to develop and sustain a collective sense of ownership should: 1) arouse one or more of the motives that underlie individual personal feelings of ownership; 2) aid collective recognition that others also have a relationship with the target; and 3) through individual action, facilitate the group's controlling, coming to know, and investing of selves into the ownership target.

Pierce, and Jussila (2010) suggest that a potential target needs to minimally be visible and attractive, since it must arouse the interest and attention of its group members, and also distinctive versus other potential ownership targets. To serve each member's need for efficacy and effectance in the group context, the target must be accessible and malleable (both individually and collectively). Further, to serve each group member's need for self-identity motive, the target needs to be jointly accessible, attractive, socially esteemed and self-revealing. Finally, to fulfill each individual's need for a place to dwell, the target must be jointly open, available, and receptive. Pierce, and Jussila conclude (2010, p. 820) that "if the target is going to satisfy each of the group member's social-identity motives it needs to be simultaneously receptive, accessible, malleable, attractive, and socially esteemed by many; its meaning must be collectively understood; and it must involve a visible and collaborative working relationship."

Psychological Ownership in Social Media

In a landmark paper, Belk (1988) described how possessions are major components of and reflections of individual consumer identities. However, this work was rooted in a discussion of *material* possessions. More recently, Belk (2013, p. 477) has suggested that:

> ... the current wave of digital technologies is fundamentally changing consumer behavior in ways that have significant implications for the formulation of the extended self.

One area in particular that seems worthy of attention from marketers in this regard is that of social media (Martinez-Lopez et al., 2016). Kaplan and Haenlein (2010) define social media as a group of applications that allow for the creation and exchange of user-generated content, and classify social media into six types of applications: blogs, social networking sites (e.g., Facebook, Pinterest), virtual social worlds (e.g., Second Life), collaborative projects (e.g., Source Forge), content communities (e.g., YouTube), and virtual games worlds (e.g., World of Warcraft). Although prior research has examined a wide variety of factors that can potentially affect social media use, relatively little work has looked at how social media usage fulfills consumers' various needs (Karahanna et al., 2013). Psychological ownership theory offers a useful lens through which to investigate this phenomenon.

Some preliminary work in this area provides support for the notion that feelings of psychological ownership and social media usage are intertwined (Hulland et al., 2015; Karahanna et al., 2015). For example, Lee and Chen (2011) found that individuals' intentions to participate in a virtual world were positively related to their sense of ownership towards that world. Xu et al. (2012) argue that individuals use online game play to fulfill their needs for building relationships with other game players (i.e., providing a sense of belonging) and mastering the game itself (i.e., efficacy). Similarly, Jenkins-Guarnieri et al. (2012) suggest that social media platforms help individuals both to develop relationships and to express a sense of self-identity. Finally, Karahanna et al. (2013) show empirically that psychological needs relating to psychological ownership are significantly associated with the extent to which individuals use social media, as well as providing some evidence that different social media applications are associated with fulfilling different psychological needs.

However, despite these promising initial studies, much more work is needed to understand how consumers use various forms of social media to enrich their lives by addressing their latent needs as described by psychological ownership theory. Using social media, consumers can express and learn more about their self-identities, find communities within which they feel a strong sense of comfort and belonging, and exert their own control over the content they share with others (i.e., user-generated content). Thus, social media applications can clearly address the needs/motives that underpin psychological ownership.

Collective Ownership and Social Media

Many social media platforms provide opportunities for collective ownership. While some aspects of social media platforms emphasize individual ownership, such as a Facebook "Wall," others encourage a sense of collective ownership. For example, in community discussion boards, where all participants are typically able to freely exchange ideas in an open forum, members are unable to segregate themselves from other members. As a result, community discussion boards have the potential for giving rise to a sense of collective psychological ownership. To some degree this depends on how the board is administered. Moderators who regularly evaluate and have the power to censor individuals' contributions to a board can undermine collective ownership. On the other hand, many discussion boards do not share this limitation. This observation suggests that organizers and companies that host community boards can influence the level of collective psychological ownership that develops over time. In our empirical study section, we focus on examples drawn from these boards.

While marketers to date have focused primarily on in-network ad placement and optimization of key search words, this collective notion of ownership provides new opportunities for marketers to strategically promote (or discourage) collective psychological ownership. As a result, marketers need to develop a better understanding of the opportunities and threats created by consumers' sense of collective psychological ownership. On the positive side, Kim and Thompson (2013) suggest that the role that representatives adopt in an online community influences how community members react to their communication attempts. Specifically, when firms' representatives assume a social role within a community, emphasizing that they share the same interests and primarily wish to interact socially, members of communities react more positively toward not just the representative but also toward the brand. On the other hand, representatives who assume other roles such as technical support or sales support are treated less favorably. This suggests that firms may be able to use collective psychological ownership to engage community members as invested, fellow stakeholders rather than as arms-length consumers.

On the negative side, the sense of collective psychological ownership that results from active consumer participation in social media contexts can lead to conflict between firms and their customers over who "owns" the platform or how the site should be managed over time. Facebook, Twitter, Instagram, and Google have been involved in a series of high profile battles with their users over control of content on their social media networks (e.g., Isidore, 2013; Ortutay, 2012). Conflicts over collective psychological ownership have given rise to consumer campaigns such as "Quit Facebook Day" (Paul, 2010). By relying on terms of service agreements which grant firms legal ownership of consumer-generated content, firms have repeatedly failed to anticipate the reaction that consumers who feel a sense of psychological ownership have to the firm's use of this content. This disagreement over ownership can occur both between firms and consumers as well as between individual consumers, as we discuss in the next section.

Contested Psychological Ownership

A common point of contention between consumers and firms is the use of "opt out" rather than "opt in" privacy policies. If the content is viewed from a legal perspective as belonging to the firm (as Facebook does, for example), allowing consumers to "opt out" appears to be a generous concession on the part of the firm. However, when viewed from a collective psychological ownership perspective, "opt out" policies appear as an egregious attempt to grab content that rightly belongs to community members. From this perspective, the ethical course of action would be for the firm to ask users to "opt in" to the use of "their" content. Thus, collective psychological ownership provides insights into consumer conflicts that have bedeviled the largest social media companies. It also suggests policies that are sensitive to psychological ownership may forestall future conflicts and enhance customer satisfaction.

The nature of connected consumers in social media settings creates an environment where products and/or services are adopted and psychologically owned by many different consumers at once. Separate from the firm, consumers generate their own strong feelings of psychological ownership, and express their self-identity, establish a preferred space, and provide stimulation and efficacy to satisfy their own needs and motivations. While this environment has the potential to develop into a shared collective sense of psychological ownership, the interactions between consumers can sometimes fracture and follow a very different (and more negative) path than that intended by firms.

Each consumer is likely to hold different conceptions of the role that social media plays in their life, in part because of their different needs and motivations. For example, consider a Facebook user who primarily interacts with other like-minded consumers, seeking a safe place for expression and interaction. She is using her social media account primarily as a means for self-identity development. In contrast, one of her social media-connected friends uses Facebook as a means to engage in political discussion and stimulation with others, seeking spirited conversation and argument. These very different personal motivations may result in conflict as the two consumers interact. Each consumer has a legitimate motivation for engaging in the social media network, but when the two interact it is likely that each will perceive the other as 'incorrectly' consuming the service, and even may perceive the other's actions as a direct attack on their personal psychological ownership of the social media platform, eventually resulting in negative attitudes and behaviors (e.g., unfriending) between the two. Furthermore, firms are increasingly finding themselves entangled in these conflicts, with consumers demanding that services such as Facebook and Twitter ban other consumers that they feel are inappropriately using their service.

These contested perspectives on the proper use of social media are made more nebulous by the intangible nature of most social media experiences. Rarely do social media platforms provide a tangible product that a consumer can point to and claim legal ownership of. However, the social nature of the services provided, coupled with firms' implicit (or even explicit) encouragement of customers to view themselves as owners of their own accounts, can foster a sense of broader consumer ownership that is at odds with the firms' and other consumers' perspectives. The final result of each consumer holding a different vision of psychological ownership is conflict over who has a greater claim to ownership, and conflict over whose version of ownership is more legitimate.

The Dark Side of Psychological Ownership in Social Media

Firms that want to encourage a sense of psychological ownership need to ensure that their marketing-related sites are attractive, visible, accessible, and customizable (Hulland et al., 2015). Many marketers have done a good job of emphasizing some of these attributes (particularly visibility and accessibility), but have lagged with respect to others. Furthermore, marketers have often focused on potential positive outcomes without considering the negative consequences. Both collective and contested ownership within social media platforms provide fertile ground for negative consumer behavior, the 'dark side' of psychological ownership.

In an effort to highlight some of these negative outcomes, we used a netnographic approach (Kozinets, 2002) to investigate a number of online communities associated with online multiplayer game products. Netnographic methodologies "adapt ethnographic research techniques to study the cultures and communities that are emerging through computer-mediated communications" (Kozinets, 2002, p. 62), and have been widely adopted within the marketing literature to study online and social media contexts. Netnographies provide access to naturally occurring behavior among members of the community. Furthermore, unlike traditional ethnographies, netnographies can be conducted almost entirely unobtrusively, eliminating the concern that the researcher may impact behavior by their presence.

Online multiplayer games are increasingly popular among consumers. The computer and video game industry has undergone explosive growth in the past ten years, with reported US revenues of $23.5 billion in 2015. Over 60% of US households play video games regularly (3 hours or more per week), and over half of those households play games with other people, either online or in person (Entertainment Software Association, 2016). As noted above, community discussion boards provide an excellent context within which to study psychological ownership, often fostering a combination of collective and contested ownership that can highlight potential dark side outcomes. Thus, threads and posts were collected from the message forums of three of the largest multiplayer online games (World of Warcraft, League of Legends, and Call of Duty).

Trolling and Cyberbullying[2]

Marketers and policymakers are becoming increasingly alarmed at the rise of *cyberbullying* and *trolling*. This has led to public campaigns aimed at curbing these behaviors (e.g. www.stopbullying.gov/cyberbullying), but these efforts are hampered by a poor understanding of why consumers engage in these activities in the first place. Psychological ownership suggests that consumers are motivated by a need to find a place to belong. This need for a place gives rise to efforts to claim control of one's surroundings in order to assert ownership. Thus, psychological ownership suggests that negative behaviors like cyberbullying and trolling behaviors may be motivated (at least in part) by a desire to claim ownership of virtual spaces such as Facebook, virtual worlds, and online communities. Furthermore, consumers who feel that their own identity is threatened through attacks on their 'owned' products may adopt toxic bullying or trolling behaviors towards others. While these attacks can take the form of external criticisms of the product, they are just as likely to be derived from the bully's perception of other consumers as embarrassing or poor representatives of the product's consumer base.

In online game products, these threats to belonging (sense of a personal place) and self-identity are often evident in the treatment of new players within the game. Online game communities have a variety of derogatory names for new players, including 'noob', 'scrub', 'spammer', 'knobhead', and 'smurf' to name a few. New players are often treated poorly by some existing product owners, who encourage new players to quit the game or repeatedly abuse them within the game itself. For example, one forum user addressed a new member by telling them to "Man up. Admit you suck. ... And L2P [learn to play]."

Although harsh, this castigation is relatively benign compared to other behaviors directed at new players. Indeed, attacks can take much more aggressive forms. In some games, consumers can engage in one of several different competitive roles within a team of fellow consumers, such as offense, defense, or support roles. Some players feel that certain ways of playing (e.g., acting as a support character) violate their invested identity in the game: "Nobody likes support i mean lets be real support is only … chicks and gay guys." Others may embrace the bully or troll role in an attempt to drive out those consumers perceived as different or as threats to their own identity. For example, a League of Legends player commented on a shift in his own self-identity resulting from his trolling behaviors: "I play super toxic but I try to be subtle like steal health packs in front of you when I don't need them, steal buffs, shop a long time, reveal my team in the bush, annoying pings. I was labeled toxic and I have embraced it, much more fun than helping dummies … ." Furthermore, this comment illustrates how consumers sometimes deny ownership of virtual objects, such as health packs, to fellow consumers despite the fact that the game was designed with the intent that such objects were collective team resources.

Consumer-to-consumer Conflict

While cyberbullying has gained widespread attention, other forms of consumer-to-consumer conflict have arisen as a result of the psychological ownership of virtual or social media products. In the context of online games, consumers often create and develop avatars that represent their identity within the game world. These avatars are manifestations of the motivation and investment in self-identity exercised by each individual consumer, and the items and features chosen to adorn avatars enhance feelings of psychological ownership. Consumers' avatars can be enriched and customized by using resources or items found within the game itself.

However, these virtual items are not equally available to all consumers and are in limited supply. As a result, consumers will often compete with one another for the right to utilize or 'own' these in-game items. It is the competition for these items that generates a state of contested ownership within the context of collective ownership. Different consumers' feelings regarding their 'rights' to a virtual item are likely to be influenced by how strong their feelings of psychological ownership are towards the game. These items are rarely awarded based on a consumer's feelings of psychological ownership, however, instead often being delivered randomly to players. When consumers feel that the virtual items they have obtained are incongruent with their investment in the game world (e.g., their feelings of psychological ownership), they sometimes resort to negative behaviors to remedy that discord.

Common examples of these types of behaviors include ninja looting, kill stealing,[3] or carrying.[4] Each of these behaviors comprises situations where consumers feel that they have a greater right to something in the game, and engage in virtual theft or violation of social norms to ensure access to these limited virtual goods. Ninja looting describes an action where one consumer steals a virtual item in game that was intended for others. Individuals who engage in ninja looting are often ostracized or stigmatized by most consumers. One forum post notes, "These guys just love to deprive others of their loot out of pure spite, and IMO [in my opinion] should not be allowed to play the game." Other consumers go so far as to accuse ninja looters of theft, "… stealing and cheating your peers. The stealing of an item that someone else deserved. Always done by a dumb-ass &★!@#."

The conflict that arises between ninja looters and other players can result from disparate feelings of ownership between consumers, or from differences in how individual consumers have integrated the virtual avatar and social media product into their own self-identity and preferred space. Despite the fact these disputes are over virtual goods, the aggrieved consumers have real feelings of theft and violation: "Sadly, this person is on my server. Like living across the street from a thief."

Psychological ownership suggests that the confluence of collective and virtual ownership results in potentially contested ownership. This can be centered not just around virtual items, but also around situations where disparate effort is expended by different consumers. This can lead to feelings of inequity: "Some people are almost afk [away from keyboard] … they kinda wait for others to do their job. I saw people sitting, doing nothing while the rest of us were killing the mobs [monsters]. Some healers don't heal. They just sit. … Is this fair?" Furthermore, contested ownership can extend beyond virtual objects to include entire virtual environments. For example, players will sometimes "camp" an area, asserting their ownership over an entire virtual space. This, in turn, leads to conflict over the psychological ownership of the space, with players heatedly denouncing others who attempt to play in the same area as "camp stealers" or "kill stealers."

Consumer–firm Conflict

Psychological ownership also highlights the often overlooked consequences that collective or shared psychological ownership of products and services can have for the relationship between consumers and firms. Although firms generally have the right to terminate or alter brands, services, and even online communities that consumers feel they own, a sense of psychological ownership can exist despite the absence of any legal right (Jussila et al., 2015). Thus, consumers may feel robbed or betrayed in the face of significant firm changes, leading to backlashes such as the one experienced by Apple after abandoning its Newton line (Muñiz & Schau, 2005).

This disjuncture between legal versus psychological ownership can be particularly problematic for online electronic services such as virtual worlds and multi-player games. Consumer attachments to the virtual product, their avatar and their virtual possessions can prompt some consumers to engage in modifications to the software code that enable them to consume the product as they desire. In many cases, these modifications are at odds with the intentions of the firm (as well as those of many other consumers). In these situations, it is not clear who has a greater "right" to dictate how a product is consumed—the firm or individual consumers. Often, firms establish oversight on shared consumption in order to ensure that a common ground of consumption exists for all their potential customers. However, these efforts can place the firm in the middle of consumer conflicts over ownership.

One common example of consumer–firm conflict in virtual world and online multiplayer games can be found in cheats or hacks installed by some consumers. Illegal software is designed and installed to bypass or circumvent the coded rules of a game. These can include software hacks to ensure perfect aiming, increased run speed, or invincibility in a multitude of different game genres. It is likely that the individuals who install and use these software hacks have a strong sense of psychological ownership over the product, to the degree that their preferred use of the product supersedes the intended use by the firm. While denounced as "cheaters" by other consumers, consumers who use such hacks often defend their actions on the basis that they "paid for the game" and therefore can play "their game" however they wish. Nonetheless, the "cheater's" actions, derived from their own sense of ownership, have implications for other consumer's feelings of ownership, and on the perception all consumers have of the product (and firm).

Responses from "non-cheaters" can vary from confusion, to frustration, to attacks against the firm. Some consumers, when faced with "cheaters", simply seek equity or fairness of some kind, as evidenced by a forum post from the popular Call of Duty series of games: "Ok, so i have a recording of a game with an obvious cheater that goes 113-0 [win-loss record]. What should i do? How do i report him?" Others simply express frustration with the situation, despite attempts by the firm to redress or resolve the problem: "Cheating in [Modern Warrior 3] is rampant. I really don't understand why the developers can't or won't get this under control. [Valve Anti-Cheat software] doesn't seem to be working … been seeing the same cheaters for months."

These outcomes are potentially frustrating for individual consumers who find their consumption of the game and their own developing sense of psychological ownership compromised by "cheaters" who disagree with the expected consumption pattern established by the firm. It is not uncommon, however, for this frustration to be converted into feelings of disappointment, frustration, and ultimately abandonment towards the firm. Consumers can interpret the presence of "cheaters" as an indictment on the quality of the product: "I'm not buying another CoD [Call of Duty] game or anything by Infinity Ward [developer]. They release substandard products and have no regard for the customer." At extreme levels, the negative interactions with "cheaters" are interpreted as negative interactions between the customer and the firm: "If this goes on for another week then this is the last of the Cod series I buy. I run my own business and if I treated my customers like this I would be out of business in no time."

The issues raised by contested psychological ownership lead to important questions for marketing managers to consider. For example, what obligations do firms incur by fostering a sense of ownership? Should firms respect the "property rights" of consumers who "own" virtual possessions? Do firms have a moral obligation to compensate consumers for the loss of possessions when a service is terminated? Should firms engage in policing activity to ensure that all customers can consume the product as designed, or should consumers have the 'right' to engage with the product however they desire? Psychological ownership not only provides a basis for understanding negative consumer behaviors, but also provides a starting point to answering these types of complicated questions regarding ownership rights in collective and contested social media contexts.

General Discussion

While the specific examples outlined above were drawn from online multiplayer gaming contexts, it is important to note that these phenomena are not restricted to the online gaming environment. These games share many of the same characteristics with other social media platforms that make them conducive to fostering psychological ownership. Attractiveness, accessibility, openness, and customizability are all present in many different social media contexts, and it is these attributes, combined with consumer motivations towards self-identity and preferred space that make social media products appealing targets for psychological ownership on the part of consumers.

Although various negative outcomes and implications are a consequence of high levels of psychological ownership, firms and consumer groups are increasingly experimenting with solutions to address these negative interactions, with varying degrees of success. For example, firms have developed formal anti-cheat systems that specifically identify cheaters and implement both temporary and permanent bans from product use for those who consistently employ cheats. Similarly, formal rules such as "PNPs" or "Play Nice Policies" that establish the rights that consumers may have to virtual goods and environments have been implemented by a number of firms. In a similar vein, consumers have devised complex and sophisticated systems to ensure fairness and equity in the distribution of virtual goods among fellow guild or clan members.[5] While negative outcomes are possible and perhaps even inevitable, firms and consumer groups who chose to spend the resources can limit the most egregious behavior. Of course, the resources required to implement and enforce such policies must be weighed by firms seeking to minimize negative behaviors against the benefits of such an investment.

Conclusion

Belk (2013) has suggested that as marketing researchers we need to revisit the notion of extended self in the face of rapid technological advancement. He proposes five areas for particular attention in future research: collecting, gift-giving, rematerialization, virtual brand communities, and digital relationships. Psychological ownership theory provides a strong and useful conceptual lens through which a number of these topics critical to social media can be studied and better understood. Furthermore, as we have outlined in the preceding pages, application of psychological ownership theory in the consumer behavior and marketing domains—particularly in the social media context—raises important new questions while also offering the promise of new and important insights. Particularly in the context of 'dark side' behaviors, psychological ownership can provide clearer understanding to help guide managerial practice. Trolls, ninja looters, and cheaters are just a few examples of the types of negative behaviors that regularly occur in social media contexts. Identifying others, and devising methodologies to manage their impact, both to the firm and to other consumers, highlights where psychological ownership theory can play an insightful and helpful role.

Notes

1 Legal ownership and psychological ownership cannot always be viewed as equivalent. In fact, they often differ. Legal ownership comprises the legal rights accorded to an individual who claims ownership over a product or service. In contrast, a state of psychological ownership does not require legal ownership over a product or service.
2 Trolling comprises posting inflammatory or off-topic messages in online communities with the intent of provoking or disrupting community discussion. In contrast, cyberbullying is simply bullying behavior using some form of electronic media. While similar, trolling is often targeted at entire groups and occurs most frequently on message boards, whereas cyberbullying is often targeted at individuals and can occur on message boards, via email, texts, and chats, as well as other media formats. While differences exist, for our current purposes both trolling and cyberbullying represent the 'dark side' of social media.
3 Kill-stealing occurs when a player attacks monsters in an online game in such a way that another player must expend the resources to defeat the monster, but credit for the kill goes to the player who expended few resources.
4 Carrying describes an action wherein a player participates in a team action, but purposely either doesn't contribute, or even walks away from the computer to allow other team members to 'carry' them through the activity.
5 Guilds and clans are formal organizations of like-minded players that are typically formed by virtue of game systems designed and implemented by the game developers.

References

Belk, R. W. (1988). Possessions and the extended self. *Journal of Consumer Research*, 15(2), 139–168.

Belk, R. W. (2013). Extended self in a digital world. *Journal of Consumer Research*, 40(3), 477–500.

Bhattacharya, C. B. & Sen, S. (2003). Consumer-company identification: A framework for understanding consumers' relationships with companies. *Journal of Marketing*, 67(2), 76–88.

Brenner, L., Rottenstreich, Y., Sood, S. & Bilgin, B. (2007). On the psychology of loss aversion: Possession, valence, and reversals of the endowment effect. *Journal of Consumer Research*, 34(3), 369–376.

Brown, G., Lawrence, T. B. & Robinson, S. L. (2005). Territoriality in organizations. *Academy of Management Review*, 30(3), 577–594.

Duncan, N. G. (1981). Home ownership and social theory. In J. S. Duncan, (Ed.), *Housing and Identity: Cross-Cultural Perspectives* (pp. 98–134). London: Croom Helm.

Entertainment Software Association. (2016). *2015 Sales, Demographic and Usage Data: Essential Facts About the Computer and Video Game Industry.*

Fuchs, C., Prandelli, E. & Schreier, M. (2010). The psychological effects of empowerment strategies on consumers' product demand. *Journal of Marketing,* 74(1), 65–79.

Hulland, J., Thompson, S. A. & Smith, K. M. (2015). Exploring uncharted waters: Use of psychological ownership theory in marketing. *Journal of Marketing Theory and Practice,* 23(2), 140–147.

Isidore, C. (2013, Sept. 5). New Facebook flap: Your Face in some product's ad. *CNN Money.* Retrieved from http://money.cnn.com/2013/09/05/technology/social/facebook-privacy/

Jenkins-Guarnieri, M.A., Wright, S.L. & Hudiburgh, L.M. (2012). The relationships among attachment style, personality traits, interpersonal competency, and Facebook use. *Journal of Applied Developmental Psychology,* 33(6), 294–301.

Jussila, I., Tarkiainen, A., Sarstedt, M. & Hair, J. F. (2015). Individual psychological ownership: Concepts, evidence, and implications for research in marketing. *Journal of Marketing Theory and Practice,* 23(2), 121–139.

Jussila, I. & Tuominen, P. (2010). Exploring the consumer co-operative relationship with their members: An individual psychological perspective on ownership. *International Journal of Co-operative Management,* 5(1), 23–33.

Kahneman, D., Knetsch, J. L. & Thaler, R. H. (1990). Experimental tests of the endowment effect and the Coase theorem. *Journal of Political Economy,* 98(6), 1325–1348.

Kaplan, A. M. & Haenlein, M. (2010). Users of the world, unite! The challenges and opportunities of social media. *Business Horizons,* 53(1), 59–68.

Karahanna, E., Zhang, N., Xu, X. & Xu, Y. (2013). Needs-oriented technology acceptance model: A Motivation-needs lens to social media use. (Working paper). Athens, GA: Terry College of Business, University of Georgia.

Karahanna, E., Xu, S. X. & Zhang, N. (2015). Psychological ownership motivation and use of social media. *Journal of Marketing Theory and Practice,* 23(2), 185–207.

Kim, M. & Thompson, S. (2013). Customer-to-Customer Relationship Management (CCRM): CCRM strategies and customer responses. (Working paper). Athens, GA: Terry College of Business, University of Georgia.

Kozinets, R. V. (2002). The field behind the screen: Using netnography for marketing research in online communities. *Journal of Marketing Research,* 39(1), 61–72.

Lee, Y. & Chen, A.N. K. (2011). Usability design and psychological ownership of a virtual world. *Journal of Management Information Systems,* 28(3), 269–308.

Martinez-Lopez, F.J., Anaya-Sanchez, R., Aguilar- Illescas, R. & Molinillo, S. (2016). *Online Brand Communities: Using the Social Web for Branding and Marketing.* Switzerland: Springer International Publishing.

Muñiz, A.M., Jr. & Schau, H. J. (2005). Religiosity in the abandoned Apple Newton brand community. *Journal of Consumer Research,* 31(4), 737–747.

Ortutay, B. (2012, Dec. 18). Users express anger at Instagram's privacy policy. *Associated Press.* Retrieved from http://www.mercurynews.com/ci_22215165/users-express-anger-at-instagrams-privacy-policy

Paul, I. (2010, May 31). It's Quit Facebook Day, Are You Leaving? *PCWorld.* Retrieved from http://www.pcworld.com/article/197621/It_Quit_Facebook_Day_Are_You_Leaving.html

Peck, J. & Shu, S. B. (2009). The effect of mere touch on perceived ownership. *Journal of Consumer Research*, 36(3), 434–447.

Pierce, J. L., Kostova, T. & Dirks, K. T. (2001). Towards a theory of psychological ownership in organizations. *Academy of Management Review*, 26, 298–310.

Pierce, J. L., Kostova, T. & Dirks, K. T. (2003). The state of psychological ownership: Integrating and extending a century of research. *Review of General Psychology*, 7(1), 84–107.

Pierce, J. L. & Jussila, I. (2010). Collective psychological ownership within the work and organizational context: Construct introduction and elaboration. *Journal of Organizational Behavior*, 31, 810–834.

Pierce, J. L. & Jussila, I. (2011). *Psychological Ownership and the Organizational Context: Theory, Research Evidence, and Application*. Cheltenham, UK: Edward Elgar.

Prahalad, C.K. & Ramaswamy, V. (2000). Co-opting customer competence. *Harvard Business Review*, 78(1), 79–90.

Shu, S. B. & Peck, J. (2011). Psychological ownership and affective reaction: Emotional attachment process variables and the endowment effect. *Journal of Consumer Psychology*, 21, 439–452.

Strahilevitz, M.A. & Loewenstein, G. (1998). The effect of ownership history on the valuation of objects. *Journal of Consumer Research*, 25(3), 276–289.

Thaler, R. (1980). Toward a positive theory of consumer choice. *Journal of Economic Behavior and Organization*, 1(1), 39–60.

Thompson, S. & Loveland, J. (2015). Integrating identity and consumption: An identity investment theory. *Journal of Marketing Theory and Practice*, 23(3), 235–253.

Vargo, S. L. & Lusch, R. F. (2004). Evolving to a new dominant logic for marketing. *Journal of Marketing*, 68(1), 1–17.

Xu, Z., Turel, O. & Yuan, Y. (2012). Online game addiction among adolescents: Motivation and prevention factors. *European Journal of Information Systems*, 21(3), 321–340.

PART III

Some Unintended Consequences for Consumers

Now that we have established some horrific and specific types of dark side behaviors that manifest via social media sites such as Facebook, Instagram, YouTube, Snapchat, Pinterest and others, is it time to consider some more unintended consequences for *consumers* who use social media. First, we establish the fact that the self that people display on Facebook is not authentic in many cases; consumers do not display their actual self. Instead, the consumer tends to implicitly or even subconsciously at times display their desired self (Chapter 6). With that fact established, it is important to look at the unintended consequence of too much social media consumption; we are flooded in it if we let ourselves get lost in all of the social media walls, messages, apps, photos, status updates, and shares. In many ways, too much social media use or an unhealthy way of using it is a function of one's emotional intelligence.

Consider someone you know who uses social media in an unpleasant way—such as promoting their narcissism, showing whenever they get drunk, using it to shame others or try to exclude people, or cyber-stalking others via social media to the point that they should and will get blocked for their perverted behavior. It is likely that these people have low emotional intelligence. Chapter 7 gets into the role of emotional intelligence. This chapter illuminates the relationship between excessive online consumption and procrastination by considering emotional intelligence as a key variable related to self-control failure. The results suggest that low levels of Emotional Intelligence (EI) interfere with a person's ability to adopt healthy online consumption patterns. Specifically, results indicate that one's ability to correctly understand emotions represents a key factor in excessive online consumption. Consumers with low levels of the understanding branch of emotional intelligence engage more in online overconsumption than consumers with high levels of the understanding branch.

6

BEING YOURSELF ONLINE

Why Facebook Users Display Their Desired Self

Adriana M. Bóveda-Lambie and Kaci G. Lambeth

The amount of information Big Data provides business is massive and growing, and it is having a large impact on social media marketing strategies (Hung, 2016). Eighty percent of the data being collected comes from sources such as social media, meaning businesses rely on the content of customers' social media stream as a guide to drive their own and better target their efforts. Content is information and social media is a must for businesses' marketing strategies (Hung, 2016). McKinsey & Company report that Big Data can improve a business's operating margins by 60%, so it is understandable why the availability of data on social media is garnering attention.

Social media ad spending is expected to garner almost 21% share of marketing budgets within the next five years, up 15% from just seven years ago (Moorman, 2016). Overall, social media ad revenue is expected to reach $15 billion by 2018, an increase of over 194% (Shukairy, 2016). With social media ad spending poised to exceed $35 billion in 2017, Facebook remains the preferred social media platform by advertisers (92%) with an 8.1x higher click-through rate and widespread usage (Shukairy; LePage, 2015); it will represent 16% of all digital ad spending (eMarketer 2015). Advertisers in the United States spent more than $50 per user in 2015 and this number will increase to $71.37 by 2017, while social network ad spending will comprise 40% of the total marketing budget (eMarketer, 2015). Hence, the reliance on customer data and the increased social ad spending makes the quality of the content put forth by users in Facebook become relevant—are they truly representing their real self?

In recent years, privacy concerns and the apprehension towards personal data being bought and sold has risen. With many people aware that they are being watched, or that they have the potential to be, socially intelligent Facebook users' profiles have appeared to become more and more guarded for fear of real-life consequences of what they are posting online. While there has been much research on Internet identity construction and self presentation, these have focused more on anonymous groups and only recently has the attention shifted to online social networks (Mehdizadeh, 2010; Zhao et al., 2008). Ellison et al. (2006) found that people will act and interact differently in these environments vs. more anonymous ones; therefore how we present ourselves online will vary depending on the setting (Zhao et al., 2008). Mostly focused on personality traits of the individual, research focusing on understanding if and how users manage their social networks impression is scant.

The main goal of this study is to address this gap and extend the identity line of research by examining if, how, and why users curate their Facebook profiles to manage their self-presentation and its implications for marketing and Big Data use.

Theoretical Framework

> You have one identity. The days of you having a different image for your work friends or co-workers and for the other people you know are probably coming to an end pretty quickly....Having two identities for yourself is an example of a lack of integrity. (Marc Zuckerberg quoted in Kirkpatrick, 2010, p. 199 as cited in van Dijck, 2013)

Social media platforms started as a way to keep in touch and maintain relationships (Boyd and Ellison 2007). However, over time their objective has changed. Platform owners are now most interested in monetizing their networks by figuring out how to provide advertisers with "truthful data" (van Dijck, 2013). This runs against users' interests as the need for a faceted self has only increased since we moved to the online space (van Dijck, 2013). The commercialization of the online social network platforms have turned what was a byproduct of connectedness—user data, reactions, and connections—into a valuable data mining resource (van Dijck, 2013).

Tufekci (2014) recognizes the "validity and representativeness" issues with Big Data analysis of social media content. Analyzed by all major stakeholders in society, social media data is often hailed as the last frontier in obtaining key insights into humans (boyd and Crawford, 2012; Lazer et al., 2009). Social media allows us to observe people's behavior at an unimaginable level such as Golder et al.'s (2011) evaluation of mood oscillations and Lynch et al.'s (2014) ideological polarization study of Syrian Twitter. While social media produces a qualitative shift in information availability and its analysis capabilities, it also allows for content gamification through human self-awareness (they *know* they are being observed), altering behavior accordingly (Tufekci, 2014). For example, in her primary research in Turkey Tufekci (2014) found how easy it was for someone to "game" the system to make data look "organic" when the Ankara mayor was able to manipulate the #cnnislying hashtag to trend in Twitter (after being retweeted more than 4,000 times) simply by asking his followers to be ready to post with the hashtag at a specific time.

Depending on the setting and audience, one has certain variables with which to form one's identity. Face-to-face interactions allow for identity manipulation through different accessible cues (mostly physical), limiting how one can represent oneself since it involves displaying one's body, which "prevents people from claiming identities that are inconsistent with the visible part of their physical characteristics (e.g., sex, race, and looks) … and personality attributes" (Zhao et al., 2008, p. 1817). In addition, the maintenance of fairly clearly defined "facets" of one's identity in person is aided by different social contexts being defined in times and places (Farnham & Churchill, 2011, p.359). The Internet has allowed many of these boundaries to be dissolved from identity construction since the physical body is detached from social interactions online, and time and place no longer exist in the ubiquitous Internet.

Traditionally, online identity was anonymous and users could have a "virtual self" (Turkle, 1995) unconstrained by their own physical characteristics. Impression formation in the online environment has been researched since the first days of the Internet (Utz, 2010). Online social networks provide a new method of self-presentation and, depending on the platform, challenge this tradition of online anonymity as they provide a space for self-presentation and the opportunity to stay in touch with friends and acquaintances (boyd and Ellison, 2007; Donath and boyd, 2004; Ellison et al., 2007). In the context of online dating, Ellison et al. (2006) showed that people do carefully construct an idealized self-presentation online. While a user's identity can remain anonymous on platforms such as Instagram and Twitter, trust-driven platforms that blend offline and online life such as Facebook and Snapchat present a challenge in identity/impression management.

Because social networking websites like Facebook encourage users to use their real name, display factual information about themselves, and connect with people they also know offline, they exist somewhere in-between the traditional face-to-face interactions, and the mostly anonymous interactions of social websites that through screen names and avatars allow users to assume an identity not necessarily compatible with their own. In this new space for social interaction, people construct their identities with a wider viewing audience than in the offline world, and face higher potential for real-world consequences than anonymous sites. They are often speaking to a large mixed audience who can view their online activity anytime, anywhere. "A socially intelligent person takes care to consider how her behavior impacts how she is perceived" (Farnham & Churchill, 2011, p.360), and behaviors facilitated through social media sites such as Facebook facilitate a way to judge someone from a distance, without the need for face-to-face interaction. Socially intelligent people therefore understand that managing how others will perceive them online is important, since others may or may not have more information to know and judge them by. This leads to people leaving out the bad, or objectively unflattering, parts of their lives and only posting the positive attributes and moments.

The "self" is defined as an identity that we subjectively perceive ourselves to be or reflect (Ahuvia, 2005; Belk, 1988; Doster, 2013; Kleine et al., 1993), and it has been extensively researched (e.g., Ahuvia, 2005; Belk, 1988; Giddens, 1991; Kleine et al., 1993; Smith, 1992). There are three domains of self: actual self, the ideal self, and the ought self (Tzeng, 2010). People are increasingly fearful of being their "actual selves" online—"the self the individual believes he/she currently is" (Ferguson et al., 2010, p.1486) and tend to display an idealized version referred to as "ideal" or "desired" self—"the self that is wished or hoped for" (Ferguson et al., 2010, p. 1486). When there is a discrepancy between versions of the self, cognitive dissonance can occur, inducing anxiety and a behavioral change to reduce the discrepancy (Tzeng, 2010, p.496). Social interaction on Facebook is likely to cause this sort of self incompatibility because it operates under, "the assumption that a single unified user identity is appropriate and sufficient" (Farnham & Churchill, 2011, p. 359).

The idea that there is a singularly defined desired self is inaccurate and fails to recognize the fact that people have multiple identities, and thereby display different parts of their actual self, depending on the social context, and these identities have generally accepted norms that should be followed (Farnham & Churchill, 2011). However, the degree of faceted identities varies by individual, and online they are usually incompatible. Social media sites like Facebook operate under the incorrect assumption that a singular and converged version of all of one's identities can exist in harmony within the view of several different facets of social audiences in one's life. There are different layers of the self (facets) such as individual, family, and community (Belk, 1988) that suit different contexts or multiple selves that are role dependent (Kleine et al., 1993). Most researchers agree that the vision of a single self is too simplistic (Doster, 2013) with some seeing the self as malleable or flexible—a narrative or story that is dynamic and can change (Ahuvia, 2005; Giddens, 1991; Hall, 1996; Nuttall, 2009)—and others arguing that identities on social network sites are performances that straddle all facets of their lives (Pearson, 2009).

In order to present the self we want and be perceived how we want, individuals engage in self-presentation, the deliberate component of identity (Goffman, 1959). Performed identities is not a new concept as it was developed by Goffman (1959). These "performances" need to be managed in reaction to the cohorts present on the platform being used and the networks that co-exist, the same as you would in face-to-face interactions.

Today's digital media presents a challenge in managing faceted identities and suppressing aspects of their identities to specific audiences. Current platforms require a more transparent identity while at the same time allowing individuals to think and reflect before posting—therefore crafting their identity and engaging in impression management (Kramer & Winter, 2008). This gives users the opportunity to be strategic about their self-presentation (Ellison et al., 2006; Kramer & Winter, 2008) and engage in impression management: defined as the process of managing how others perceive one's self in order to produce desired social outcomes (Farnham & Churchill, 2011, p.360).

Online social networks can be sites where users, employers and platform owners struggle to control online identities (van Dijck, 2013). Although initially institutionally bound, Facebook users had to learn to manage a public profile that all their audiences would be exposed to: close friends, family members, acquaintances, colleagues, and employers. On Facebook, though, all audiences including family, friends and co-workers tend to converge. It becomes hard to discern the appropriate way to portray oneself when all audiences are looking. People want to post things based on how they want others to perceive them, including people they don't know very well in real life. The issue gets conflated when people are connected with people they are close with in real life, people they are acquaintances with in real life, and those that they only know through online interaction. It is not until there is a certain closeness in a relationship that people begin to feel comfortable to share more personal or embarrassing aspects of themselves (Bargh et al., 2002, p.45), and what is considered desirable or appropriate behavior to one audience, may be stigmatized and ridiculed by another. This makes online sharing difficult depending on the degree to which their offline selves are faceted. Authentic online sharing on Facebook can be difficult for users "because users are not always aware of or in control of their audience, and do not have the tools to segment their contacts into the faceted areas of their lives" (Farnham & Churchill, 2011, p. 360).

Some research has shown these profiles/home pages to be "surprisingly accurate" as people claim not to be interested in playing the identity game (Buten, 1996; Machilek et al., 2004). Nevertheless, one of the most important motives for having home pages is for impression management (Kramer & Winter, 2008). As is common knowledge, the online and offline world are far from being separate and without consequences (Clark, 1998; Zhao, 2008). As the online world continues to be more permeable and the offline and online converge, there is the potential for more undesirable outcomes as results of juggling faceted identities. Self expression through comments and visual images can turn into self censoring so that facets of our identities do not conflict. Many individuals have their "friends" from multiple contexts in Facebook, creating the possibility of awkward situations. Online social networks bound the limits of how far one can self present an idealized self as the individual's friends can express doubts on the validity of the information being presented (Kramer & Winter, 2008).

We explore—within the context of Facebook—if users curate their profiles, what strategies they use, and why they engage in impression management of their selves and the facets of their offline lives.

Methods

To find out how users manage their identity in online social networks we decided to target Facebook for context as it is the network with the largest and widest membership base. This would ensure that we could sample different ages that use Facebook. We opted to follow a more qualitative approach and created a survey of open ended questions regarding users' behavior and identity portrayal in Facebook.

The data were collected by propositioning a pool of Facebook users to participate in a "study on social media behavior." Both authors published the link to an online survey on a public post on their Facebook profiles and asked viewers to complete the survey and share it with their friends. A voluntary snowball sample of co-workers, peers, friends, and friends of friends over 18 years of age was collected during a period of 40 days. The only other information provided to them was that their responses would remain anonymous and their name would not be used. As an incentive for participation, we disclosed that five $10 Amazon gift cards would be raffled among those who completed the survey. Forty Facebook users (30 female, 10 male) ranging in age from 19 to 57 years old voluntarily completed in the survey. Each responded to the same ten questions via a link to an online survey created in Qualtrics.

Procedure

Subjects were told the study was about social media behavior, and that they would be asked to answer some questions regarding their social media use. The questions included a combination of multiple choice and free response questions. Only completed surveys were used in analysis. The survey asked about the accuracy of their and others' presentation in Facebook, the content of their posts, whether they edit pictures and/or untag/delete posts, and about their concern of how they are viewed/judged by others. Lastly, the survey asked demographic questions related to gender, age, ethnicity, profession, and income.

Analysis

Following the collection of the data, graduate students free coded and developed a coding scheme to locate key concepts in the data with an inter-coder reliability rating of 90%. Once a coding scheme had been developed with high inter-coder reliability, the authors then coded the data with the coding scheme as well as some free coding. When disagreements in coding arose—whether between the students coding or between the authors—these were resolved through author discussion. The full sample was coded; coded data was analyzed to find relationships and common themes in the data. Three main themes emerged: *authenticity*, *facet management*, and *impression management*.

Results

All of the respondents were, to varying degrees, critical of what they post on Facebook. Therefore, they all seem to engage in some level of identity management, by presenting mostly a desired self that they believe is "safe" or "appropriate." Their answers to our interview questions were thoughtful and never displayed haste or apathy. Three main themes emerged about Facebook users' identity management online: *authenticity, facet management,* and *impression management.* Authenticity refers to the accuracy of the representation of the user profile, and the consistency between a user's Facebook profile and how the user presents him/herself offline. It covers both how the users see themselves and how they see others. This was addressed both on self report and on how "authentic" they view others' profiles to be. *Facet management* relates to how users manage their Facebook identity presentation based on the different audiences from different facets of their lives who can view the user's Facebook profile. Lastly, *impression management* covers the actions that users take to make sure their identity in Facebook stays true to how they want to be perceived. While the three areas relate to each other, we separated them in our results to be able to present a better context for the results. In reality people's online persona or "performance" is a compilation of all three—but in reviewing them separately, we are able to discover and present more nuanced answers and a better overall picture of how users manage their Facebook identity.

These findings seem to be a result of an attempt at identity management in a social context that includes many different types of audiences. Users fear and respond to ridicule of their online profiles, and actively work to avoid such criticism. As one user perfectly stated it: "I am less afraid of people thinking I'm weird, strange, dorky or ugly than I am of people thinking I'm trashy or inappropriate".

Authenticity

None of the respondents felt as if their Facebook self was an entirely accurate representation of themselves nor did they believe they were accurate representations of others.

> I think that everyone's profiles, including my own, are more often than not "highlight reels" of a person's life … usually omits truly embarrassing, painful or ugly parts of yourself.
> I feel that my online presence/image is not my true self. I never post about a mistake I made or about a time I hurt someone's feelings. I only show people my good side.

Facebook users seem to take their social media profiles to be a reflection of their desired identity, by actively filtering out significant parts of their actual selves that are not considered "positive" for online viewing. Almost all of the respondents mentioned left out things about themselves that they found negative, unappealing, unattractive, or only showed their "good side" as one put it. They seem to feel this way not because they are attempting and failing to put forth a completely accurate representation of themselves on the Internet, but instead they are in fact trying to put a positive light on themselves for viewing by friends and strangers alike. Multiple respondents stated that one of their goals is having a positive online identity or image.

> my social media output inadvertently reflects my idealized self by filtering out negative aspects of my life.
> yes I edit the images I post online … make pictures a little better … wanting to put your best foot forward online.

Something else important to note here is that most of the respondents do not take other's social media profiles to be an accurate representation of themselves either. They understand that what they are seeing is generally a carefully constructed identity that is meant for viewing, rather than a glimpse into another person's diary or subconscious. There seems to be no assumption of authenticity, yet it is all still taken fairly seriously. This is likely to be because what someone posts online about themselves is still a deliberate process that can reflect different characteristics if not explicitly displaying them.

> It is a curated portrayal of my individuality … contingent upon a self-conscious awareness of public perception, my social media output inadvertently reflects my idealized self by filtering out negative aspects of my life.
> … people portraying themselves online are, whether consciously or unconsciously, providing at most the same level of accuracy at which they portray themselves in the public sphere. This may include compensating for weaknesses or fears they might have or exemplifying aspects of their personality they champion.
> I don't think anyone is truly willing to post an entirely accurate representation of themselves online.
> I think that they are at least a reflection of who they are, even if the mirror is bent.

Most believe that even the curated profile can give a glimpse into a person's identity—the content that they *choose* to post allows others to make a judgment of their "true" identity. By looking past what a user shares, and attempting to understand their motivations (why someone decided to post a photo or a status) rather than just what the content is, one can get a glimpse of how they feel about, and how they see, themselves, and what they fear being seen as. One participant infers that people "compensate for weakness" on online profiles, and another notes that what people post, whether accurate or not, is "within itself a representation of who they are as a person." As much as they report carefully crafting their online identities, being misinterpreted or having false impressions made about them are still of high concern. So the care shown in constructing the Facebook desired self can tell secrets of the actual self.

Impression Management

The expressions of the desires to make "a positive online impression", to make "a positive impact", and to put "your best foot forward online" all reflect the idea that people want to be seen in an attractive light when viewed online, motivating the use of impression management. The overwhelming majority of respondents engaged in impression management in some capacity. They are aware not only that they are being viewed by others, but that "others" can be a very wide audience. This results in them carefully thinking about the content they will post, how often they do it, and seems to serve as a main driver to ensure that others see them the way they want to be seen. To an extent, they also manage what others post/comment on their profiles, by deleting or "untagging" themselves in posts that do not match their desired online image. Many also report deleting their own past posts if they "no longer reflect my interests or activities" or "are no longer accurate of who I am currently." As discussed earlier, this makes it difficult to share parts of one's self that could be viewed by everyone with whom one is connected with online.

> ... my focus is more on making a positive impact by sharing my experiences with others. I have also used social media for clubs I'm involved in on campus as well as ways to get involved.
>
> I think about what others will think of me all the time. ... While in "real life" I might swear, or make a crude joke, and drink and party, I am very cautious and prefer to maintain a more wholesome image online. I also don't want the people who "know me" first and foremost through social media to make false assumptions.
>
> I don't want someone to think I am lame because I post lame things. Only photos of the most interesting things usually make the cut. I generally try and post pictures of things I'm doing rather than just pictures of myself, by myself, because that would make me seem like a lonely, narcissistic loser who only takes selfies all day.

At the same time, users reported overly curating or managing their posts to the extreme of "only post something if I feel I have something post-worthy". They are conscious of what the content, and reactions to the content, implicitly says about them and this extends the theme we saw in authenticity of putting our best self forward. If it is not interesting or worthy enough it will not make the cut and get posted. Many users reported being "more aware of what I post", "picky" about their posted content, aware of how it would reflect on them or how others would react. Some users even attempt to avoid conflict or hurting others by refraining to post what they view as controversial or "hot" material.

> I do not post anything about my political or religious beliefs.
> Don't put things that would cause discussion.
> If someone is going to take it the wrong way - I usually don't post.

So it is not only about how it reflects on them that drives impression management, but also consideration of others' feelings or reactions that, at the same time, can reflect negatively on the poster.

In addition to this, one respondent reported not posting things out of fear that not "enough people will like it," or in other words, her post not being well received by her audience because it would not be popular enough. This is another example of how the view of others drives how users curate their profile, in this case fear of not being liked "enough". This user engages in impression management to maintain a veil of popularity or being "well liked" by her peers that is carefully assembled.

> I want people to like me and like my post. Sometimes even if I want to post something, I won't do it just because I'm afraid not enough people will like it.
> I worry about looking too lonely. … show when I am with people.
> It's important to me to have other people with me in pictures so I don't look super alone all the time because I'm not.

By attempting to shape others' perception, when users remove unflattering photographs or embarrassing content, or even only posting things based on the number of "likes" they expect to get, they are participating in impression management—and continuing on the theme of presenting or maintaining a positive image.

Facet Management

Social media users today encounter the situation that their audiences collide in Facebook. They have friends, family, acquaintances, co-workers, employers, and universities with access to their profiles and now have to manage these faceted identities with care so as to be able to maintain the impression they want to put forth in front of all audiences.

To deal with this, many of the respondents reported deleting things on their profiles in order to maintain their online image. A majority of the respondents admitted to deleting or "untagging" content they did not want to be associated with, or a particular person to see. This could stem from privacy concerns, and the fear of a permanent online record being kept, reviewed, and having negative "real" life consequences.

> most people I know tend to hold back as much as I do simply because of all the people that can view our profiles. Such as colleges & employers.
>
> I have deleted pictures and or posts that I find do not portray me in a positive light or that I feel are too politically charged.
>
> Back in college days, I had pictures of me drinking and not looking quite sober. ... Now I work for a school ... delete them to protect myself.

This also supports the findings that Facebook users often delete old posts, and untag photos of themselves that they no longer find congruent with their current self-image. Their online Facebook identity is constantly changing, as is their self-concept, and many freely exercise the ability to delete and edit what others can view of their past in order to shape others' impressions of them. This also supports the view that identity is dynamic and malleable.

> Because of my husband's job
> > Things I wouldn't post myself
> > "Unattractive" or "Unflattering" pictures

Some respondents are aware of how they can be perceived, but are not concerned. Their true concern only comes with specific audiences for whom they do actively curate their profile. The three main audiences of concern when engaging in facet management were: colleges, employers, and family members. For some, it isn't even *their* audience but the audience of a close relation such as in the case of the "husband's job" where the user has to manage an audience that is not hers and keep an online identity out of concern for how her husband's work relations may view or perceive her.

> However, I do worry about future employers or universities falsely reading into something I have posted, so I try to be very careful that nothing could be misconstrued against my favor in that way.
>
> ... my family and friends seem to have very different opinions about my social media and what it means about my personality.

Interestingly, one way respondents manage the different facets of their identity is through multiple social media platforms. On Facebook they deal with multiple audiences through impression management and the deletion/untagging of posts, and multiple respondents mentioned portraying different parts or versions of themselves depending on the social media site and their audience on each. In short, they show the facet of themselves that is most congruent with the platform being used and their audience on that specific platform.

> I know each social media site has different tools to display information, different etiquette, and a different audience. I might post the same picture on different social media sites with different captions.
>
> On Facebook I think I'm perhaps more selective about what I post because everyone can see what I share on Facebook. On Twitter for example I hardly have any followers, so I feel less reserved.
>
> I can better control who sees my instagram and my facebook needs to be more professional ...
>
> I am more liberal with Instagram bc my family is not on it.

The participants reported one strategy they engage in for facet management is to use different sites for different audiences, one even commenting on the size of her following on each respective site affecting how "reserved" she felt in posting. Others reported using Facebook for more family or wholesome matters, while Twitter or Instagram was used more for viewing by their friends and peers. This is further evidence of the idea that people seek to maintain faceted parts of their lives, and need to maintain a happy existence in multiple social worlds.

> My older family uses Facebook so I don't post very often ... twitter is more fast paced and has a younger audience so I post more often ... am more laid back with what I post
>
> My Facebook is a little more about the happier things ... because I'm friends with family and coworkers ... tumblr is more a safe space to vent

By tweaking content to be "appropriate" or "happy" or even their frequency of posting they manage their audiences in combination with having different audiences in different platforms. For the most part, the three audiences of concern seemed to all be in Facebook, so this is the platform they are more careful with and use a higher degree of planning.

Discussion

Our findings build on the accepted identity formation theories, exploring them in the context of online social networks on one of the most popular social media sites—Facebook. Identity seems to definitely be dynamic and have some fluidity and we all have more than one identity or a faceted identity. And when it comes to posting on social media platforms, it seems we mostly present our "desired" or "idealized" self, not our true self; we present an idealized and carefully constructed and curated version of ourselves.

There seems to be a clear divide in opinion between the respondents on the topics of authenticity, impression and facet management online. Most of our sample is of the opinion that online profiles are not entirely authentic, that people post content best suited to the audience that will be viewing it, and that people are mindful of how this audience will judge said content. There were a few respondents, however, that claim that they and most people they know are just as authentic online as they are in person, and post mostly the same content across all of their social profiles regardless of audience. However, every respondent did express some hesitation and skepticism when asked about the authenticity of others' profiles. We may be able to attribute this divide to the concept of social intelligence—the degree to which a person takes care to consider how their behavior reflects on them and how it is perceived (Farnham & Churchill, 2011).

As a whole, most users do engage in impression management—ensuring they are seen or perceived as they intend to be and not as what they fear. This theme of "positive image" was a big driver of not only what content gets posted but how it gets posted. Users reported that they carefully craft a Facebook persona that puts their "best foot forward", posting only positive, non-controversial, and sanitized content. One user even reported that her mother posted pictures of someone else's food as her own to give an impression of a healthy lifestyle. They also admitted they will and do go back and delete pictures that they feel either no longer identifies them or that will be viewed by the wrong audience, as well as untagging themselves, and editing pictures for aesthetic purposes. While there is some degree of inauthenticity going on, users reported they only alter pictures for light purposes or to hide the occasional blemish—due in part to a lack of skill in making such alterations and inconsistencies with their real live self.

It is clear that most everyone is aware that their profiles can be viewed by unintended audiences, or that they have facets of their identity that they wish to keep hidden from specific audiences. Also, since everyone seemed concerned with posting only positives or giving a positive impression, the authenticity of the content posted comes into question. As Big Data, re-targeting marketing, and even ad schemes within Facebook, employ user and user content data for their marketing strategies and to drive their own content (i.e., sentiment analysis), a caveat emerges. While some of the information being presented is authentic, as a whole the identity being presented is a half truth—a carefully designed and planned performance by users who are very aware of their public viewing. Hence, profile data harnessed for marketing purposes is not mistake-proof. It is common knowledge that online profiles generated by web searching/browsing behavior have a degree of error that everyone has come to accept; the behavior in itself is real while the assumptions made on demographics and some psychographics may not be. On Facebook, some of the information that is presented is real—the user's name for the most part and some general assumptions such as gender, some school information—but the rest is not necessarily trustworthy. Our findings were consistent across all ages, not just millennials, on Facebook.

Marketers should continue to understand that the data they receive about social media users is not 100% accurate and that mistakes will be made; also that results may not be as expected depending on what their efforts entail. An automated system or query will not be able to truly get a "whole" picture of a Facebook identity. They will get only a facet of it, so marketers need to be careful with the assumptions made about the user profile based on the content that they post. They should also understand that Facebook ad preferences may be off, and consider that there may be a larger percentage of waste than initially estimated. When spending money on targeted advertising based on social media profile data, marketers must keep in mind the purpose that the profiles serve for the actual people behind them—an aspirational, idealized self. Brands that do not engage with or enhance this version of the self may have difficulties utilizing social media and its data to market to consumers.

The findings in this study are not generalizable due to the smaller and convenient sample, but it does yield a view of or a peek into how users manage and sometimes manufacture their identity on social media. The results may not be entirely reliable since some of the questions may be considered personal by some respondents, and therefore could have been affected by social desirability bias. This study also looks at only one aspect of identity—its construction and management on Facebook.

Future research should look at how identity management changes—if at all—by gender, race/ethnicity, and age. In addition, understanding more about the motivations behind the identity management and how it contrasts, if at all, with real-life identity management would be of interest to better understand social media identity construction. Finally, since our research only looked at Facebook, exploring how this phenomenon unfolds in other social media platforms (if at all), how users' strategies/tactics differ, and how their presentation differs across platforms would yield interesting insights for the identity construction literature. By learning more on how and why users construct and manage their social media identities, marketers can hope to learn how to interpret and use the data being mined into successful strategies and tactics that speak to their target audience.

References

Ahuvia, A. C. (2005). Beyond the extended self: Loved objects and consumers' identity narratives. *Journal of Consumer Research*, 32(1), 171–184.

Bargh, J. A., McKenna, K. A. & Fitzsimons, G. M. (2002). Can you see the real me? Activation and expression of the "true self" on the internet. *Journal of Social Issues*, 58(1), 33.

Belk, R. W. (1988). Possessions and the extended self. *Journal of Consumer Research*, 15(2), 139–168.

boyd, d. m. & Ellison, N. B. (2007). Social network sites: Definition, history, and scholarship. *Journal of Computer-Mediated Communication*, 13(1) 210–230.

boyd, d. & Crawford, K. (2012). Critical questions for big data: Provocations for a cultural, technological, and scholarly phenomenon. *Information, Communication & Society*, 15(5), 662–679.

Buten, J. (1996). Personal home page survey. *Washington Post Cybersurfing Column*.

Clark, A. (1998). *Being There: Putting Brain, Body, and World Together Again*. MIT press.

Donath, J. & boyd, d. (2004). Public displays of connection. *BT technology Journal*, 22(4), 71–82.

Doster, L. (2013). Millennial teens design and redesign themselves in online social networks. *Journal of Consumer Behaviour*, 12(4), 267–279.

Ellison, N., Heino, R. & Gibbs, J. (2006). Managing impressions online: Self-presentation processes in the online dating environment. *Journal of Computer-Mediated Communication*, 11(2), 415–441.

Ellison, N. B., Steinfield, C. & Lampe, C. (2007). The benefits of Facebook "friends:" Social capital and college students' use of online social network sites. *Journal of Computer-Mediated Communication*, 12(4), 1143–1168.

eMarketer (2015) *Advertisers in North America spend the most to be social*. (www.emarketer.com/article/social-network-ad-spending-hit-2368-billion-worldwide-2015/1012357 Accessed on May 2016

Farnham, S. D. & Churchill, E. F. (2011, March). Faceted identity, faceted lives: Social and technical issues with being yourself online. In Proceedings of the ACM 2011 conference on Computer supported cooperative work (pp. 359–368). ACM.

Ferguson, G., Hafen, C. & Laursen, B. (2010). Adolescent Psychological and Academic Adjustment as a Function of Discrepancies Between Actual and Ideal Self-Perceptions. *Journal of Youth & Adolescence*, 39(12), 1485–1497. doi:10.1007/s10964-009-9461-5

Fisher, E. (2015) You media: Audiencing as marketing in social media. *Media, Culture & Society*, 37(1), 50–67.

Giddens, A. (1991). *Modernity and Self-identity: Self and Society in the Late Modern Age*. Stanford, CA: Stanford University Press.

Goffman, E. (1959). *The Presentation of Self in Everyday Life*. Garden City: Doubleday.

Golder, S.A. & Macy, M.W. (2011). Diurnal and seasonal mood vary with work, sleep, and daylength across diverse cultures. *Science*, 333(6051): 1878–1881.

Hung, D. (2016). Impact of big data on social media marketing strategies. tech.co/impact-big-data-social-media-marketing-strategies-2016-01. Accessed May 2016.

Kleine, R. E., Kleine, S. S. & Kernan, J. B. (1993). Mundane consumption and the self: A social-identity perspective. *Journal of Consumer Psychology*, 2(3), 209–235.

Kramer, N.C. & Winter, S. (2008) Impression Management 2.0 The relationship of self-esteem, extraversion, self-efficacy, and self-presentation within networking sites. *Journal of Media Psychology*, 20(3), 106–116. Doi: 10.1027/1864-1105.20.3.106

Lazer, D. et al. (2009). Life in the network: The coming age of computational social science. *Science (New York, NY)*, 323(5915), 721–723.

LePage, E. (2015). *A Long List of Social Media Advertising Stats*. Hootsuite Blog, (blog.hootsuite.com/social-media-advertising-stats/). Accessed May 2016

Machilek, F., Schütz, A. & Marcus, B. (2004) Self-presenters, or people like you and me? Intentions and personality traits of owners of personal websites. *Zeitschrift für Medienpsychologie*, 16(3), 88–98.

Mehdizadeh, S. (2010) Self-presentation 2.0: Narcissism and self-esteem on Facebook. *Cyberpsychology, Behavior, and Social Networking*, 13(4), 357–364.

Moorman, C. (2016) The social media spend impact disconnect, *Forbes*. www.forbes.com/sites/christinemoorman/2016/02/16/the-social-media-spend-impact-disconnect/#333908d7417b. Accessed July 2017.

Nuttall, P. (2009). Insiders, regulars and tourists: Exploring selves and music consumption in adolescence. *Journal of Consumer Behaviour*, 8(4), 211–224.

Pearson, E. (2009). All the World Wide Web's a stage: The performance of identity in online social networks. *First Monday*, 14(3), http://firstmonday.org/ojs/index.php/fm/article/view/2162. Accessed July 2017.

Sherry, T. (1995). Life on the screen: Identity in the age of the internet. *NY etc.: cop.*

Shukairy, A. (2016) Social media ad spending. Invespcro www.invespcro.com/blog/social-media-ad-spending. Accessed July 2017.

Smith, W. P. & Kidder, D. L. (2010) You've been tagged! (then again, maybe not): Employers and Facebook. *Business Horizons*, 53, 491–499.

Toma, C. L. & Hancock, J. T. (2013) Self-affirmation underlies facebook use. *Personality and Social Psychology Bulletin*, 39(3), 321–331.

Tufecki, Z. (2014). Big questions for social media big data: Representativeness, validity and other methodological pitfalls. In ICWSM'14: Proceedings of the 8th International AAAI Conference on Weblogs and Social Media.

Turkle, S. (1995). *Life in the Screen: Identity in the Internet*. New York: Simon.

Tzeng, J. Y. (2010). College students' self-discrepancy on the internet, from the perspectives of desktop practices, self-control, and academic training. *Cyberpsychology, Behavior, and Social Networking*, 13(5), 495–502.

Utz, S. (2010). Show me your friends and I will tell you what type of person you are: How one's profile, number of friends, and type of friends influence impression formation on social network sites. *Journal of Computer-Mediated Communication*, 15(2010), 314–335.

Walther, J.B, Van Der Heide, B., Kim, S.Y., Westerman, D. & Tong, S.T. (2008). The role of friends' appearance and behavior on evaluations of individuals on Facebook: are we known by the company we keep? *Huan Communication Research*, 34 (2008), 28–49.

van Dijck, J. (2013) You have one identity: Performing the self on Facebook and LinkedIn. *Media, Culture & Society*, 35(2), 199–215.

Vignoles, V. L., Golledge, J., Regalia, C., Manzi, C. & Scabini, E. (2006) Beyond self-esteem: Influence of multiple motives on identity construction. *Journal of Personality and Social Psychology*, 90(2), 308–333.

Zhao, S., Grasmuck, S. & Martin, J. (2008). Identity construction on Facebook: Digital empowerment in anchored relationships. *Computers In Human Behavior*, 24(5), 1816–1836. doi:10.1016/j.chb.2008.02.012Appendix. Accessed July 2017.

APPENDIX

Survey Questions

1) Do you feel your online social media profiles/presence are/is an accurate representation of yourself? Discuss why or why not. Please provide examples.
2) Do you consider OTHER people's social media profiles to be accurate representations of themselves? Discuss why or why not. Give examples (Friends, family, etc.)
3) Do you display different aspects of yourself across different social media platforms?
   ☐ Yes (1)
   ☐ No (2)
4) What type of things (content) do you usually post about on social media? Please give examples.
5) Do you post different types of things (content) across different social media? For example, does your content in FB vary from your content in Instagram. Please discuss your reasons and give examples.
6) On a scale from 0-10, with 0 being not at all and 10 being highly, how concerned are you about how others perceive you based on the content that you post in social media?
6a) Why or why not? Please discuss and give examples of when you are concerned and when you are not.
7) On a scale from 0-10, with 0 being not at all and 10 being highly, how concerned are you about how OTHERS perceive YOU based on how frequent/often you post in social media?
7a) Why or why not? Please discuss and give examples of when you are concerned and when you are not.

8) Have you deleted old posts or photos that YOU posted in social media sites?
- ☐ Yes (1)
- ☐ No (2)

8a) Can you give examples of why or why not? How does it vary by social media platform?

9) Have you ever edited or photoshopped your photos before you post them?
- ☐ Yes (1)
- ☐ No (2)

9a) Please discuss why you do or do not edit photos before posting.

10) Please select your gender
- ☐ Male (1)
- ☐ Female (2)
- ☐ Other (3) _____

10a) What is your age?

10b) What is your highest education level?
- ☐ High School (1)
- ☐ Some College/Bachelors (2)
- ☐ Graduate (Master's, PhD, JD, MD, etc.) (3)

7

EMOTIONAL INTELLIGENCE, BEHAVIORAL PROCRASTINATION, AND ONLINE (OVER)CONSUMPTION

Paula C. Peter and Heather Honea

The indispensability of the Internet for consumers is undeniable; it is a necessity in people's lives, a ritualized part of daily routines—akin to a product one cannot do without (e.g. Hoffman et al., 2004). Of the key categories where individuals spend time online, social networking captures the greatest percentage of activity, but people spend almost as much time in search, reading content, and engaging in communication; users spend slightly less time with multi-media and engaged in commerce ("How People Spend Their Time Online", 2012). The critical role the Internet now plays in consumption across these categories creates unique challenges for understanding what behaviors are simply the next phase in consumer social and information interactions or what actually might represent maladaptive consumption behavior.

The advent of widespread usage of the Internet initially brought about concerns of social displacement through Internet use—a theory that time online was largely an asocial activity that would compete with, rather than complement, face-to-face social time (Nie et al., 2002). Predictions were that Internet usage would serve to weaken real-world ties, reduce community involvement, local knowledge, and interest in living in the local area (Kraut et al., 1998, 2002). However, research quickly emerged which suggested a positive relationship between Internet consumption and life satisfaction for people with healthy Internet consumption patterns (Kraut et al., 2002). Today, there is increasingly the perspective that the Internet allows for individuation or transformation of community social relationships, so that relationships may be formed on shared values, interests, and outcomes, which largely serves to enhance social connectivity (Castells, 2014).

However, there are signs of problematic consumption regulation relative to Internet use, particularly in key activity categories of online consumption such as social networking (Kuss & Griffiths, 2011). So while it is not necessarily a weakening of social connection that is an issue with online consumption, it is the level of use, feelings of a lack of control relative to consumption, and the neglect of other activities that represent a dark side to online and social media consumption (hereafter referred to simply as *online consumption*). According to Pew Research Center, 73% of Americans report going online daily, but over one-fifth of Americans (21%) now report going online "almost constantly" based on a metric that began to be collected in 2015 (Perrin, 2015). Constant use of the medium may purely be a function of how indispensable the Internet is relative to social networking, and to the utilitarian and social aspects of searching, reading, communicating, and shopping online. Or it may be a signal of overuse and compulsive activity (e.g., Baumer et al., 2015) that leads users to neglect school, work, and social responsibilities due to a failure to control their Internet use, despite goals or intentions that are otherwise (e.g., Widyanto & McMurran, 2004; Fitzpatrick, 2008).

Delay or avoidance of intended action due to a failure in self-regulation, defined as procrastination (Steel, 2007), may be an important correlate to determine whether the nature of constant Internet use is more or less adaptive. Moreover, with an indispensable technology, you cannot obviate its use, only identify interventions that might palliate the dark side of usage. Emotional Intelligence (EI), defined as an individual's ability to recognize, employ, understand, and control emotions (Salovey & Mayer, 1990; Kidwell, et al., 2008), is a critical component of consumer well-being (Kidwell et al., 2015; Peter & Brinberg, 2012) that might serve to reduce or redirect impulsive and excessive consumption (Peter & Krishnakumar, 2015; Peter & Brinberg, 2012). The present study builds on current research related to excessive online consumption, behavioral procrastination, and EI by exploring the relationship between these variables. The goal is to understand whether EI may be a potential focus of interventions aimed at reducing the impact of behavioral procrastination on excessive use of the Internet.

Excessive Online Consumption

There has been significant work to try to understand excessive consumption relative to activity on the Internet. This work has labeled overuse variably as addiction, addicted disorder, pathological use, and high dependency, but in general the literature has characterized excessive online consumption in terms of a mental disorder (Byun et al., 2014). Based on a meta-analysis of this literature, Byun borrowed Beard's 2005 definition of excessive consumption of the medium, suggesting an impairment of the individual's psychological, mental and emotional states, as well as everyday behavior in scholastic, occupational, and social interactions (Beard, 2005). Byun et al. (2014) also summarized key attempts to measure overuse as: amount of time spent online (the most frequently reported predictor), dependency, desire relative to usage, and impulse-control.

However, with an indispensable technology, time spent and dependency may be somewhat imperfect indicators of addicted or excessive behavior. In addition, a lack of consensus in the measurement instruments of addicted behavior has prompted scales that focus on the examination of issues relative to overuse as opposed to a core focus on more pathological issues of addicted mental disorders. Widyanto and McMurran (2004) explore the psychometric properties of Young's Internet Addiction Test and qualify that beyond excessive time, overuse relates to neglect of work and social life, and involves a salience of the Internet. They suggest this salience is characterized by a preoccupation with the medium, feelings of desire—fantasizing about engaging in online activity, a sense of anticipation about going online, and feeling a lack of control regarding engaging in its use. So, excessive online consumption is linked to neglect of key intentions and postponement of other activities as well as an emotional or non-rational salience of the Internet in terms of desire to use, anticipation of use, and self-control relative to use.

Behavioral Procrastination

Behavioral procrastination refers to the act of postponing one's intended course of actions despite the acknowledgement of consequences resulting from that delay (Steel, 2007). It entails a self-regulation style that involves deferral in the start and/or completion of a task (Ferrari & Tice, 2000). Key in behavioral procrastination, is the postponement of *intended* action or the avoidance of the implementation of an intention, (Van Eerde, 2000) not planned avoidance of action (Lay & Silverman, 1996; Milgram, 1991; Silver & Sabini, 1981; Anderson, 2003). If actual intent does not exist relative to an action, then postponing it is not procrastination (Van Hooft et al., 2005). Thus, procrastinators do not differ from non-procrastinators in their intent to perform a behavior; instead they differ in their ability to take action on their intentions (Sirois, 2004).

Still, procrastination has consequence akin to avoidance because it is associated with poor performance across domains (Steel et al., 2001) including health (Sirois et al., 2003), academics (Klassen et al., 2008; Tice & Baumeister, 1997), and economics (Kasper, 2004). Kasper (2004) reports the results of an H&R Block survey where procrastination led to an average overpayment of $400 on taxes because of rushing and consequent errors. Relative to personal well-being, procrastinators delay seeking care for their health problems and have challenges regulating consumption, eating healthily and getting exercise (Sirois et al., 2003).

Steel's (2007) meta-analytic study reveals that key predictors of procrastination are task aversiveness and delay, low self-efficacy, lack of self-control (control issues in terms of distractibility, organization and achievement motivation), and impulsiveness. When these drivers of procrastination are considered along with the aspects that characterize excessive online consumption (neglect of intentions, postponement of activities, and non-rational salience of usage in terms of desire, anticipation, and lack of self-control) the overlap between procrastination and overuse of the Internet is notable. Thus, a positive relationship between behavioral procrastination and excessive online consumption is expected. We predict that individuals lead by their impulse and desires that lack self-control, will engage in excessive online consumption, and exhibit higher levels of behavioral procrastination.

> *H1.* Excessive online consumption is positively related to behavioral procrastination.

Emotional Intelligence

Given that the literature on excessive online consumption and procrastination points heavily to issues regarding control of feelings of desire, anticipation, and impulsiveness, this indicates a more non-rational or emotional explanation for the relationship between Internet overuse and behavioral procrastination. Exploratory research has suggested a positive relationship between low levels of emotional intelligence and impulsiveness (Peter & Krishnakumar, 2015; Peter & Brinberg, 2012; Peter, 2009).

Emotional intelligence (EI) as originally defined by Mayer and Salovey (1997) is an individual's ability relative to four particular intelligences: perception of emotions, use of emotions, understanding of emotions, and regulation of emotions in self and others (Salovey & Mayer, 1990). EI positively contributes to one's own well-being (Mayer & Salovey, 1997). With high levels of EI comes the ability to correctly perceive, understand, use, and regulate emotions in oneself and others (Salovey & Mayer, 1990). Whereas, low levels of EI is positively associated with several problematic or excessive consumption behaviors, such as smoking (Trinidad et al., 2004), alcohol and drug abuse (Riley & Schutte, 2003), and the overall adoption of unhealthy behaviors, such as excessive calorie intake and impulse buying (Peter & Brinberg, 2012; Peter & Krishnakumar, 2015).

According to Mayer and Salovey (1997), the four different branches of EI are organized from basic psychological processes related to emotions (such as expression and recognition) to more psychologically integrated processes (such as understanding and regulation). *Perception* of emotions consists of the ability to accurately recognize and express emotions in oneself and others. It is related to nonverbal reception and expression of emotions. According to the ability model of EI (Mayer & Salovey, 1997), individuals high on this ability should be able to recognize emotions in faces, pictures and cultural artifacts. This ability provides an important starting point for more advanced understanding of emotions and associated skills in emotional expression. Research has shown a positive relationship between this EI ability and successful interaction (Elfenbein et al., 2007; Rubin et al., 2005).

Use of emotions helps prioritize thinking in terms of directing cognitive processes in the right direction. For example, an emotionally intelligent individual who needs to elicit creative ideas, will recognize happiness as an important emotion in order to promote creativity. Relatedly, the act of writing about meaningful aspects of life seems to help individuals cope with negative emotional states (Baikie & Wilhelm, 2005). Therefore, people who are capable in their use of emotions, recover faster from negative emotional states because they are able to generate positive memories (Limonero et al., 2015).

Understanding of emotions helps individuals use emotions to convey information. It encompasses the ability to be sensitive to slight variations between emotions, and the ability to recognize and describe how emotions evolve over time. Individuals who score highly on EI Understanding are the ones who have a very rich emotional vocabulary and understand nuances and relationships among different emotions. For instance, they might understand that despair, over time, might give away to anger and then to sadness, and then ultimately resolve in a state of acceptance. In the context of risk management, Yip and Côté (2013) demonstrated that individuals with lower emotion-understanding ability, tended to be excessively influenced by incidental anxiety and could not separate their anxiety from an unrelated decision, even though it would enhance their well-being.

Regulation of emotions implies the understanding of emotions and the willingness to stay open to emotional signals as long as they are not too painful or overwhelming. Once an individual has found his/her emotional comfort zone, he/she is able to regulate and manage his/her own or others' emotions in order to achieve desired goals. Research has shown that individuals with greater ability to regulate their emotions can experience improved personal outcomes and relationships (Lopes et al., 2005). For example, an emotionally intelligent consumer who struggles with indulgent food consumption should be able to recognize the urge to consume unhealthy food and find coping mechanisms to deal with the emotions experienced (e.g. take a walk instead of consuming).

Given excessive online consumption is associated with an overwhelming desire to use, intense feelings of anticipation relative to use, and a sense of lack of self-control regarding use, it parallels the non-rational emotional challenges of impulsiveness and control associated with behavioral procrastination. Thus, we expect emotional intelligence to moderate the relationship between behavioral procrastination and excessive online consumption. Specifically, we expect that low levels of EI will exacerbate the relationship between behavioral procrastination and excessive online consumption.

> *H2.* Emotional Intelligence moderates the relationship between behavioral procrastination and excessive online consumption such that low levels of EI will serve to increase the impact of behavioral procrastination on excessive online consumption.

Method

A study was conducted to explore the hypothesized relationships among behavioral procrastination, excessive online consumption, and emotional intelligence.

Participants

Participants were 131 students (57 males and 74 females) from a large southwestern university in the US. The mean age of the students was 22 (SD = 1.88), ranging from 20 to 29. All the students were enrolled in an introductory marketing course in their second year at the university and were awarded extra credit for their participation in the study.

Procedures and Measures

Students were invited to participate in a 20-minute online study in a controlled lab environment for extra credit. Each student took the study on a personal computer in a room with 15 other students completing the same task. During the study, respondents were first asked to recall their online and social media behaviors. Then they were asked to respond to three scales regarding such behavior.

Excessive online consumption was measured with the Internet Addiction Test (IAT), a 20-item scale developed by Young (1998), which allows for the identification of excessive and problematic online consumption. The scale is comprised of 20 items that use a five-point Likert scale (from 1 – not at all, to 5 – always) to measure the extent of individual's problems due to Internet use in their daily routine, social life, productivity, sleeping patterns, and feelings (Cronbach's alpha = .92).

Behavioral procrastination was measured with a scale by Lay (1986). The scale is comprised of 20 items that use a five-point Likert scale (from 1 – extremely uncharacteristic, to 5 – extremely characteristic) where individuals describe themselves and their behaviors relative to planning and task orientation. The scale has shown high reliability and for our sample the Cronbach's alpha was .86.

Emotional Intelligence was measured with the Consumer Emotional Intelligence Scale (CEIS, Kidwell et al., 2008), which is an 18-item questionnaire related to EI and individual abilities (perception, use, understanding, regulation). The CEIS originates from the Mayer-Salovey-Caruso Emotional Intelligence Test (MSCEIT; Mayer et al., 2003) but it is optimized for consumer behavior.

Analyses and Results

All participants in the study spent time online and engaged in a range of online consumption behaviors, include the use of social media. In order to test our first hypothesis (H1) that behavioral procrastination and excessive online consumption are positively related, a simple correlation analysis was performed. Next, to test the role of EI as moderator of behavioral procrastination in excessive online consumption (H2), a stepwise regression analysis was conducted.

Excessive Online Consumption and Behavioral Procrastination

Results of a correlation analysis suggest that excessive online consumption is positively related to behavioral procrastination ($r = .38$, $p < .001$). Table 7.1 reports the results of the correlations among the variables of interest. Our results confirm our first hypothesis (H1) and show that an increase in behavioral procrastination is positively related to an increase in excessive online consumption. The results also suggest a negative relationship between excessive online consumption and EI ($r = -.20$, $p < .05$).

EI as Moderator of Behavioral Procrastination

To further investigate the process underlying excessive online consumption and explore potential interventions that might support adaptive online consumption, we examined the expected role of Emotional Intelligence (EI) as a moderator between behavioral procrastination and excessive online consumption. The overall model of the stepwise regression analysis was significant ($R = .460$, R-square $= .212$, $F (3, 92) = 8.23$; $p < .001$). Behavioral procrastination and the behavioral procrastination by EI interaction were the only significant behavioral determinants related to excessive online consumption (both $p < .05$). EI does not directly predict excessive online consumption ($p =$ ns). However, EI significantly moderated the relationship between behavioral procrastination and excessive online consumption ($p = .05$). The results confirm our second hypothesis (H2).

TABLE 7.1 Correlations

	Mean	SD	1	2	3	4	5	6	7
1. Excessive online consumption	48.44	19.10	1.00						
2. Behavioral Procrast.	55.21	11.39	.38**	1.00					
3. EI	8.44	3.38	−.20*	−.14	1.00				
4. EI_Perception	1.73	.63	−.23*	−.11	.22*	1.00			
5. EI_Use	1.13	.72	.19*	−.08	.15	−.00	1.00		
6. EI_Understand	3.1	1.15	−.13	−.08	.37**	.13	.13	1.00	
7. EI_Regulate	2.39	3.08	−.08	−.08	.87**	−.01	−.11	−.02	1.00

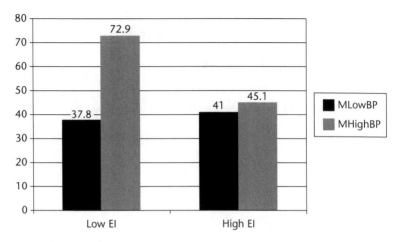

FIGURE 7.1 EI as Moderator

To further explore this result, we examined the moderation of behavioral procrastination with high and low levels of EI (25 and 75 percentiles). This procedure has been adopted in previous EI studies (e.g. Peter & Brinberg, 2012). Results from the general linear model analysis confirm the significance of the product term interaction of behavioral procrastination by EI (F(3, 36) = 7.701, p < .05). Thus, EI moderates the relationship between behavioral procrastination and excessive online consumption. Specifically, ANOVAs reveal that for people with high levels of EI (75 percentile), an increase in behavioral procrastination does not correspond to a significant increase in excessive online consumption (M_{LowBP} = 41.00 vs. M_{HighBP} = 45.10 p = ns). However, for people with low levels of EI (25 percentile), an increase in behavioral procrastination does correspond to a significant increase in excessive online consumption (M_{LowBP} = 37.80 vs. M_{HighBP} = 72.90, p < .05). Figure 7.1 illustrates the effect.

These results suggest an important role for EI relative to managing excessive online consumption. In particular, the ability to correctly perceive, understand, use, and regulate emotions might represent a key component to facilitating the management and healthy regulation of online consumption. To explore potentially valuable interventions, we explore which particular branch of EI ability might play the most significant role in the relationship between behavioral procrastination and excessive online consumption.

Emotional Intelligence Abilities

The same analysis as outlined above for the role of overall EI on excessive online consumption was performed using the individual EI abilities: perception, use, understanding, and regulation. The analysis reveals that the EI ability of understanding is the core branch of EI that interacts with behavioral procrastination

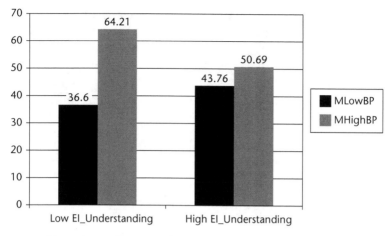

FIGURE 7.2 EI_Understanding as moderator

relative to excessive online consumption. Specifically, the overall model of the stepwise regression analysis was significant (R = .465, R- square = .216, F (3, 92) = 8.45; p < .001). Behavioral procrastination, EI understanding, and the behavioral procrastination by EI understanding all significantly related to excessive online consumption (p < .05). The results suggest that EI understanding significantly moderates the relationship between behavioral procrastination and excessive online consumption (p = .01). Next, we explored the moderation of the relationship between behavioral procrastination and excessive online consumption via EI, in the case of high and low levels of EI (25 and 75 percentiles). Results from the general linear model confirm the significance of the interactions between behavioral procrastination and EI understanding (F(3, 36) = 4.09, p = .049). EI understanding moderates the relationship between behavioral procrastination and excessive online consumption. Specifically, ANOVAs reveal that for people with high levels of EI Understanding (75 percentile), an increase in behavioral procrastination does not correspond to a significant increase in excessive online consumption (M_{LowBP} = 43.76 vs. M_{HighBP} = 50.69, p = ns). However, for people with low levels of EI (25 percentile), an increase in behavioral procrastination does correspond to a significant increase in excessive online consumption (M_{LowBP} = 36.60 vs. M_{HighBP} = 64.21, p < .05). Figure 7.2 illustrates the effect.

Discussion

The present study explores the relationship between behavioral procrastination and excessive online consumption and is the first to consider Emotional Intelligence (EI) as a potential moderator between these two variables of interest. Results reveal a positive relationship between behavioral procrastination and excessive online consumption, and indicate that EI acts as moderator between the two variables. Specifically, for people with low levels of EI, an increase in behavioral procrastination corresponds to an increase in excessive online consumption, while individuals with high levels of EI (75 percentile) are not differentiated in their degree of excessive online consumption relative to behavioral procrastination. These findings suggest that low levels of EI interfere with a person's ability to use the Internet in appropriate doses due to behavioral procrastination, while high levels of EI might help people to use emotional knowledge to manage their online activity to appropriate levels. Specifically, considering two individuals who engage equally in behavioral procrastination, our results suggest that low vs. high levels of EI will differentiate them in the degree to which they engage online in a problematic or healthy manner.

EI understanding seems to be the key EI ability driving the effect. Emotional understanding is the ability to recognize and describe how emotions evolve over time based on past, current, or forecasted events. It is the ability to analyze cause-effect relationships between emotions and events. This intelligence involves fully understanding the meaning of emotions, coupled with the capacity to reason about those meanings. This skill represents a mindful approach to the experience of emotions as they contribute to thinking and decision-making.

Individuals who score highly on EI understanding are able to separate incidental emotions from their decisions and behavior (Yip & Côté, 2013). They are capable of differentiating the emotions they experienced as related or unrelated to particular tasks to be accomplished and therefore, unrelated emotions do not serve to inappropriately influence their decisions and behavior. In contrast, individuals low in EI understanding seem to miss emotional cues or misread their own, so it is not surprising that EI differentiates usage of the Internet when behavioral procrastination is taken into account. Our results suggest that low EI Understanding individuals may not be able to make sense of variations in their emotions, thus may be challenged in understanding their feelings of desire and impulsiveness, as well as their capacity to recognize how these emotive states give way to a lack of control. Thus, low ability level in terms of EI understanding, exacerbates the relationship between behavioral procrastination and excessive online consumption. This is an important finding since it points toward the importance of a specific EI ability that might be the focus of interventions (e.g., Peter & Brinberg, 2012) to help individuals who engage in behavioral procrastination and struggle with excessive online consumption.

Conclusion and Implications

Worldwide, Internet users have increased from approximately 361 million in 2000 to approximately 3.6 billion in 2016 (www.internetworldstats.com). The most widely adopted online communication and social interaction tool, Facebook, has roughly 1.71 billion monthly active users in 2016 (statista.com). There is no debate that the Internet, in particular social media, has transformed consumers' lives and become indispensable, but the implications of this impact need further research. Several researchers have looked at ways to support healthier consumer lifestyles in the modern age of ubiquitous connection to the Internet but no study, to our knowledge, has recognized the need to consider Emotional Intelligence (EI) to promote the adoption and maintenance of healthy online consumption patterns.

According to our results, excessive online consumption is related to behavioral procrastination. So, individuals with low levels of EI and low EI understanding engage in more behavioral procrastination and pursue excessive online consumption due to their inability to correctly *understand emotions*. Thus, the ability to distinguish between emotions and explain how emotions evolve over time, seems to represent an important variable to consider when addressing excessive online consumption. EI understanding underlines the importance of a mindful approach toward consumption (Bahl et al., 2016) and therefore offers a potential path to manage the experience of emotions and, in turn, tame behavioral procrastination and excessive online consumption. Once a person can identify, describe and understand the evolution of their emotions, the capacity to reason with and about those emotions becomes a key behavioral determinant for managing tasks (e.g. surfing or connecting online). The study presented here supports EI as an activator of mechanisms that could direct cognitive processes in a healthy direction.

These results heed valuable theoretical and practical implications to the study of the dark side of the Internet and social media. People with low levels of EI might be more at risk of excessive online consumption than people with high levels of EI, especially when their "understanding" of emotions is impaired. Future studies should also explore the impact of *EI understanding* training on the relationship between behavioral procrastination and excessive online consumption. The development of specific EI skills (especially understanding of emotions) may play a critical role in preventing detrimental (over)consumption of the Internet. As such, training for healthy online consumption should be based on understanding of emotions related to behavioral procrastination rather than simply those related to minimizing excessive online consumption.

Our study leveraged the Internet Addiction Test (Young, 1998) to examine excessive online consumption. Future research should try to capitalize on multiple measures that consider excessive online consumption and a range of problematic online and social media consumption behaviors when considering the role of EI. In this vein, studies should consider the emotive states associated with behavioral procrastination such as anxiety (Spada et al., 2006), mindfulness (Bahl et al., 2016) and impulsiveness (Ferrari, 1993) as it relates to EI and EI understanding.

Most importantly, due to indispensability of the Internet, future studies should work to examine the relationship between healthy consumption patterns, different levels of EI, and online consumption. Our findings are applicable to any online situations where desire, impulse and personal control are challenged. Thus, attention to and intervention relative to EI and EI understanding that have successfully managed other failures in self-regulation for necessary or needed activities and products, might offer opportunities to improve overall life satisfaction relative to online usage in addition to supporting adaptive online and social media consumption patterns.

References

Anderson, C. J. (2003). The psychology of doing nothing: Forms of decision avoidance result from reason and emotion. *Psychological Bulletin*, 129, 139–167.

Baumer, E. P., Guha, S., Quan, E., Mimno, D. & Gay, G. K. (2015, July 03). Missing photos, suffering withdrawal, or finding freedom? How experiences of social media non-use influence the likelihood of reversion. *Social Media Society*, 1(2), 1–14.

Bahl, S., Milne, G. R., Ross, S. M., Mick, D. G., Grier, S. A., Chugani, S. K., Chan, S., Gould, S. J., Cho, Y. N., Dorsey, J. D. & Schindler, R. M. (2016). Mindfulness: The transformative potential for consumer, societal, and environmental well-being. *Journal of Public Policy & Marketing*, 35(2), 198-210..

Baikie K. & Wilhelm K. (2005). Emotional and physical health benefits of expressive writing. *Advances in Psychiatric Treatment* 11(1), 338–346.

Beard, K. W. (2005). Internet addiction: A review of current assessment techniques and potential assessment questions. *CyberPsychology & Behavior*, 8(1), 7–14.

Byun, S., Ruffini, C., Mills, J. E., Douglas, A. C., Niang, M., Stepchenkova, S., Lee, S.K., Loutfi, J., Lee, J., Atallah, M. & Blanton, M. (2009). Internet addiction: Metasynthesis of 1996–2006 quantitative research, *CyberPsychology & Behavior*, 12(2), 203–207.

Castells, M. (2014). The impact of the internet on society: A global perspective, Change: 19 Essays on How the Internet is Changing Our Lives. In M. Castells (Ed), *Change: 19 Key Essays on How Internet Is Changing our Lives* (BBVA Annual Series), Madrid, Spain: Turner Publicaciones, S.L., 127–148.

Diener, E., Emmons, R. A., Larsen, R. J. & Griffin, S. (1985). The satisfaction with life scale. *Journal of Personality Assessment*, 49(1), 71–75.

Elfenbein, H., Beaupré, M., Lévesque, M. & Hess, U. (2007). Toward a dialect theory: Cultural differences in the expression and recognition of posed facial expressions. *Emotion (Washington, D.C.)*, 7(1), 131.

Ferrari, J. R. (1993). Procrastination and impulsiveness: Two sides of a coin? In W. G. McCown, J. L. Johnson, & M. B. Shure (Eds.), *The Impulsive Client: Theory, Research, and Treatment*, pp. 265–276. Washington, DC: American Psychological Association.

Ferrari, J. R., & Tice, D. M. (2000). Procrastination as a self-handicap for men and women: A task-avoidance strategy in a laboratory setting. *Journal of Research in Personality*, 34(1), 73–83.

Fitzpatrick, J. J. (2008). Internet addiction: Recognition and interventions. *Archives of Psychiatric Nursing*, 22(2), 59–60.

Hoffman, D. L., Novak, T. P. & Venkatesh, A. (2004). Has the Internet become indispensable? *Association for Computing Machinery*, 47(7), 37–44.

"How People Spend Their Time Online." (2012). In *Go-gulf.com Web Technologies*. Retrieved August 20, 2016 from http://www.go-gulf.com/blog/online-time/

Kasper, G. (2004, March 30). Tax procrastination: Survey finds 29% have yet to begin taxes. Retrieved September 16, 2016, from http://www.prweb.com/releases/2004/3/prweb114250.htm

Kidwell, B., Hardesty D. M. & Childers, T. (2008). Consumer emotional intelligence: Conceptualization, measurement and the prediction of consumer decision making. *Journal of Consumer Research*, 35(1), 154–166.

Kidwell, B., Hasford, J., & Hardesty, D. M. (2015). Emotional ability training and mindful eating. *Journal of Marketing Research*, 52(1), 105–119.

Klassen, R. M., Krawchuk, L. L. & Rajani, S. (2008). Academic procrastination of undergraduates: Low self-efficacy to self-regulate predicts higher levels of procrastination. *Contemporary Educational Psychology*, 33(4), 915–931.

Kraut, R., Patterson, M., Lundmark, V., Kiesler, S., Mukopadhyay, T. & Scherlis, W. (1998) Internet paradox: A social technology that reduces social involvement and psychological well-being. *American Psychologist*, 53(1), 1017–1031.

Kraut, R., Kiesler, S., Boneva, B., Cummings, J., Helgeson, V. & Crawford, A. (2002). Internet paradox revisited. *Journal of Social Issues*, 58(1), 49–74.

Kuss, D. J. & Griffiths, M. D. (2011). Online social networking and addiction-A review of the psychological literature. *International Journal of Environmental Research and Public Health*, 8(9), 3528–3552.

Lay, C. H. (1986). At last, my research article on procrastination. *Journal of Research in Personality*, 20(1), 474–495.

Lay, C. & Silverman, S. (1996). Trait procrastination, anxiety, and dilatory behavior. *Personality and Individual Differences*, 21(1), 61–67.

Limonero, J. T., Fernández-Castro, J., Soler-Oritja, J. & Álvarez-Moleiro, M. (2015). Emotional intelligence and recovering from induced negative emotional state. *Frontiers in Psychology*, 6(1), 816.

Lopes, P. N., Salovey, P., Côté, S., Beers, M. & Petty, R. E. (2005). Emotion regulation abilities and the quality of social interaction. *Emotion (Washington, D.C.)*, 5(1), 113.

Mayer, J. D. & Salovey, P. (1997). What is emotional intelligence? In P. Salovey & D. J. Sluyter (Eds.), *Emotional Development and Emotional Intelligence: Educational Implications*, pp. 3–34. New York: Harper Collins.

Mayer, J. D., Salovey, P., Caruso, D. R. & Sitarenios, G. (2003). Measuring emotional intelligence with the MSCEIT V2. 0. *Emotion*, 3(1), 97.

Milgram, N. (1991). Procrastination. In R. Dulbecco (Ed.) *Encyclopedia of Human Biology* (Vol. 6), pp. 149–155. New York: Academic Press.

Nie, N. H., Hillygus, D. S. & Erbring, L. (2002). Internet use, interpersonal relations, and sociability: A time diary study. In B. Wellman & C. Haythornthwaite (Eds.), *The Internet in Everyday Life*, pp. 215–243. Oxford: Blackwell.

Perrin, A. (2015). One-fifth of Americans report going online 'almost constantly'. Retrieved August 20, 2016 from http://www.pewresearch.org/fact-tank/2015/12/08/one-fifth-of-americans-report-going-online-almost-constantly/

Peter, P. C. (2009). *Emotional Intelligence and Health: An Empirical Investigation of the Role of Emotional Intelligence in the Adoption and Maintenance of a Healthy Diet/Weight*. Verlag, Germany: VDM.

Peter, P. & Brinberg, D. (2012). Learning emotional intelligence: An exploratory study in the domain of health. *Journal of Applied Social Psychology*, 42(6), 1394–1414.

Peter, P., and Krishnakumar, S. (2015). Experiential and strategic effects of emotional intelligence on impulse buying and self-esteem considering two ability measures of EI. In S. Raz. & L. Zysberg (Eds), *Emotional Intelligence: Current Evidence from Psycho-physiological, Educational, and Organizational Perspectives*. Hauppauge, NY: Nova Publishing.

Riley, H. & Schutte, N. (2003). Low emotional intelligence as a predictor of substance-use problems. *Journal of Drug Education*, 33(4), 391–398.

Rubin, R. S., Munz, D. C. & Bommer, W. H. (2005). Leading from within: The effects of emotion recognition and personality on transformational leadership behavior. *Academy of Management Journal*, 48(5), 845–858.

Salovey, P. & Mayer, J.D. (1990). Emotional intelligence. *Imagination, Cognition, and Personality*, 9(1), 185–211.

Silver, M., & Sabini, J. (1981). Procrastinating. *Journal for the Theory of Social Behavior*, 11(1), 207–221.

Sirois, F. M., Melia-Gordon, M. L., & Pychyl, T. A. (2003). "I'll look after my health, later": An investigation of procrastination and health. *Personality and Individual Differences*, 35(1), 1167–1184.

Sirois, F. M. (2004). Procrastination and intentions to perform health behaviors: The role of self-efficacy and the consideration of future consequences. *Personality and Individual Differences*, 37, 115–128.

Spada, M. M., Hiou, K. & Nikcevic, A.V. (2006). Metacognitions, emotions, and procrastination. *Journal of Cognitive Psychotherapy*, 20(3), 319–326.

Steel, P. (2007). The nature of procrastination. *Psychological Bulletin*, 133(1), 65–94.

Steel, P., Brothen, T. & Wambach, C. (2001). Procrastination and personality, performance, and mood. *Personality and Individual Differences*, 30(1), 95–106.

Tice, D. M. & Baumeister, R. F. (1997). Longitudinal study of procrastination, performance, stress, and health: The costs and benefits of dawdling. *Psychological Science*, 8(6), 454–458.

Trinidad, D. R., Unger, J. B., Chou, C. P., Azen, S. P. & Johnson, C. A. (2004). Emotional Intelligence and smoking risk factors in adolescents: Interactions on smoking intentions. *Journal of Adolescent Health*, 34(1), 46–55.

Van Eerde, W. (2000). Procrastination: Self-regulation in initiating aversive goals. *Applied Psychology*, 49(3), 372–389.

Van Hooft, E. A. J., Born, M. P., Taris, T. W., van der Flier, H. & Blonk, R. W. B. (2005). Bridging the gap between intentions and behavior: Implementation intentions, action control, and procrastination. *Journal of Vocational Behavior*, 66(1), 238–256.

Widyanto, L. & McMurran, M. (2004). The psychometric properties of the internet addiction test. *CyberPsychology and Behavior*, 7(4), 443–450.

Yip, J. & Côté, S. (2013). The emotionally intelligent decision maker: Emotion-understanding ability reduces the effect of incidental anxiety on risk taking. *Psychological Science*, 24(1), 48.

Young, K. S. (1998). Internet addiction: The emergence of a new clinical disorder. *CyberPsychology and Behavior*, 1(3), 237–244.

PART IV

Some Unintended Consequences for Brands/Business

With the consumer aspect considered in Part III, this section (Part IV) now shifts focus from the consumer and social media to brands or businesses and social media with a specific focus on some unwanted or unintended consequences for the brand, business, or organization. Consider the case of brands and how some consumer activists use brands, businesses, or organizations to make a point that actually goes against what the entity stands for.

Namely, consider Greenpeace's use of generated content on YouTube, the "LEGO: Everything is NOT awesome" video. In this case, we learn about some consequences faced by the brands Shell and Lego. Chapter 8 specifically examines consumers' emotional responses to this video through sentiment analysis of online comments from YouTube. It is found that, in general, consumers respond positively to Greenpeace's YouTube campaign and exhibited high levels of joy in response to the video. Greenpeace's implementation of this viral marketing strategy in conjunction with its other efforts successfully raised the public awareness of Shell's impending Arctic drilling operations and placed pressure on Lego to dissolve its cobranding relationship with the multinational oil company. So, there may even be some outcomes that companies may not want, but a point here in Chapter 8 points to the power of consumers via activism on social media, which IS awesome.

Meanwhile, in Chapter 9, the "organization" of interest is the news media in general. Social media has been pretty aggressive at being a server of the news. The problem to the news outlets is that some is fake news plagued with alternative facts and some questionable, proprietary algorithms that show certain news content in select order. Are there unintended effects to news organizations? Yes, they are dropping in consumer trust and credibility. Chapter 9 takes a twist to this and thinks about how social media news sources expose consumers to news that fits in their own personal bubble.

It sadly reinforces what they already think if the news component of the social media site makes it less broad and more catered to keeping the consumer in their bubble. Why do we as consumers stay in our news bubble? It reduces cognitive dissonance and a need for conflict or counter-arguments or a felt desire to get worked up or engage in some digital drama. Because, sleeper-effect aside, are you really going to change your high school friends mind about who to vote for in a presidential election with a Facebook post? Probably not—because that person stays in their bubble and social media sites have made it quite easy to do so. Chapter 9 helps explain how exposure to more diverse news sources can actually both hamper and enable consumer sense-making.

The findings reveal a non-beneficial aspect of social media-enabled news consumption, namely, the potential for a "filter bubble". What does this mean? It means that while news-like information is abundant on social media such as Facebook, converting it to knowledge requires the consumer to engage in sense-making, all the while dealing with massive information overload. This leads the user to make choices with respect to how much information they are willing (and able) to process and what strategies they use to make sense of the news or information garnered on social media. A second finding is that social media plays a nuanced role in online or social media news consumption and identifies both its benefits and its "dark side". The findings in Chapter 9 reveal a non-beneficial aspect of social media-enabled news consumption, namely, the potential for a "filter bubble".

8

WHEN CORPORATE PARTNERSHIPS ARE NOT AWESOME

Leveraging Corporate Missteps and Activist Sentiment in Social Media

B. Yasanthi Perera, Ryan E. Cruz, Pia A. Albinsson, and Sarita Ray Chaudhury

> The modern day forum for unrest and disagreement is social media. What makes social media different than traditional protests is the speed, scope and intensity of the reaction ... As we have seen with Black Lives Matter, social media can quickly start and organize a national or global response. John Foley (2015)

Today's consumers, especially those in the developed world, live in media-saturated societies characterized by "a large number of competing media, a large number of channels within those media, and a large variety of messages on those channels" (Sherry, 2002, p. 208). Ever developing technology and social media platforms, as indicated by the quote above, have facilitated consumers' engagement and participation in various societal discourses. However, social media presents both challenges and opportunities for the parties involved. For businesses, it presents "a revolutionary new trend" (Kaplan & Haenlein, 2010, p. 59) which, if utilized effectively, is an excellent tool for connecting with the public, courting new consumers, and presenting the firm's desired brand image. However, social media is also a challenge because while firms traditionally controlled the information about themselves in the public sphere (Kaplan & Haenlein, 2010), now, any individual or organization can share information with millions of others with a single key stroke. Given the public's interest in social issues, especially as they relate to businesses, individuals and activist organizations often share information, which may or may not be accurate, about businesses' practices on various social media platforms, all of which have the potential to become viral. It is extremely difficult for businesses to curate all this information about them in cyberspace. Thus "firms have been increasingly relegated to the sidelines as mere observers, having neither the knowledge nor the chance—or, sometimes, even the right—to alter publicly posted comments provided by their customers" (Kaplan & Haenlein 2010, p. 60). Therefore, at times, firms are placed in the unenviable position of having to respond to various claims made about them by other organizations, including activist organizations, as well as by individuals and consumer groups.

Without a doubt, online activism has increased in popularity and its presence can be found on social media platforms such as Twitter, Facebook and YouTube. Thus, given its popularity and relative newness, it is important to study activists' use of social media and the impact of their digital activities on corporations, brands, and consumers. Extant research includes time-series analysis of Twitter and Facebook streams on protests (Bastos et al., 2015), corporate boycotts on Facebook (Kang, 2012), and shareholder activism on Twitter (Orangburg, 2015). However, there are two gaps that must be addressed. First, there is limited research about online activism conducted through YouTube. This is surprising in that YouTube videos have the potential for rapid dissemination (Berger, 2013; Leonhardt, 2015) which makes this platform ideal for activists' purposes. Second, the existing research on YouTube video largely adopts a content analysis approach and ignores consumer sentiment (consumer comments). While content analysis of singular videos (or media) yields information on the message, its appeals, strategies, and characteristics that might be useful in content generation, such an approach largely ignores or provides speculative predictions of the message's impact on consumers. Thus, as YouTube permits users to like, comment on, and share video content in addition to uploading, viewing, rating, and sharing user or brand-generated content (e.g., video and audio clips, video blogs), this social media platform is a useful research tool for studying media content, peer responses to specific content, and interaction effects of media and text (peer comments). Doing so is important because, given that a key aim of posting on social media is to begin conversations, it provides insight on what resonates with the public.

Given these gaps and the ever increasing popularity of online activism, in this chapter, we discuss the dark side of social media through examining a case that entailed Greenpeace, the environmental activist organization, disseminating a video titled "LEGO: Everything is NOT awesome" through YouTube. The case involved four parties: Greenpeace, Lego, Royal Dutch Shell, and consumers who participated in Greenpeace's activist efforts. In particular, we focus on the online consumer and the peer-to-peer communication that occurred in response to Greenpeace's video to illustrate how social media can be leveraged by online activists to raise awareness about their causes and how negative content generation and virality can result in undesired outcomes (depending on the perspective adopted) with respect to corporate relationships.

Online Activism

We'll only ask you to do a little, and in return you get to feel as though you are making a difference. (Eaton, 2010, p. 187)

To be effective, activist organizations must continuously engage more participants and maintain sustained activist efforts. As such, they may appeal to consumers through various means of fast activism (Eaton, 2010). Fast activism is referenced as such first because "it simply takes less time to participate in click through petitions and online donations than marches and sit-ins" (p. 187), and second because such efforts are similar to speedy services such as those offered at fast food eateries (Eaton, 2010). Fast activism, also known as clicktivism, slacktivism, convenience activism, (Albinsson & Perera, 2012) and armchair activism (Montgomery et al., 2004) can be facilitated through social media platforms where consumers click petition links, send automated messages, and view and share activist content. While it allows easy access and participation, fast activism does not foster social ties among activists and activist organizations (Albinsson & Perera, 2012; Fabian & Reestorff, 2015). This drawback of fast activism must be noted, given that e-petitions (e.g. Change.org and MoveOn.org) and online information sharing are standard practices within activist campaigns (Karpf, 2010). While such activist approaches serve the underlying organization's goals, they neglect the communal and relational components incumbent of activist organizations. However, community can be fostered and encouraged on social networking platforms such as Facebook, Twitter, and YouTube which feature embedded dialogue or conversation functions, such as comments and replies. The following section discusses how online activism can result in publicity crises for targeted businesses.

Marketplace Crises, Consumer Sentiments, and Firms' Crises Management Efforts

An organization's reputation is its stakeholders' "aggregate evaluation" of how it is meeting their expectations (Wartick, 1992). It is reasonable to suggest that all businesses want to develop and maintain a strong, positive reputation in the marketplace. While the traditional view of business as operating on the principle of profit maximization within the law places the stockholder/ shareholder as the key stakeholder (Friedman, 1970), the stakeholder perspective defines a stakeholder as "groups and individuals who benefit from or are harmed by, and whose rights are violated or respected by, corporate actions" (Freeman, 2001, p. 41). In a similar vein, the Stanford Research Institute defines a stakeholder as any group "on which the organization is dependent on for its continued survival" (Mitchell et al., 1997, p. 856). To this end, "persons, groups, neighborhoods, organizations, institutions, societies and even the natural environment are generally thought of as actual or potential stakeholders" (Mitchell et al., 1997, p. 855). As such, the perspectives of multiple groups ranging from consumers and employees to activists, competitors, and unions matter in the management of reputation.

Research conducted in Europe indicates that managers regard risks to firms' reputation as a major threat to firms, operations, and market value (AON, 2007). However, unexpected online activism can potentially damage firms' reputations.

Depending on the contextual factors, such an occurrence may be deemed as an organizational crisis which is "a low-probability, high-impact event that threatens the viability of the organization and is characterized by ambiguity of cause, effect, and means of resolution" (Pearson & Clair, 1998, p. 60). With specific reference to brands, crises "threaten a brand's perceived ability to deliver expected benefits thereby weakening brand equity" (Dutta & Pullig, 2011, p. 1281). These crises are either performance-related or values-related: the former relates to defective products and the inability to deliver on expected functional outcomes whereas the latter pertains to "social or ethical issues surrounding the values espoused by the brand" (Dutta & Pullig, 2011, p. 1282).

When crises occur, firms engage in crisis communication which entails them collecting, processing, and disseminating information to address the situation (Coombs, 2010). While the early literature on crisis communication was largely based on case studies (Coombs, 2007), the more recent literature includes conceptual models such as the Situational Crisis Communication Theory (SCCT) (Coombs, 2007, 2010).

This model includes emotions and attributions of whether the firm involved in the crisis has a measure of responsibility in creating the situation and is informed by Attribution Theory (Weiner, 1986, 2006). People attribute responsibility for an event and display emotional reactions, anger and sympathy being core responses, to it. Thus, in a crisis, stakeholders will assess which party or parties might be responsible for the event (Coombs, 2007). According to the SCCT, the reputational threat to an organization is based on the following: 1) the initial crisis responsibility (the extent to which stakeholders perceive the organization as being responsible for the crisis); 2) history (whether or not the organization has faced a similar crisis in the past); and 3) prior relational reputation (how the organization has treated its stakeholders in the past) (Coombs, 2007). Some of this, especially assessing initial crisis responsibility, is influenced by how pertinent messages are framed.

Framing is to "select some aspects of a perceived reality and make them more salient in a communicating text, in such a way as to promote a particular problem definition, causal interpretation, moral evaluation, and/ or treatment recommendation for the item described" (Entman, 1993, p. 52). Crisis communication involves framing on two levels: frames in communication, and frames in thought (Druckman, 2001). The former is about how information is presented to highlight or minimize certain aspects, whereas the latter concerns how people interpret the information shared based on their personal scripts, schemas, or mental models (Coombs, 2007). Frames in communication, and frames in thought are related in that how a situation is presented will influence others' understanding of it which, in turn, influences attributions of responsibility, determining possible solutions, and decisions (Coombs, 2007). Thus, with respect to activism efforts, message framing is relevant in that it would likely influence recipients' reactions, including their willingness to take action and contribute to the activists' aims.

Attributing responsibility for the crisis elicits emotional reactions such as anger, schadenfreude, and sympathy and can present a potential risk to the organization's reputation (Coombs, 2007) as some emotions, in particular anger and fear, can result in negative word-of-mouth communications. Thus, Gopaldas' (2014) suggestion that examining marketplace sentiments would expand social marketing research through including consumers' psychological and emotional insights applies to online activism. With respect to marketplace sentiment or emotion, Gopaldas (2014) contends that: 1) emotions are present in consumer expressions; 2) that Greenpeace's YouTube video serves as an attitudinal object and marketplace element at which emotions are targeted; 3) and a group of actors (video viewers, activists, and consumers) apportion emotions towards the marketplace element. While Gopaldas (2014) does not specifically discuss Greenpeace's use of the "LEGO: Everything is NOT awesome" video, one can extend this research to information shared in any given crisis situation stemming from activism efforts, including that faced by Lego due to Greenpeace's efforts.

A firm's response to a crisis shapes attributions of responsibility, improves perceptions of the organization, reduces negative emotions, and influences consumers' reactions (Coombs, 2007). Four crisis response strategies were proposed by Coombs (2007): deny, diminish; rebuild; and bolster. With denial, the organization refuses to acknowledge a connection between itself and the crisis; through diminishing, the organization downplays the crisis and depicts it as being less negative; rebuilding entails the organization attempting to develop a more positive reputation by presenting new, positive information about itself and undertaking positive actions to counter the negative perceptions stemming from the crisis; finally, bolstering draws upon goodwill stemming from positive interactions with stakeholders in the past to reinforce the firm's reputation in the present (Coombs, 2007). In terms of effectiveness, regardless of the type of crisis, denial is the least effective strategy in restoring brand confidence among stakeholders (Dutta & Pullig, 2011). Instead, it appears best for organizations to assume complete responsibility for the situation and/or promise on remedial measures to address it (Dean, 2004). While the appropriate response is undoubtedly influenced by contextual factors, in this research, we examine the case of Greenpeace targeting Shell through an intermediary, Lego, with whom Shell maintained a longstanding co-branding relationship, with the aim of disrupting the collaboration while raising awareness of the environmental concerns associated with Shell's operations.

Lego: A Pawn in Greenpeace's Chess Match with Shell

The Royal Dutch Shell Corporation, a multinational oil company founded in 1907, is as of February 2016, the second largest oil company in the world (Katakey, 2016). Greenpeace, founded in 1971 in Vancouver, British Columbia, is a non-governmental environmental organization that engages in highly visible direct action in order "to ensure the ability of Earth to nurture life in all its diversity" ("Our Core Values", n.d.). The two organizations have collided on several occasions through the decades. For example during the 1990s, Greenpeace vehemently opposed Shell's plan of sinking an obsolete 14,500 ton North Sea-based oil platform, the Brent Spar, into the Atlantic Ocean (Greenpeace, n.d.). The most recent iteration of the tension between Greenpeace and Shell came to the public's attention on July 8, 2014 when Greenpeace released a short parody video, titled "LEGO: Everything is NOT Awesome" as part of a larger campaign that included several offline activities and protests. The video, which depicted the Arctic landscape, and Lego figures such as polar bears, Santa Claus, and characters from Harry Potter, Game of Thrones and the Lego movie, drowning in oil to the soundtrack of "Everything is awesome" (but played slowly in a somber tone) from the popular 2014 Lego Movie, eventually became the most viral Greenpeace video of all time (Reestorff, 2015). This video clip was clever in that it integrated multiple ideas: the oil spill referenced Shell's intention, stated in August of 2013, to drill for oil in the Arctic region; the presence of characters, objects, and indeed the entire landscape made of Lego referenced Shell's longstanding relationship with Lego; the title "LEGO: Everything is NOT awesome" connected this video to the Lego Movie. Greenpeace made the video to put pressure on Shell after the news of Arctic drilling was released. The video, which ended with the caption: "SHELL IS POLLUTING OUR KIDS' IMAGINATIONS. TELL LEGO TO END ITS PARTNERSHIP WITH SHELL" ("LEGO ends 50-year tie-up with Shell after anti-Arctic oil campaign by Greenpeace", 2016), included a link to a petition. On YouTube, the video was accompanied by the following statement (Starr, 2014):

> We love LEGO. You love LEGO. Everyone loves LEGO. But when LEGO's halo effect is being used to sell propaganda to children, especially by an unethical corporation who are busy destroying the natural world our children will inherit, we have to do something … Help us stop Shell polluting them by telling LEGO to stop selling Shell-branded bricks and kits today.

Upon signing the petition, consumers had the option of sending Lego an automated email asking that the company stop its collaboration with Shell. By early October 2014, over one million consumers had signed the petition urging Lego to end its partnership with Shell (Hansegard, 2014).

Greenpeace initially disseminated the video through YouTube (Reestorf, 2015); however, a few days and about six million views later, it was briefly removed, due to possible violation of Warner Brothers' copyright ("How LEGO Got Awesome," n.d.). At that point, Greenpeace changed its strategy and began sharing the video through its various Facebook pages, Vimeo, etc. (Greenpeace UK, 2004; Reestorff, 2015) and other groups and individuals reposted/retweeted it with their networks. Once alerted about YouTube's decision to remove the video, as illustrated in Figure 8.1, Greenpeace tweeted: "Did we offend someone? Banned on YouTube, back up on Vimeo" (Child, 2014)). Eighteen hours later, YouTube reposted the video due to Warner Brothers dropping its copyright complaint (Child, 2014) and possibly in response to the significant public backlash ("How LEGO Got Awesome," n.d.).

The partnership between Lego and Shell, based on a $110 million contract, entailed Lego creating Shell logo branded playsets, such as gas stations, tanker trucks, and race cars, which were then sold online and at Shell filling stations ("LEGO ends 50-year tie-up with Shell after anti-Arctic oil campaign by Greenpeace", 2016). To date, over 16 million Shell branded playsets have

 **Greenpeace UK** ✓
@GreenpeaceUK

Did we offend someone? Banned from YouTube, back up on Vimeo. Watch our LEGO video bit.ly/1jwSJ7V #BlockShell

RETWEETS 399 LIKES 168

3:55 AM - 11 Jul 2014

↩ 18   ♺ 399   ♥ 168

FIGURE 8.1 Greenpeace's Twitter Response to Having "Lego: Everything is NOT awesome"YouTube Video Temporarily Banned.

either been sold or given away at gas stations in 26 countries ("It's time for LEGO to block Shell", 2016). Through this partnership, Lego earns monetary compensation while Shell attains a sense of legitimacy (Motion et al., 2016) with a broader base of consumers due to its positive brand association with a beloved toy company.

On the day that Greenpeace launched its campaign (July 1, 2014), Lego's CEO, Jørgen Vig Knudstorp, released a statement indicating that Lego would honor its contract with Shell, that it did not agree with Greenpeace's strategy, and that Greenpeace and Shell should confer directly (Trangbaek, 2016). Knudstorp emphasized that Lego operates in a socially responsible manner and lives up to its long-standing motto, "Only the best is good enough." He noted that Lego had a desire to contribute positively to society and the earth, especially as children will inherit the earth. He believed that the cobranding relationship allowed the company to "bring Lego bricks into the hands of more children" (Trangbaek, 2016). He made note that Lego receives inspiration from many stakeholders such as their fans, children, parents, and NGOs in addition to traditional stakeholders. The Lego CEO notes that these interested parties have very high expectations as to the way Lego does business; he reiterates that they also have high expectations of themselves (Trangbaek, 2016). For instance, Knudstorp notes how the LEGO brand was used as a tool in an argument between organizations, citing conflict between Shell and Greenpeace:

> The Greenpeace campaign focuses on how Shell operates in a specific part of the world. We firmly believe that this matter must be handled between Shell and Greenpeace. We are saddened when the LEGO brand is used as a tool in any dispute between organizations …

Thus, Lego's initial response was denial (Coombs, 2007; Dutta & Pullig, 2011) or resistance (Spar & La Mure, 2003), which is contrary to research indicating that firms should resist denying involvement or responsibility in a crisis (Dutta & Pullig, 2011).

Greenpeace's online campaign was accompanied by multiple offline gatherings. For example, protests were held at Legoland, and in front of Shell's HQ where children built giant Arctic animals from Legos (Duff, 2014), and on July 22, 2014, Greenpeace attempted to deliver a petition signed by 115,000 individuals calling for Lego to end its partnership with Shell to the company's UK headquarters but were denied access ("LEGO refused 115,000 UK petition calling on them to ditch Shell Greenpeace UK", 2016). Elena Polisano, Greenpeace's Arctic campaigner said ("LEGO refused 115,000 UK petition calling on them to ditch Shell | Greenpeace UK", 2016):

> … LEGO is a trusted brand, but it's trying to dodge its responsibility. As long as LEGO keeps on helping Shell clean up its image, it's helping it get

away with aggressively hunting for oil in the extreme and fragile Arctic …
It's time for LEGO to take a stand …

On August 4, 2014, Greenpeace published a second video on YouTube titled "I
dream of the Arctic" with the tagline, "LEGO: Help children save the Arctic."
The video, which once again comprises Lego people, animals, and landscapes,
features children speaking of their Arctic dreams, of visiting with the Arctic with
their families and seeing whales, penguins, and even riding a polar bear. The
video, which ends with the captions "*Imagination is precious*" and "*Keep our Arctic
dreams alive,*" calls for viewers to sign Greenpeace's petition.

Three months later, after over one million consumers had petitioned Lego to
dissolve its co-branding relationship with Shell, Lego's CEO, Jørgen Vig
Knudstorp, released a second online statement on October 8, 2014 ("Comment
on Greenpeace campaign and the LEGO® brand – About Us LEGO.com",
2016)" which reiterated information from his July 1 statement. He once again
emphasized that Lego did not agree with Greenpeace's tactics and that it would
honor the contract with Shell; however he stated the contract, which ends in
2016, would not be renewed (Freisleben, 2015). They did *not* want to be a part
of Greenpeace's campaign ("Comment on Greenpeace campaign and the
LEGO® brand – About Us LEGO.com", 2016). In response, Greenpeace UK's
executive director, John Sauven, stated that the extraordinary public response to
the campaign was indicative of a shift in the public's attitude towards oil companies (O'Reilly, 2014). This case illustrates how Greenpeace implemented a successful activist campaign utilizing a contemporary marketing technique, namely
content generation, through social media platforms (Facebook, Vimeo, Twitter
and YouTube, etc.) to strain the co-promotion and branding relationship
between two organizations. Next we engage in sentiment analysis, also known
as opinion mining, to illustrate consumers' response to Greenpeace's "Lego:
Everything is NOT awesome" video.

Method

Data

As of July 1, 2016, Greenpeace's "LEGO: Everything is NOT awesome"
video had received 7,658,721 views, 62,292 likes, and 12,833 comments. It
was rated the second highest of 49 videos posted on Greenpeace's YouTube
account and at the time of this analysis was the most liked video by the organization. As this research examines consumers' sentiments, the data consisted of
consumer-generated responses, i.e. online comments to the video. All data
were publically available and were not treated as personal data (Fu & Chan,
2013), but all identifiers (e.g. user names) were removed to ensure anonymity
within the sample.

The data were collected through customized web-crawling techniques, specifically a Javascript enabled search using YouTube API 3.0 and multiple relevant keywords including "Greenpeace", "Lego", "Shell", "Arctic", and "Drilling." YouTube allows users to form multiple word search strings using words like 'and' to combine multiple terms but limits search results to 500–1,500 comments per query. The search results are based on what Google's algorithm deems as being relevant at that point in time. It does not allow comments to be queried and mined outside the Google architecture. To bypass these limitations, multiple searches were generated with combinations of keywords over a period of four months in 2016. The search results were combined to only include unique comments in the sample, yielding a total 6,221 comments, or 48% of the comments posted on YouTube.

Data Analysis and Results

To determine the polarity of consumers' sentiment responses to the video, a computer-generated sentiment analysis was conducted on the data. Automated sentiment analyses relate to natural language processing, computational linguistics, and text mining (Hogenboom et al., 2015). While there are multiple well-documented methods of performing sentiment analysis within the domains of computer science and marketing practice (Wang et al., 2015), the technique has yet to be widely adopted by marketing scholars. Given the proliferation of data availability stemming from marketing initiatives on social media platforms, text analytics and sentiment analysis may provide brands and organizations with a competitive advantage in engaging consumers, fostering brand communities and brand relationships.

Sentiment and Sentiment Analysis

When analyzing social media data, researchers typically focus on quantitative measures such as consumer approval (number of likes), conversation rates (number of comments), and amplification rates (number of consumer shares). While such metrics provide information on consumer engagement with the media, the brand, or the brand community, researchers often overlook sentiments in their analysis. As noted, Gopaldas (2014) indicates the value of examining marketplace sentiments for cultural and consumer research. Online activism, like ethical consumerism, is shaped largely by activists' interests, and the environmental and ethical implications of brand activity and the activities of co-branded products (Kozinets & Handelman, 2004). If regarded as a marketplace for media consumption, production of consumer experiences, and consumer identity, consumer-generated responses to market products (i.e. media) would benefit from sentiment analysis. Based on Gopaldas (2014), we consider consumer and activist expressions as cultural patterns of emoting and regard such expressions as components of the online activist culture. While Gopaldas (2014) extends this work to ethical consumerism, we limit our analysis to consumer sentiment, specifically sentiment polarity, emotional categorization, sentiment-word association, and word frequency to emphasize the role of Greenpeace's video and subsequent consumer sentiment in the dissolution of the Lego–Shell partnership.

Sentiment analysis is an automated method of analyzing written text excerpts for the purpose of extracting subjective information within text documents (Feinerer et al., 2008). In marketing research, sentiment analysis is used to determine attitudes, judgements, and evaluations of the emotional states of consumers who have performed a type of written communication to an intended reader (Homburg et al., 2015). Thus, sentiment analysis may be performed on textual data originating from letters, emails, consumer product reviews, and social media comments, such as those in response to Greenpeace's video.

To perform the sentiment analysis, the data was pre-processed by removing all punctuation, numbers, and HTML links. Next, every word was transformed to lower case (i.e. 'Car', "CAR", and 'car' are now treated as the same word), extra whitespace was eliminated from text strings (i.e. extra spaces between texts or paragraphs), stop words were removed (i.e. a, the, of, for, if), and only English words were retained in the data set.

To generate our variable of interest, sentiment, from consumer-generated comments, an unsupervised sentiment analysis was conducted to determine sentiment polarity, emotion, word-association, and frequency within our sample. We used R version 3.2.2 (R Core Team, 2016) to conduct text mining, provided by the following packages: 'tm' (Freiner et al., 2008), 'sentiment' (Jurka, 2012), 'word cloud' (Fellows, 2014), 'plyr' (Wickham, 2011), 'ggplot2' (Wickham, 2009), 'RColorBrewer' (Neuwirth, 2014), and 'SnowballC' (Bouchet-Valat, 2014).

Comment Polarity

First, sentiment polarity (i.e. emotional valence) of each online comment was determined by using the *classify polarity* function within the *sentiment* package (Jurka, 2012). This approach allows for determining the directionality and magnitude of the sentiment of a comment using a naïve Bayes classifier with the following measure:

$$Polarity = \frac{positive\ emotions}{negative\ emotions}$$

In this equation, *positive emotions* indicate the absolute log likelihood of the comment expressing a positive sentiment, and *negative emotions* indicate the absolute log likelihood of the comment expressing a negative sentiment. Polarity is expressed as the ratio of the absolute log likelihoods between positive and negative sentiment scores, where a score of less than 1 denotes negative sentiment and a score greater than 1 denotes positive sentiment. Because comments may contain both negative and positive sentiment words, the polarity measure may not accurately capture the

TABLE 8.1 Sample of emotional category and associated words used for sentiment analysis and emotion categorization of words.

Emotion Category	Associated Words
Joy	happy, confident, love, content, safe, ...
Sadness	dejected, unhappy, discouraged, depressed, confused, ...
Anger	tense, irritate, furious, mad, upset, ...
Surprise	amazed, shock, dismay, fascinate, confuse, ...
Fear	terrified, scared, panic, horrified, worry, ...
Disgust	displeasure, annoy, repulse, hate, bored, loathe, ...

degree of emotionality of the comments, resulting in a neutral sentiment or a polarity value equal to 1.

Emotional Categorization

Next, the emotional classification of each online comment was determined using the *classify emotion* function within the *sentiment* package (Jurka, 2012). The emotions lexicon contains 1,500 words classified into one of six emotional categories (see Table 8.1 for an example of emotional categories and associated words). Each emotional category is the absolute log likelihood of a particular emotion (i.e. anger, disgust, fear, joy, sadness, or surprise) being expressed in a given comment and the *classify emotion* function implements a naïve Bayes classifier to sort words within a dataset into these categories.

The emotional lexicon employed comprises a small set of terms relative to lexicons such as the Hu and Liu's (2004) sentiment dictionary. Any words within our data set that were not included in the emotions lexicon generated "NA" and were classified as "unknown" and represented a seventh option within the emotional categories. Given that an average adult has a vocabulary ranging from 20,000–35,000 words (Johnson, 2013), it is likely that we were unable to fully capture the emotionality of every individual; however, for the purposes of this analysis, it extends typical sentiment analysis metrics reporting of polarity and is of added value when analyzing consumer activist sentiment.

Word Cloud and Word Frequency

In a word cloud, content that occurs at a greater frequency is depicted as being larger in size. This allows the viewer to easily identify and interpret the most significant language and content phrases utilized by YouTube users that engaged with the Greenpeace video (Brennan & Croft, 2012; Wang et al., 2015). The word cloud of this analysis indicates the most frequently occurring words and their likely association with emotions.

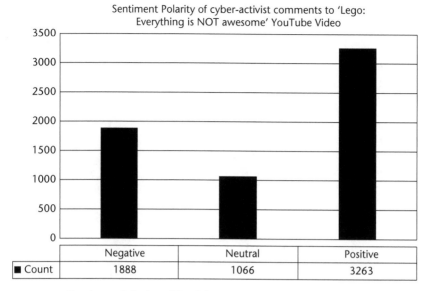

FIGURE 8.2 Sentiment Polarity of YouTube Comments

Our analysis indicates consumer sentiment surrounding the discussion of the YouTube video, which includes responses to others' online comments, is approximately 52% positive, 30% percent negative, and approximately 18% neutral. Thus, as illustrated in Figure 8.2, the prevailing sentiment detected from our analysis is positive. Examples of positive, negative, and neutral polarity can be found within our sample and are indicated in Table 8.2. This indicates the vast majority of user-generated comments contained positive words directed at the video or at other consumer comments, which supports the popularity and virality of the video and its use by the Greenpeace campaign.

Following the polarity assessment, categorization of consumer language stemming from the discussion about the Greenpeace video, represented in Figure 8.3, indicated that of the 2,500 correlated words matching the emotion lexicon used, consumer expressions were as follows: *joy* for 54%, *sadness* 21%, *anger* 12%, *surprise* 4%, and *disgust* 1% of consumer word use within our sample. Additionally, word frequency count was performed for instances where the comment utilized organization-dominant terms (i.e. Greenpeace used at a higher degree than Shell or Lego). The results are reported in Table 8.3. As one may expect, the dominant term or comment topic involved "oil", the three organizations, and referenced the video. Additionally, the consumers discussed the role of 'plastic', 'children or kids', the organizational 'partnership', and the environment. When 'Greenpeace' was the dominant organization discussed, the topic involved 'Lego', 'oil', 'Shell', and was frequently accompanied by action words such as 'stop', 'using', and 'drilling'. When 'Lego' was the dominant organization

TABLE 8.2 Examples of Online-activist Comment Polarity and Emotion

User Generated Comment	Emotion	Polarity
everything is awesome when we stick together wow that was clever	joy	positive
awesome video portraying the reality in the arctic	joy	positive
wow that was incredible no anticorporate video has given me that much feels ever and it didn't even show any actual living things whoever came up with that surely deserves a raise and big rewards or they deserve a better job but yeah it was so powerful it almost seems like bullying really i mean poor defenseless shell … how can they compete with feels like that again srsly nicely done	joy	positive
good video greenpeace	joy	positive
i never knew that shell was doing this to the arctic im really not happy anymore i knew shell was a oil company but thats just wrong	unknown	positive
well there goes my childhood	unknown	neutral
we need the master chief minifigure	unknown	neutral
i totally support this but im pretty sure that the only way to dispose of that stuff involves polluting water so	unknown	neutral
so whos singing that version of everything is awesome	unknown	neutral
halp should I like or dislike this plz halp	unkown	neutral
including my not finsihed childhood thanks green peace im gonna cry under my bed and burn all my legos now thanks bareek obamapeace	anger	negative
guilt by association banning lego is dumb but them dumb over emotional is what greenpeace does best	sadness	negative
holy fuck that was depressing jesus	sadness	negative
this should play on the climax of thelego movie in the time when all hope is lost during the disastrous duplo dictatorship	unknown	negative
i hate lego its stupid and boring	anger	negative

discussed, the topic was 'shell', 'oil', 'plastic' in reference to the video, and the partnership between Lego and Shell was often associated with the action word 'stop'. When 'Shell' was the dominant organization discussed, it was used in conjunction with Lego, mentioned in reference to the video, and featured action words such as 'think', 'more', 'stop', and 'now'. Considered together, the results indicate that Greenpeace's YouTube video was met with positive consumer sentiment polarity and thus was instrumental in the success of its campaign. Qualitatively, while the comments included much praise for the campaign, there were many instances of consumers responding negatively against the activist organization. For example, some consumers blamed Greenpeace for destroying their positive view of Lego.

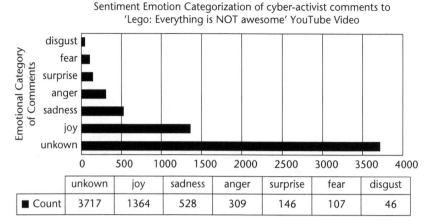

FIGURE 8.3 Emotion Categories of Terms used in YouTube Comments

Discussion and Conclusion

In modern social-media-steeped societies, information flows in multiple directions as individuals or groups can easily collaborate with others to generate and share content on public platforms such as YouTube. Social media has empowered activist organizations and individual consumers to take a stand on issues of personal importance. Activists can manage campaigns wholly online or utilize the virtual medium to support real-life actions such as coordinating demonstrations, boycotts or sit-ins. They are no longer solely reliant on traditional media outlets to publicize their causes. Additionally, consumers who might not participate in traditional forms of activism such as protest marches can now engage in discourse about various issues under contention utilizing social media. Thus, now, individuals like Vani Hari, the blogger who alerted the public about the "yoga mat" chemical additive in Subway sandwich bread ("No more "yoga mat" chemical in our bread," n.d.), start campaigns, often directed at businesses, in order to change prevailing practices. Additionally, activism conducted on social media is highly visible to the public which increases the likelihood of positive outcomes. For example, the Greenpeace "Detox Challenge," initiated in 2011 to reduce toxic chemical use in the supply chains of major global brands, resulted in Puma, Adidas, and Nike pledging to do so ("Timeline: Follow the toxic trail," n.d.). However, this also means that individual consumers and activist organizations can generate crisis situations for firms through the use of social media.

In this regard, Coombs' (2010) assertion that, "no organization is immune from a crisis … even if that organization is vigilant and actively seeks to prevent crises" (p. 17) certainly applies to Lego, the beloved toymaker, which found itself embroiled in a Greenpeace-generated crisis during the summer of 2014. Lego aims to "Inspire and develop the builders of tomorrow" through adhering to six

8

TABLE 8.3 The Representativeness of Comments Terms by Organization

Greenpeace (N=1665)		Shell (N=2021)		Lego (N=1855)		All Comments (N=6221)	
Words	Freq.	Words	Freq.	Words	Freq.	Words	Count
Greenpeace	1012	shell	1774	lego	1841	oil	2110
Lego	759	lego	1350	shell	957	lego	1404
Oil	712	oil	988	oil	824	shell	1355
Shell	653	video	401	plastic	329	greenpeace	1199
Video	317	greenpeace	308	video	313	video	1003
People	261	people	209	greenpeace	307	people	704
World	185	plastic	230	people	221	plastic	557
Stop	160	think	226	out	199	think	502
Plastic	160	more	217	partnership	180	think	502
Company	134	company	211	think	179	out	497
Fuck	130	legos	206	stop	164	world	474
Arctic	124	stop	203	company	162	stop	412
Kids	111	partnership	202	kids	157	company	396
Partnership	101	kids	196	arctic	145	kids	370
Energy	92	arctic	189	world	129	partnership	333
Environment	91	use	182	use	118	drilling	246
Using	91	world	182	drilling	105	used	245
Drilling	89	drilling	133	stupid	92	environment	236
Used	86	gas	125	need	88	money	233
Children	82	now	126	children	87	children	221
Stupid	78	using	109	using	83	stupid	203
Against	78	logo	105	bricks	76	energy	198
Propaganda	77	fuck	102	time	76	gas	196
Time	70	used	101	toys	76	fuck	192
Care	70	children	101	logo	74	arctic	178

N = *Total count of terms in entire document*
Freq = Count of terms where organization name is dominant

core values: imagination, creativity, fun, learning, caring, and quality (The Lego Brand, n.d.). The company also notes that "through environmental sustainability, we want to make a positive impact on the world our children will inherit" (The Lego Brand, n.d.). Without warning, Lego found its values being challenged by a viral Greenpeace video titled "LEGO: Everything is NOT awesome."

Greenpeace, through creating a parody of the popular Lego movie, brought the co-branding relationship between Lego and Shell to the public's attention. This long-standing partnership delivers multiple benefits to both parties including monetary gains and, for Shell, which operates in an industry characterized by environmental damage, pollution, etc., a sense of legitimacy and respectability. Greenpeace's objective in releasing the video was to raise the public's awareness, and persuade them to take action, about Shell's intention to drill for oil in the Arctic. Thus, though Greenpeace created a crisis for Lego in this particular case, from a broader and longer term perspective, Lego was simply a proxy through which Greenpeace targeted Shell. In the midst of this triad between Greenpeace, Lego, and Shell, are the consumers who utilize Shell and Lego products. They use fuel, some of which is most likely produced by Shell, for transportation purposes, and many children play with the much beloved Lego bricks. However, the vast majority of consumers are little, if at all, aware of the decades old Lego–Shell collaboration that produces Shell-logo-embossed Lego playsets sold online and at Shell gas stations. As consumers, and the public in general, represent important business stakeholders, especially in terms of maintaining positive reputation, their sentiments or emotional reactions to brand and brand related claims matter to businesses' success. Therefore, this research focused on consumers' sentiment regarding Greenpeace's video and, by extension, the Lego–Shell collaboration.

The results of our campaign-specific sentiment analysis within YouTube go beyond 'likes' to explore the thoughts, motivations, and opinions of consumers engaged with the "LEGO: Everything is NOT awesome" video. This includes *a posteriori* descriptive analysis of the overarching consumer sentiment polarity and emotionality gleaned from the YouTube video user comments. Activist brands that maintain a presence on social networking sites to leverage their causes are likely to benefit from a 'real-time' sentiment analysis to monitor and gain an overview of public opinion as campaign initiatives are implemented. For instance, as Baker and Wurgler (2007) find, individual investor sentiment shifts can have rapid effects on stock prices. This can be extended to sentiment surrounding activist initiatives on social media. Implementing and using sentiment analysis may provide organizations with a method to rapidly recognize and capitalize on emerging positive sentiment towards activist responses against corporate deviance. Similarly, organizations targeted by activist organizations may utilize sentiment analysis to determine whether to response to activist claims and if so, determine from sentiment analysis, how to structure their messages to ameliorate negative sentiment towards their organization.

Beyond sentiment analysis, Greenpeace demonstrated a sophisticated understanding of marketing strategy. It understood the 'ethos' of the Lego brand and created the parody video and other engagement events based on a thorough research and deep understanding of the company and for what it stands (Reestorff, 2015). Greenpeace's campaign did not offer new creative messages but instead played on Lego's existing branding efforts. Additionally, it utilized Game of Thrones and Harry Potter in the video to garner the interest of those franchises' audiences (Reestorff, 2015). Thus, Greenpeace appears to understand the modern marketing landscape well in terms of how today's consumers acquire information, with video consumption seeing a tremendous increase in recent years (Miners & Miners, 2016). Additionally, Greenpeace appears to understand content marketing as it developed a type of video that is likely to be shared and made viral by the general public. Besides utilizing marketing tools, Greenpeace collaborates across various stakeholder groups to build and sustain a narrative. For instance, a YouTube video published on June 19, 2016 shows Ludovico Einaudi, the acclaimed composer, playing his composition on the Arctic Ocean (Greenpeacespain, 2016). By July 27, 2016, this video had been viewed 1,120,688 times with 18,705 likes. Such ongoing collaborative efforts, combined with individual consumer activists' actions like signing petitions, and writing emails, further the long-term goals of non-profits like Greenpeace. Considered together, such efforts are formidable and it would behove firms to pay close attention to stakeholder groups like activist organizations, as well as consumers, that can affect their brands, operations and, ultimately, their success.

Limitations and Future Research

This analysis is not without limitations. There are a few factors that limit the generalizability and usability of textual analysis methods such as sentiment analysis. First, the context dependency of word usage varies by users, positive or negative sentiment words can have varying levels of connotation depending on the context of its use, which sentiment analysis cannot detect. Second, the presence of a positively or negatively associated language may be used in an ambiguous manner and express no sentiment, and certain nuanced or implied sentiment cannot be detected (i.e. "this video took up a lot of time", although this post doesn't contain any sentiment words, its implications are negative). Third, it has been widely noted that sarcasm can switch word sentiment. Finally, language can have different sentiment and meanings depending on its application and relationship to slang, dialects, elaboration style, as well as language variations (i.e. 'bad' can have multiple meanings based on the context, tone and language, relationship between the message sender and recipient, and can also carry clear linguistic codes to 'in-group' members).

Future research on online activism can benefit from the inclusion of time-series analysis of social media content in conjunction with sentiment analysis (emotion and polarity) and traditional marketing metrics (likes and shares). Such an approach may be of interest to marketing managers and activist organizations to determine emotional and polarity trends of consumer sentiment. Including a time element into the research paradigm may provide insight into the formation, persistence, and decay of consumer sentiment responses to online activists' efforts. Additionally, it would be of benefit to include media analysis of video content to determine what content elements contribute to the success of media used on YouTube for such online activism (i.e. why did Greenpeace have considerably greater success with this particular video than their previous efforts?). Future studies could also examine traditional media and its coverage of the campaign in terms of sentiments and/or framing used in the reporting of events. These efforts would provide a more global view of the role of social media in consumer activism and may elicit new and novel approaches to content generation for brand administrators and activists.

References

Albinsson, P.A. & Perera, B.Y. (2012). Consumer activism through social media: Carrots vs. sticks. In A. Close (Ed.), *Online Consumer Behavior: Theory and Research in Social Media, Advertising, and E-Tail*, New York: Routledge (pp.101-132).

AON (2007). *Corporate Reputation - Not Worth Risking.* Economist Intelligence Unit (EIU).

Baker, M. & Wurgler, J. (2007). Investor sentiment in the stock market. *Journal of Economic Perspective*, 21(2), 129–151.

Bastos, M.T., Mercea, D. & Carpentier, A. (2015). Tents, tweets, and events: The interplay between ongoing protests and social media. *Journal of Communication*, 65(2), 320–350.

Berger, J. (2013). *Contagious: Why things catch on.* New York: Simon & Schuster.

Bouchet-Valat, M. (2014). SnowballC: Snowball stemmers based on the C libstemmer UTF-8 library. R package version 0.5.1. https://CRAN-R-project.org/package= SnowballC.

Brennan, R. & Croft, R. (2012). The use of social media in B2B marketing and branding: An exploratory study. *Journal of Consumer Behaviour*, 11(2), 101–115.

Child, B. (2014). *Warner Bros allows Greenpeace parody Lego video back on YouTube. The Guardian.* Retrieved 22 July 2016, from https://www.theguardian.com/film/2014/ jul/14/lego-lets-greenpeace-parody-video-back-on-youtube

Coombs, W. T. (2010). Parameters for crisis communication. In Coombs, W. T. & Hollday S. J. (Eds.). *The Handbook of Crisis Communications.* United Kingdom: Wiley-Blackwell.

Coombs, W. T. (2007). Protecting organization reputations during a crisis: The development and application of situational crisis communication theory. *Corporate Reputation Review*, 10(3), 163–176.

Dean, D. H. (2004). Consumer reaction to negative publicity. *Journal of Business Communication*, 41(2), 192–211.

Druckman, J. N. (2001). The implications of framing effects for citizen competence. *Political Behavior*, 23(3), 225–256.

Duff, I. (2014, October 9). How LEGO got awesome to #SaveTheArctic. Retrieved July 22, 2016, from http://www.greenpeace.org/international/en/news/Blogs/ makingwaves/save-the-arctic-lego-dumps-shell/blog/50917/.

Dutta, S. & Pullig, C. (2011). Effectiveness of corporate responses to brand crisis: The role of crisis type and response strategies. *Journal of Business Research*, 64(12), 1281–1287.

Eaton, M. (2010). Manufacturing community in an online activist organization: The rhetoric of MoveOn.org's e-mails. *Information, Communication & Society*, 13(2), 174–192.

Entman, R. M. (1993). Framing: toward clarification of a fractured paradigm. *Journal of Communication*, 43(4), 51–58.

Environment (n.d). Retrieved June 13, 2016, from http://www.lego.com/en-us/aboutus/ responsibility/environment.

Fabian, L. & Reestorf, C. M. (2015). Mediatization and the transformations of cultural activism. Conjunctions. *Transdisciplinary Journal of Cultural Participation*, 2(1), 1–20.

Feinerer, I., Hornik, K. & Meyer, D. (2008). Text mining infrastructure in R. *Journal of Statistical Software*, 25(5), 1–54.

Fellows, I. (2014). Wordcloud: Word Clouds. R package version 2.5. https://CRAN. R-project.org/package=wordcould.

Foley, J. (2015). Beware of social media backlash. *Huffington Post*. Retrieved July 16, 2017, from http://www.huffingtonpost.com/john-foley/beware-of-social-media-ba_b_8039358.html

Freeman, R. E. (2001). Stakeholder theory of the modern corporation. In Hoffman, W. M.,

Frederick, R. E. & Schwartz, M.S.(Eds), *Business Ethics: Readings and Cases in Corporate Morality*, Fourth Edition. Boston: McGraw Hill. http://academic.udayton.edu/LawrenceUlrich/Stakeholder%20Theory.pdf

Freisleben, C. (2015, August 6). How online activism can be harmful to established brands: An example of Lego and Greenpeace [Web blog post]. Retrieved July 16, 2017, from http:www.brandBa.se/blog/online-activism-lego-greenpeace

Friedman, M. (1970). The social responsibility of business is to increase its profits. *New York Times Magazine*, September 13: 32-33, 122-124.

Fu, K. & Chan, C. (2013). Analyzing online sentiment to predict telephone poll results. *Cyberpsychology, Behavior & Social Networking*, 16(9), 702–707.

Gopaldas, A. (2014). Marketplace sentiments. *Journal of Consumer Research*, 41(4), 995–1014.

Greenpeace (n.d.). 1995 – Shell reverses decision to dump the Brent Spar. Retrieved July 22, 2016, from http://www.greenpeace.org/international/en/about/history/Victories-timeline/Brent-Spar/.

Greenpeace UK (2014, July 11). Did we offend someone? Banned from YouTube, back up on Vimeo. Watch our LEGO video http://bit.ly/1jwSJ7V#BlockShell. Retrieved from https://twitter.com/greenpeaceuk/status/487550841306759168.

Greenpeace UK (2014, July 22). LEGO refused 115,000 UK petition calling on them to ditch Shell. Retrieved from http://www.greenpeace.org.uk/media/press-releases/lego-refused-115000-uk-petition-calling-them-ditch-shell-20140722.

Greenpeace International (n.d.). Our core values. Retrieved July 22, 2016, from http://www.greenpeace.org/international/en/about/our-core-values/.

Greenpeace International (2016, July 22). It's time for LEGO to block Shell. Retrieved from http://www.Greenpeace.org/international/en/news/Blogs/makingwaves/save-the-arctic/blog/49773/.

Greenpeacespain (2016, June 19). Greenpeace holds a historic performance with pianist Ludovico Einaudi. [Video File]. Retrieved from https://www.youtube.com/watch?v=dHpHxA-9CVM

Greenpeace Video (2009, April 21). Greenpeace – inspiring action. [Video File]. Retrieved from https://www.youtube.com/watch?v=zVu9eawb1QY.

Greenpeace Video (2009, January 29). Catching tuna Maldivian style. [Video File]. Retrieved from https://www.youtube.com/watch?v=HP6rYThJWUg.

Greenpeace Video (2014, June 8). LEGO: Everything is NOT awesome. [Video File]. Retrieved from https://www.youtube.com/watch?v=qhbliUq0_r4.

Greenpeace Video (2014, August 4). LEGO: Help children save the Arctic. [Video File]. Retrieved from https://www.youtube.com/watch?v=Ci4I-VK9jew

Hansegard, J. (2014, October 9). Lego to stop making Shell Play Sets after Greenpeace campaign. Retrieved from http://www.wsj.com/articles/lego-to-end-shell-collaboration-after-greenpeace-campaign-1412845373.

Hogenboom, A., Frasincar, F., De Jong, F. & Kaymak, U. (2015). Using rhetorical structure in sentiment analysis. *Communications of the ACM*, 58(7), 69–77.

Homburg, C. Ehm, L. & Artz, M. (*2015*) Measuring and managing consumer sentiment in an online community environment. *Journal of Marketing Research*, 52(5), 629–641.

Hu, M. & Liu, B. (2004). Mining and summarizing customer reviews. In *Proceedings of the Tenth ACM SIGKDD International Conference on Knowledge Discovery and Data Mining*, Seattle, 22–25 August (pp.168-177). New York, NY: ACM.

Johnson, S. (2015, May 29). Vocabulary size: Lexical facts. *The Economist*. Retrieved from http://www.economist.com/blogs/johnson/2013/05/vocabulary-size.

Jurka, T. P. (2012). Sentiment: Tools for Sentiment Analysis, 2012. URL http://CRAN.R-project.org/package=sentiment. R package version 0.2.

Kang, J. (2012). A volatile public: the 2009 Whole Foods boycott on Facebook. *Journal of Broadcasting & Electronic Media*, 56:4, 562-577, DOI: 10.1080/08838151.2012.732142

Kaplan, A. M. & Haenlein, M. (2010). Users of the world, unite! The challenges and opportunities of social media. *Business Horizons*, 53(1), 59–68.

Karpf, (2010). Measuring the success of digital campaigns. In: M. Joyce (editor). *Digital Activism Decoded: The New Mechanics of Change*. New York: International Debate Education Association, pp. 151–164.

Katakey, R. (2016, February 15). Shell surpasses Chevron to become No. 2 oil company. *Bloomberg*. Retrieved from http://www.bloomberg.com/news/articles/2016-02-15/shell-surpasses-chevron-to-become-no-2-oil-company-chart.

Knudstorp, J.V. (2014, October 8). Comment on Greenpeace campaign and the LEGO® brand - About Us. *Lego.com*. Retrieved from http://www.lego.com/en-us/aboutus/news-room/2014/october/comment-on-the-greenpeace-campaign-and-the-lego-brand.

Kozinets, R.V. & Handelman, J.M. (2004). Adversaries of consumption: Consumer movements, activism, and ideology. *Journal of Consumer Research*, 31(4), 691–704.

LEGO ends 50-year tie-up with Shell after anti-Arctic oil campaign by Greenpeace. (2014, October 10), RT News. Retrieved from https://www.rt.com/business/194800-lego-partnership-shell-greenpeace/.

Leonhardt, J. M. (2015). Going viral on YouTube. *Journal of Digital & Social Media Marketing*, 3(1), 21–30.

Miners, Z. & Miners, Z. (2016). *Facebook will be mostly video in 5 years, Zuckerberg says*. PCWorld. Retrieved 1 August, 2016, from http://www.pcworld.com/article/2844852/facebook-will-be-mostly-video-in-5-years-zuckerberg-says.html

Montgomery, K., Gottlieb-Robles, B. & Larson, G. O. (2004). Youth as e-citizens: Engaging the digital generation (Report). Retrieved from the Center for Social Media, School of Communication, American University, http://www.issuelab.org/resources/837/837.pdf.

Motion, J., Heath, R. L. & Leitch, S. (2015). *Social Media and Public Relations: Fake Friends and Powerful Publics*. New York: Routledge.

Neuwirth, E. (2014). RColorBrewer: ColorBrewer palettes. R package version 1.1-2. https://CRAN.R-project.org/package=RColorBrewer.

O'Reilly, L. (2014, October 9). Here's the chilling Greenpeace video that ended Lego's $116 million deal with Shell. *Business Insider*. Retrieved from http://www.businessinsider.com/lego-ends-shell-deal-after-greenpeace-viral-video-2014-10

Orangburg, S. C. (2015). A little birdie said: How twitter is disrupting shareholder activism. *Fordham Journal of Corporate & Financial Law*, 20(3), 639-716.

Pearson, C. M. & Clair, J. A. (1998). Reframing crisis management. *Academy of Management Review*, 23(1), 59–76.

Reestorff, C. M. (2015). 'Lego: everything is not awesome!' a conversation about mediatized activism, Greenpeace, Lego, and Shell. *Conjunctions*, 2(1), 22–43.

R Core Team (2016). R: A language and environment for statistical computing. R Foundation for Statistical Computing, Vienna, Austria. https://www.R-project.org/.

Sherry, J. L. (2002). Media saturation and entertainment—Education. *Communication Theory*, 12(2), 206–224.

Spar, D. L., and La Mure. L. T. (2003). The power of activism: Assessing the impact of NGOs on global business. *California Management Review* 45, no. 3 (2003): 78–101.

Starr, M. (2014). Lego ends partnership with Shell over Greenpeace campaign. CNET. Retrieved 2 August, 2016, from http://www.cnet.com/news/lego-ends-partnership-with-shell-over-greenpeace-campaign/

Subway: No more "yoga mat" chemical in our bread. (n.d.). Retrieved August 01, 2016, from http://www.cbsnews.com/news/subway-no-more-yoga-mat-chemical-in-our-bread/

The Lego Brand. (n.d.). Retrieved June 13, 2016, from http://www.lego.com/en-us/aboutus/lego-group/the_lego_brand).

Timeline: Follow the Toxic Trail. (n.d.). Retrieved August 1, 2016, from http://www.greenpeace.org/international/en/campaigns/detox/water/detox/Detox-Timeline/

Trangbaek, R. (2016, July 22). Comment on Greenpeace campaign using the LEGO brand - About Us. *Lego.com*. Retrieved from http://www.lego.com/en-gb/aboutus/newsroom/2014/july/lego-group-comment-on-greenpeace-campaign

Wang, X. S., Bendle, N. T., Mai, F., & Cotte, J. (2015). The Journal of Consumer Research at 40: A historical analysis. *Journal of Consumer Research*, 42(1), 5–18.

Wartick, S. (1992). The relationship between intense media exposure and change in corporate reputation. *Business & Society*, 31, 33–49.

Weiner, B. (2006) *Social Motivation, Justice, and the Moral Emotions: An Attributional Approach*, Mahwah, NJ.: Lawrence Erlbaum Associates, Inc.

Weiner, B. (1986) *An Attributional Theory of Motivation and Emotion*. New York: Springer Verlag.

Wickham, H. (2009). *Ggplot2: Elegant Graphics for Data Analysis*. New York: Springer-Verlag.

Wickham, H. (2011). The split-apply-combine strategy for data analysis. *Journal of Statistical Software*, 40(1), 1–29.

9

IS MORE LESS, OR IS LESS MORE?

Social Media's Role in Increasing (and Reducing) Information Overload from News Sources

*David G. Taylor, Iryna Pentina,
and Monideepa Tarafdar*

The Internet has given rise to an explosion of available news and information sources, from online content from traditional mainstream media to fringe conspiracy websites, as well as user-generated news content outside of the domain of media altogether. The average Internet user has access to literally thousands of news sources at his or her fingertips. This has created the ability to find news anytime, anywhere, from any source. However, it has also created an environment in which consumers of news are overwhelmed with the sheer volume of news reports, are exposed to unreliable, biased, or even fabricated news reports, and, lacking trust in the veracity of the mainstream media, may insulate themselves in a "media bubble" in which they are only exposed to news and opinions that reflect their own viewpoints.

The growth in the number of available information sources has fundamentally affected how consumers consume and interpret news in several ways. First, the loss of advertising revenue among traditional print and broadcast media has negatively impacted the quality of their journalistic endeavors (Bruns & Highfield, 2012). Second, new Internet-based media such as blogs, political forums and social media have acquired legitimacy in the eyes of their users, incorporating voluntary contributions by broad networks of self-selected participants that report, share, and distribute news. In these environments, consumers curate news for their social networks, selecting and sharing those most worthy of attention, and filtering out irrelevant stories and items, or those that do not confirm their previously held views. These forms of bottom-up news "produsage" (Bruns, 2008), where consumers collaboratively create and curate news stories, offer a novel socially negotiated informational product that heavily relies on opinions, and substitutes the journalistic ideal of objectivity with that of balance or "multi-perspectivity" (Gans, 1980).

Third, the tsunami of information from the soaring number of sources—much of it unverified, biased or simply false—floods individual media spaces, potentially causing such negative consequences as information overload, suboptimal knowledge formation, and biased worldview. In connection with these developments, some writers caution against the so-called "filter bubble" (Pariser, 2011), when those attempting to overcome news information overload and to make better sense of the contemporary events, increasingly rely on information curated by like-minded others populating their virtual social networks. According to this view, an unintended consequence of such "social filtering" may ultimately undermine civic discourse by confirming our preexisting views and limiting our exposure to challenging beliefs.

These trends have the potential to powerfully and significantly affect political knowledge formation, civic discourse, social and civic awareness and the individual's worldview (Pew Research Center, 2012). Thus, it is critical for news organizations, policymakers and marketing strategists to understand how and why people choose their media sources and consume news. Researchers on information curation have examined the interactivity of curated content (Chung et al., 2012) and engagement (O'Brien, 2011), and their impact on information credibility. Other research includes case studies on the role of individual social media sites such as Twitter in promoting citizen journalism (Greene et al., 2011). To the best of our knowledge, only a single study has addressed the role of the news delivery platform in impacting information overload (Holton & Chyi, 2012). However, no studies so far have attempted to explore or explain the mechanism of news consumption processes among socially connected interactive consumers, nor the consequences of these processes on information/news acquisition and societal or civic knowledge formation. To address this gap, we conducted a qualitative investigation of news consumption practices. We used information overload and sense-making theories to explore how the consumption of online news fueled by social media affects information overload and sense-making.

Information Overload

Possibly the most prominent characteristic of today's news environment is the sheer amount of information to which consumers are exposed. A single Sunday edition of *The New York Times* today contains more information than typical 19th-century citizens faced in their entire lifetime and more new information has been produced in the last 30 years than in the last 5,000 (Pollar, 2003). The soaring number of sources that provide news via print, broadcast, and interactive modes are constantly feeding a steady stream of news, text and video. As a result, we must sift through extra information, often unrelated to our interests and needs, including spam and scams (Denning, 2006). We receive news and information from different sources simultaneously, while multi-tasking on multiple devices (Kelly & Bostrom, 1995). Too much news arriving in too many different formats creates the potential for *information overload*, which in turn leads to news-related suboptimal information processing and decision-making.

Information overload occurs when information-processing demands on individuals exceed their capacity to process the information (Klausegger et al., 2007; Rogers & Agarwala-Rogers, 1975; Schick et al., 1990). The point at which information overload occurs depends on two factors – the information-processing capacity of the individual and the information-processing requirements of the task (Eppler & Mengis, 2004). The amount of information to be processed can be too large to process in the time available (Grise & Gallupe, 1999; Schick et al., 1990). The information may also be of low quality or little relevance to the individual (Ackoff, 1967; Ho & Tang, 2001; Pollar, 2003). News overload may also occur when the information has high entropy, i.e. it is not organized or formatted to be recognized as a significant or important part of the information processing context (Hiltz & Turoff, 1978; Ho & Tang, 2001; Jones et al., 2004), or when the information pertains to many different and diverse domains and ideas (Grise & Gallupe, 1999).

Individuals have limited capacity for information processing (Thorson et al., 1985) and when the above conditions exist, people are subject to cognitive constraints that lead to information overload. Related terms include: information flood/surplus (van de Ven & van Vliet, 1995); information avalanche (Lee, 1998); data trash, data smog (Shenk, 1997); information burden (Harrison & Rosenthal, 1988); and data explosion (Marcusohn, 1995, Wilhelm, 2000). Key consequences of information overload include: information fatigue, where the individual is simply tired of receiving and processing information (Oppenheim, 1997); cognitive strain, characterized by excessive and ineffective attempts to analyze all of the information (Malhotra et al., 1982; Stanley & Clipsham, 1997); terminated or incomplete information processing (Rogers & Agarwala-Rogers, 1975); and decreased accuracy in decision making (O'Reilly, 1980).

Coping with Information Overload

Information processing theory (Galbraith, 1974) suggests two approaches to handling information overload—load adjustment strategies and complexity handling strategies (Grise & Gallup, 1999). The first category consists of activities that *reduce* the amount of information needed to be processed by the individual. It includes information pruning, i.e. reducing the number of information sources (Pollar, 2003) or ideas that the consumer considers (Grise & Gallup, 1999; Carver & Turoff, 2007). It also includes filtering, where individuals choose to receive only the information that they perceive as relevant or important (Kiesler & Sproull, 1982; Lehtonen, 1988; O'Reilly, 1980; Schultz & Vandenbosch, 1998) or that reduces dissonance with existing information (Waller et al., 1995; Pennington & Tuttle, 2007), while ignoring other information. Load adjustment strategies seek to minimize the effort required to process information, which can result in consumers processing lower-quality information or ignoring relevant information (Pennington & Tuttle, 2007; Liang et al., 2007).

The second category includes three types of activities that help the individual to more *effectively* process information. The first relates to organizing information by tagging, sorting, indexing (Carver & Turoff, 2007), and thus making it searchable. The second pertains to prioritizing information and determining the order in which it should be processed (Carver & Turoff, 2007). The third deals with accelerated information processing whereby information is simply processed faster (Pennington & Tuttle, 2007), possibly through new information management techniques (Jones et al., 2004).

In online news consumption, information overload can be attributed to the sheer number and variety of news sources, the increasingly limited amount of time available to process them, and the unorganized and unverified content available from peer-produced and peer-curated sources such as blogs and social networks (Pollar, 2003). Since information processing mediates the relationship between media use and its outcomes (Eveland & Dunwoody, 2002), the linkage between online news media usage and knowledge is influenced by how the individual attempts to address information overload (Beaudoin, 2008). Tools are available to consumers for content personalization and customization to reduce the amount of information in order to limit information overload (Davenport & Beck, 2000). Additionally, the use of social media appears to address both the reduction of information stream via human-mediated filtering, and curation.

Social Media's Role in Information Overload

Social media appear to play an important role in perpetrating news-related information overload. The amount of time spent using social media continues to grow around the globe, with 20% of our computing time and 30% of our mobile time now spent on social media (Nielsen, 2012). In addition to sharing personal information, social users increasingly post links to external content and express their opinions about the world, national and local news. Consumers with frequent exposure to news on their computers, e-readers and on Facebook perceive greater information overload than those exposed to news via TV and iPhones (Holton & Chyi, 2012).

However, social media can also offer tools to address information overload. Social media allow individuals to create, share, and search content, communicate with each other, identify and choose to communicate with specific people, and "pull" the relevant information (Lee & Ma, 2012). Social media also enable specific types of interactions between individuals. They can connect people based on similar needs, tastes and backgrounds, and facilitate the building of information networks where information publishers can deliver content to a set of information consumers, addressing current concerns or interests (Denning, 2006). Such human-mediated information processing helps individuals to identify which information is of value and to whom. Social media can thus gather, select, and value information for individuals. They can expose individuals to selective sources of news while delivering greater cognitive variety and diversity. They can also enable the individual to engage in social interactions, directly with members of the immediate network, and indirectly with members of related or connected networks. These tools can potentially address the problems of information overload by enabling the consumer to make *sense* of it—with the help of social filtering and collectively negotiated sense-making.

We are thus faced with a paradox in contemporary news consumption, one that is expected to persist. On the one hand, use of social media fuels information overload by exposing the individual to an ever-increasing barrage of news content. On the other, it has the potential to help the news consumer deal with information overload through socially-mediated information selection and organization. But these processes, which may reduce information overload, can be problematic in their own way. For instance, there is a concern that because of social filtering, exposure to alternative and challenging views can be limited. In his recent book *The Filter Bubble*, Pariser (2011) argues that the increasing customization of search and personalization of social media experiences may undermine civic discourse by providing more information that confirms our pre-existing views and limits our exposure to challenging beliefs. His opponents disagree, saying that "information bubbles" have always been imposed on news consumers by commercial TV networks and local newspapers that demonstrated narrow consensus. They argue that current reality, such as the role of Twitter in the Arab Spring events, in fact, confirms the enriching function of social media (Weisberg, 2011).

Research on online news consumption is emerging and limited. Studies show that higher levels of Internet use are associated with higher levels of interpersonal trust and lower levels of information overload (Beaudoin, 2008). We also know, based on uses and gratification theory, that higher levels of socializing, information seeking and prior social media experience are associated with higher levels of intention to share news online through social media (Lee & Ma, 2012). On the other hand, it is reported that consumers with frequent exposure to news on their computers, e-readers and on Facebook perceive greater information overload than those exposed to news via TV and iPhones (Holton & Chyi, 2012). These somewhat contradictory findings suggest that new media may play a more nuanced role in news consumption.

Traditionally, newsgathering was mainly considered a purposeful, directed activity (Tewksbury et al., 2001), and assumed some level of intention behind most news exposure. The Internet and social media, with their limitless possibilities of content integration, co-creation and sharing, have intensified more incidental news exposure, whereby individuals "stumble upon" news as a byproduct of their other online activities. In fact, current multi-functional digital media provide hitherto unparalleled access and exposure to both specific and precise sought-after information and to unsolicited content (including news and advertising).

Therefore, the distinction between purposive (active) and incidental (passive) news information acquisition in the digital space may explain diverse findings of the role of social media in affecting information overload, news sense-making, or the resulting civic knowledge. Based on the above, understanding the role of social media in addressing (or perpetrating) information overload and problems of sense-making that so compellingly characterize the context of news consumption in contemporary times presents an interesting and important research topic. Given that academic research in the area is almost non-existent, this study initiates an academic discussion of the role of social media in news consumption. Noting that key characteristics of current online news consumption are information/source overload and socially-mediated sense-making, we utilize the theoretical lenses of information overload and sense-making from the information processing literature as the explanatory background for our study. Specifically, we integrate these concepts to analyze qualitative data collected from a diverse cross-section of 112 news consumers in the U.S. Our analysis identifies several categories of coping strategies that contemporary news information consumers use to overcome information overload while making sense of news. We discuss these categories and specifically show how news consumers use new media to implement these strategies. Based on our findings, we conclude with practical implications for news producers and marketers, and directions for future research.

Sense-making

Sense-making can be defined as a process of transforming the acquired news information into new knowledge by incorporating it into the pre-existing cognitive framework of an individual. It involves understanding a situation or circumstance such that this understanding can form the basis of an action or knowledge (Weick et al., 2005). "Sense making is about the question: What does an event mean? In the context of everyday life, when people confront something unintelligible they ask, 'What's the story here?'" (Weick et al., 2005, p. 412). By interacting with their environments over time and through experience and by communication with others (for learning and teaching) (Fiske & Taylor, 1991), individuals build cognitive frameworks that are a basis for future interactions. The development of these frameworks is thus path dependent. Individuals' pre-existing cognitive frameworks affect each component of a sense-making process (Daft & Weick, 1984). They influence what is *noticed* by making some stimuli more salient than others, they provide rules and logic that influence the *interpretation* of what is noticed, and they suggest what *actions* should be taken by individuals (Galambos et al., 1986).

Two key factors aid in this process. First, increased cognitive diversity, defined as the number of concepts in a cognitive framework and the number of relationships between concepts, is required for more effective sense-making in environments that have high turbulence. This is because greater complexity of pre-existing associations allows more stimuli to be noticed and responded to, leading to greater adaptability (Weick, 1995; Bogner & Barr, 2000). At the same time, some overlap in individual frameworks is necessary for a group of people to generate a collectively coherent framework of understanding about a set of events or circumstances (Fiol, 1994; Nonaka, 1994). Second, individuals create meaning out of different situations by situating that meaning in a "structure of meaning" (Berger & Luckmann, 1966; Schütz, 1970; Weick et al., 2005). Because lone individuals find it difficult to obtain sufficient knowledge to understand everything that takes place, the "structure of meaning" provides the individual with simplifications of reality. The structure of meaning is influenced by social construction and is informed by patterns of thought that the individual adopts through various socialization processes (Schütz, 1945). These socialization processes can take place through the individual's immediate and direct social relationships or, more indirectly, through shared norms at the societal level (Schütz, 1970).

Applied to the context of online news consumption, sense-making would entail the individual identifying the news source on which to focus, constructing meaning from the information provided by that source, and informing and refining one's view of civic society based on that interpretation. The socially mediated news consumption process can *both* facilitate and hamper sense-making. In terms of facilitation, the possibility of exposure to unlimited and diverse sources of news can potentially promote cognitive diversity and *facilitate* sense-making. On the other hand, however, the path-dependent nature of sense-making requires forming associations to a certain pre-existing structure, as well as to the socially constructed cognitive frames. This may limit the amount of informational stimuli being noticed, depending on the context, thus hampering sense-making. Research (e.g., Aldoory & Van Dyke, 2006) shows that consumers often experience information overload due to excessive media coverage during news consumption. This results in cognitive strain and information fatigue, such that they might stop further information seeking, instead relying on their social networks for further information, or even denying or purposely remaining ignorant of the existence of specific news. This *obstructs* sense-making.

Thus, we observe that exposure to diverse sources of news can both hamper and enable sense-making, and thus has the potential to influence sense-making for online news consumption in nuanced and complex ways. While some studies do point to concepts such as the filter bubble, implying a possible deficiency of sense-making introduced by social media, research has not adequately articulated its role in online news consumption.

The Qualitative Study

Our study employed a qualitative research design, deemed appropriate for generating new insights and research evidence about complex and new phenomena that are relatively under-researched (Miles & Huberman, 1994), as is the case with this subject. We used the information-overload and sense-making perspectives to understand how social media affects online news consumption. Our approach follows the interpretive tradition of qualitative inquiry, wherein phenomena are interpreted through theories that can potentially provide insight about them. We followed a combination of inductive and deductive approaches. The former helped to maintain openness and understand the data in an emergent fashion, while the latter helped us to fruitfully inform the data with relevant existing theoretical perspectives (Walsham, 2006).

Research Design

The data and interpretations were derived from 112 interviews with a cross-section of news consumers in the U.S. Midwestern regions. The respondents were identified in two ways. First, trained graduate students of the business management program from a large metropolitan university interviewed their associates and acquaintances for extra points in an online marketing course. In all, 79 interview transcripts were submitted through this process. Second, 33 attendees of an annual Internet Marketing conference in a large Midwestern city, who were internet marketing professionals, were interviewed by the authors and trained graduate students of the same program.

Convenience sampling was used because at this exploratory qualitative stage we sought an understanding of the phenomenon, not its generalization to a population (McCracken, 1988). The respondents ranged in age from 20 to 57 years old and equally represented both genders. Over 90% had at least a bachelor's degree and two thirds reported a household income over $60K. The following questions were asked: "How do you receive your personal, local, national and world news? Please describe the role of newspapers, magazines, radio, TV, the Internet, mobile apps, and other communication media in your news consumption. Please describe the role of Facebook, Twitter and other social media that you use in getting your news and information. Compare the importance of the social media to other modes of your news consumption." Each interview lasted for 15–20 minutes, and was subsequently transcribed by the interviewer. Member checks were done by summarizing a respondent's answer at the end of each interview to confirm its accuracy with the respondent. Each author carefully evaluated the obtained data for possible inconsistencies in the length and pattern of responses, since they were obtained by different individuals and under different conditions. No inconsistencies were identified in the length of the text or the number of paragraphs. Additionally, it was noted that virtually all responses contained an introductory part that explained the respondent's degree of interest in the news information in general and their motivations for reading, listening to, or watching news. Although not specifically included in the questions, this information was also analyzed.

Content analysis (Kassarjian, 1977; Kolbe & Burnett, 1991) was used to analyze the data. All transcripts were coded by each author individually, with new
code categories added as they emerged from the text. The textual data was organized into units of analysis at the sentence level, since each sentence contained
exhaustive information that informed various coding categories. As a result,
responses to different questions were coded simultaneously, using the same set of
codes (Kassarjian, 1977). Data analysis consisted of identifying emerging themes
by noticing instances and patterns of responses (LeCompte & Schensul, 1999). A
combination of open and axial coding was employed to identify and arrange
emerging themes (Miles & Huberman, 1994). Open coding was employed to
identify text associated with new themes and to arrive at categories in an inductive and grounded fashion. Based on these categories, a code book was created by
the authors that was subsequently used for axial coding. Axial coding was applied
toward two ends. First, it was used to deductively situate the identified categories
in the context of the study, interpreted through the theories of sense-making and
information overload. Second, it was used to relate emerging codes to existing
codes. The analysis process iterated between axial and open coding (Strauss &
Corbin 1998, pp. 101, 123), which allowed the authors to understand the concepts and relationships as they emerged and relate them to the literature elements
that informed the study. The inter-coder reliability, measured by Perrault and
Leigh's (1989) I_r, was 92%, which corresponds to the acceptable range of >80%.
Differences were resolved through discussion.

As the coding progressed, particular themes depicted by codes based on the
information overload perspective repeatedly co-occurred with those based on the
sense-making perspective. This prompted the authors to consider relating sense-
making aspects with information overload strategies. Accordingly, the identified
categories of sense-making and information overload strategies were placed into
corresponding cells in a table.

Study Findings

The results of our investigation reveal that sense-making of contemporary news
and its subsequent transformation into civic knowledge (and/or action) is reliant
on the information overload coping strategies that increasingly employ new
technology and new media capabilities. For each aspect of news sense-making
by contemporary consumers, a separate set of information overload strategies is
effective, as described below and illustrated with examples from the data in
Table 9.1. We find that contemporary news consumption is characterized by
two distinct aspects of sense-making. The first, *screening news stimuli*, involves
determination by the news consumer of channels, sources, and content of the
news that he or she would consider attending to. Paucity of time and busy lifestyle, as well as general attitude towards the news are the contextual factors
affecting the choice of information overload strategies (e.g. news avoidance,

TABLE 9.1 Examples of Information Overload (IO) Coping Strategies for News Sense-Making

Sense-making aspect	Screening News Stimuli
Information Overload Coping Strategies	
News avoidance	– Most "news" is just full of garbage propaganda that I don't want or need to be influenced by. And at this point in my life, I have neither time nor brain space to take it all in and sort it all out. (Female, 25, medical student)
	– My busy life does not usually leave time for the news … I really just feel overwhelmed at times and I think that the news stations and papers telling me what I need to know are just too much. (Male, 28, account manager)
	– I do not have a lot of free time and I do not want to waste it on watching some boring news broadcasts. (Female, 21, full time student)
Reducing the number of information sources	– I don't remember the last time I picked up a newspaper; I do enjoy watching morning news shows but I no longer have time for these, either. (Male, 36, financial planner)
	– I get the news from the local newspapers. I don't look other places for the news because all that really affects me is the local news. (Male, 48, sales agent)
	– I am not interested in most things that the news has to talk about, so unless the first thing to pop up on my homepage is an interesting story I care about, I do not bother. (Female, 22, service professional)
Reducing information volume	– Twitter allows me to read a short excerpt of what the news stories are to get a general idea and if I am more interested, they give links to click into for more information. (Female, 21, student)

Filtering news information based on relevance	Looking at Facebook helps by showing me what others feel is relevant. I hear a lot more from Facebook than any other media. There are stories that my friends post that I probably wouldn't have read on my own … It is an effortless way for me to find out what is going on and it is almost always information that I actually want to hear about because my friends have similar tastes to mine. (Female, 23, service professional)
	For the majority of my news I use online aggregator sources. Websites like reddit.com, theregister.com, and fark.com provide me the ability to sort through popular news stories based on my interests. Using a site that gathers stories from multiple places over the Internet allows me to get the most recent and interesting news stories without having to search for them. (Male, 28, engineer)
	I get the news from news sources I follow on Facebook and from my friends that post news stories they follow. I feel the news is more targeted to my interests and views. It is targeted more to me than a newspaper or half-an-hour news program. (Male, 34, marketing professional)
	I use Facebook extensively to find out … what people are talking about. I am increasingly using it for links provided by my friends because I am sick of reading and seeing vacant house fires, car crashes, and the other stuff local TV wastes my time showing. (Female, 24, service professional)
	The news I hear on the radio is usually heard inadvertently. I listen to the radio every day for the music, but almost every station gives some form of news. Certain stations have more pertinent news than others. If I hear something that sounds interesting or might affect me, I will either search online … or watch the news that evening. (Female, 25, graduate student)
Filtering based on privacy concerns	I look at headlines, but I won't ever read further into a Facebook link, because of privacy concerns. I don't want people to see what I am reading, as well, but that doesn't mean it's not a useful tool. (Female, 24, housewife)
	Many of the people I follow on Twitter are politically active citizens, politicians, or pundits, so Twitter can be a source of news for me. However, due to the word limit on tweets, I have rarely gained much insight on world news by scrolling my Twitter feed, and for some reason I am disinclined to click on an article link posted on Twitter. (Male, 47, real estate agent)

(Continued)

TABLE 9.1 Examples of Information Overload (IO) Coping Strategies for News Sense-Making (Continued)

Sense-making aspect	Screening News Stimuli
Source and content personalization and customization	I think that is ultimately the appeal of social media for news: it will "ping" you when news happens as opposed to you going out to look for it. In today's society the convenience of getting a "ping" when big news happens is something that could be very attractive given our busy pace of life. (Male, 28, sales professional)
	Apps, apps, and more apps are the main source of how I receive my news. BBC, CNN, ONN, Aljazeera, HuffPost, WSJ and USA Today are all of my go to news apps, with Twitter a close second. (Male. 35, IT professional)
	I have the USA Today app on my iPad. I started reading *USA Today* because my mother and father read it and it seems to provide the information that they find important. (Male, 31, teacher)
Selecting "pull" over "push" media and topics	I do not watch the news on TV. It can be extremely boring and I have to listen to everything, even the things that I do not want to hear. The newspaper gives me the option to pick out what I want to know and what I do not. (Female, 23, high school teacher)
	I do not subscribe to any online sites to receive information or news. Not all news is important to me, so that is why I choose to do my own search for news rather than getting bombarded by online news websites. (Female, 43, salesperson)
	With television, I don't get a choice of what news I want to see, and the big stories are repeated over and over again. Also, television news only airs a few times a day. With the Internet, I can get breaking news any time I check. (Female, 39, accountant)
	The Internet is my most important source of news. I check a number of news sites daily or semi-daily, ranging from Yahoo News to ABC to Breitbart. My absorption is highly active, because I must devote my full attention to reading articles and watching online videos. It is also very selective because I must deliberately identify which sites and articles I read. (Male, 25, graduate student)
	I do a lot of independent searches on the Internet, that way I can research both sides and try to come up with a conclusion on my own. I do not want to be another mindless zombie who believes every word I hear or read as truth. (Female, 25, housewife)

Relying on socially curated information	In all honesty, the place I hear about most of my news is on Facebook … For example, the way I first found out about the Batman shooting was through Facebook the morning after it happened … Whenever I see something newsworthy written on Facebook, I am always curious if it is in fact true, so I usually go to CNN.com or another news webpage to double-check the story. (Male, 22, student, part-time employed)
	I guess, my main news source is what I hear second hand through my co-workers, my family and my friends. Obviously most of this is in person, but a lot of it also comes through Facebook. I don't always have time to scroll through Facebook's news feed … but there are usually comments made that bring something to my attention. (Female, 23, factory worker)
Categorizing and sorting news topics, sources, and channels	My apps are all located within two folders on the first page of my phone. The social media folder contains my Facebook, Twitter, and LinkedIn apps which I check throughout the day. I also have the other social media apps located in the folder, such as Google+, Instagram, Pinterest, and Wordpress, but these apps are used much less. My news folder was maxed out at one point, but I had to make some tough decision when going through my phone and not all of the news apps made it through the clean-up. The most popular news app that I use is Huffington Post app. Followed by CNN and USA Today. (Male, 34, software developer)
	When I want to get more in-depth, editorial content I listen to radio programs like Glenn Beck, Rush Limbaugh, and occasionally NPR. (Male, 29, engineer)
	I get my news from different places depending on if it is local, national, or world news. I use the local news channel, WTOL's website to keep up on local events. About the national and global news, it is easy to get them from TV and Internet. (Male, 22, student)
	When I look for sources to get local news, I definitely use the local newspaper called The Blade, for when it comes to looking up information about local sports highlights, community issues, and new business ventures… (Female, 26, business owner)
	When it comes to national and world news, I definitely rely on network television, and channels such as MSNBC and CNN. I feel these channels are not as biased as some conservative channels that really rub me the wrong way … (Female, 30, HR professional)
	Other shows that I avidly watch to get news are from the Daily Show and the Cobert Report on Comedy Central. Yes, these shows are satire in a sense about real news, they still deliver reports thoroughly and entertaining that keeps my attention and breaks it down for me so that I really understand it well. (Female, 28, graduate student)

(Continued)

TABLE 9.1 Examples of Information Overload (IO) Coping Strategies for News Sense-Making (Continued)

Sense-making aspect	Processing and Interpreting News Information
Information Overload Coping Strategies	
Evaluating source and content reliability	I believe that there are both credible and non-credible or biased news posts on Facebook, Twitter and other social media sites, but the same can be said for the traditional news entities. It is up to the person reading the news posts, watching the news on TV, or reading the paper, to be objective and to conduct their own research to find out all of the information. (Male, 32, IT professional)
	There are certainly many flaws in technology and people have to be very cautious with reading false information. However, if you are following a "verified" account on Twitter, it is expected to be a real account which tweets quality information (Female, 22, student)
	The political news right now is poisoning the news and I have no need to read a newspaper or watch news on TV. Both are either backed by one side or the other and do their best to push their own opinions onto the people who watch and trust them. (Female, 25, account manager)
Resisting news source bias	I tend to view mainstream news sources as biased (somebody is contributing dough for Fox News to be on television, thus they are able to select which stories they want, slant those stories however they so choose, and completely avoid other facts/viewpoints altogether … propaganda, I tell ya!). But the Internet is, for the most part, free game! And I think that's what everyone should do; educate yourself by pulling from different sources, reflect, then form your own opinion on what you believe to be the truth. (Female, 29, accountant)
Assessing news information trustworthiness	I use Google quite a bit, actually. When I read about certain topics on the Yahoo front page, I will Google them to learn more. My main source of news comes from the Yahoo.com front page. It includes daily for me news from around the nation, around the world, science, health, and local news. I like to make my own conclusions from news and do my own research on topics that I find interesting. You can't always trust what you hear, that is why I look up information on my own. (Female, 33, buyer)

Seeking news timeliness	I feel that social media sources help with having access to the news quicker and with having more information in which to make a decision about the news easier. (Male, 33, small business owner)
	Some days Facebook will be my only connection with the Internet, so I won't see any of the news if it's not on Facebook. So I like having the "trending articles" to keep me informed. Facebook is the most convenient way for me to gather information. It is just natural for me to open my laptop and open up Facebook immediately. (Female, 24, financial planner)
	In my opinion, I get more current news from social media than the actual news channels. (Male, 37, social media manager)
Acknowledging subjectivity of socially-curated content	The big reason I don't see social media as a great place for news is you are getting someone's opinion, as opposed to an unbiased account of the events. Now, I understand that major media outlets are not completely unbiased, either. However, I will take my chances with journalists as opposed to my neighbor's cousin's friend on Facebook. (Male, 40, graduate student)
	Social media are more like the opinions of news from traditional media, such as newspapers, magazines, radio, TV, and online news. Social media can't be considered as the credible sources, unlike other media. (Female, 23, secretary)
Seeking Social Legitimacy	I enjoy the fact that Facebook posts articles that people read. It catches my attention and, although I don't like the fact that people can see what I am reading, I feel more connected with the news of the world (Female, 38, college advisor)
	On the news feed Facebook will post a catchy headline that at times does catch my attention …. A neat thing is that on that article page there will be images of your "friends", and if you scroll over their picture it will show you the articles that they read. Therefore I will continuously click on interesting articles that I would like to read. (Female, 28, city government employee)
Seeking social support	Facebook seems to be a way to mobilize groups of people, useful for nurturing a base of people via social connections and emotions. (Female, 44, freelance writer)

(*Continued*)

TABLE 9.1 Examples of Information Overload (IO) Coping Strategies for News Sense-Making (Continued)

Sense-making aspect	Processing and Interpreting News Information
Sharing and co-producing content	I think Facebook does play an important role – though maybe not the most accurate role – in getting the news out. It's an online extension of the social atmospheres at work and in our personal lives. It's how we share information. (Female, 23, factory worker) I would say that I do get a lot of information from Facebook. I like to hear and see the opinions of my family and friends and see how they feel about the news going on around them. I also get the chance to give people my opinion on the topics that I find interesting. (Female, 53, nurse) I think that Facebook is a preferred site to share news stories because people are free to voice their opinions, concerns, suggestions, etc. and more than likely to strike discussions with other Facebook users about these topics. People love to voice their opinions no matter what channel of communication is used, and computers and phones just happen to be the most popular right now. (Male, 42, teacher)
Expanding cognitive diversity	Facebook has "trending articles" for my public interest topics that I read, and I see people's political stances and values by what they post on their wall. It gives me the opportunity to view a wide variety of different views and news because my Facebook friends mostly all have different opinions from one another. (Female, 22, cashier) I feel Facebook is important compared to other forms of media because so many people use it. It gives an insight to many different cohorts and allows people to see what their friends think. (Female, 39, professor) Social media allows us access to all kinds of news and differing opinions. This isn't just news processed through a news organization, but rather it comes directly from a normal person, who finds this or that topic interesting enough to share to his or her friends. It's an amazing new dissemination method not inherently controlled by the media, but rather through a person's acquaintances. (Female, 65, dog breeder)
Seeking independence from institutional media	The primary social media site I use is Facebook. I am a fan of a few politicians and pundits and friends with some politically active people, so I often happen to see news-oriented statuses or links to articles. If these pique my interest, I will investigate further. While I do not usually get much info in this fashion, I have on occasion benefited greatly from scanning the newsfeed. I recall that I first learned about the death of Osama bin Laden in 2011 from someone's Facebook status. More recently, I gained much information about the Muhammad video controversy by reading the statuses of Facebook friends who are scholars of religion. (Male, 27, employed part-time)

information load adjustment, information complexity handling, etc.) employed by news consumers in the process of screening news stimuli. Social media enable these strategies by providing timely and relevant information that is socially curated by like-minded network participants. However, social media also complicate the news stimuli screening process by contributing to information overload due to their exposure to unverified, anonymous and overwhelmingly subjective sources of news.

The second sense-making aspect, *processing and interpreting news information*, involves path-dependent and socially mediated negotiation of meaning of the acquired news and its conversion into knowledge. It is characterized by a separate set of strategies to overcome information overload. In particular, evaluating reliability and trustworthiness of the news sources and content acquires prominence, with social media again playing an ambiguous role. On the one hand offering views and opinions that are independent of the mainstream news media, social media present subjective opinions and comments as well as unverified facts. However, social media have a strong advantage over other types of news media in providing social legitimacy to the news-related opinions and aiding in incorporating the incoming information into preexisting mindsets. Thus, by helping situate the new events in the context of pre-existing political preferences and positions of familiar individuals, social media assist in reducing information overload and facilitating sense-making. Social media also play an important role in providing the diversity of opinions a news consumer is exposed to, thereby expanding their mental associations and facilitating greater assimilation of news information.

Below, we detail the information overload coping strategies pertinent to each sense-making aspect and highlight the role of social media in these processes. These results are summarized and illustrated with examples in Table 9.1.

Screening News Stimuli

To determine, which channel, source, and what specific content of the ubiquitous news stream facing each person today to focus upon, our respondents use the path-dependent heuristics determined by their prior experiences and cognitions about news consumption. Thus, the salience of the news stimuli on which to pay attention is affected by the processes of source and content filtering (including outright news avoidance), as well as categorizing and sorting the available sources and content. The *filtering* and *avoidance* strategies mainly concern the respondent-side processing constraints, while *sorting, prioritizing and categorizing* news refer to the complexities of analyzing or understanding the available content. Other strategies employed by news consumers to cope with information overload in identifying the news stimuli for further processing include *personalization/customization*, *selecting "pull" over "push" news acquisition mode*, and *relying on socially curated news content*.

Numerous respondents mention paucity of time, busy professional and family life, lack of interest towards events and developments outside their immediate environment, and resentment towards biased reporting and political spinning. As a result, the adopted coping strategies focus on load adjustment and seek to reduce the amount of news consumed. These range from reducing the number of sources, media, and volume to be exposed to (with the extreme cases of avoiding news altogether) to filtering the information to be processed. Frequently, discussions of the *news avoidance strategy* are accompanied by negatively valenced emotional and affective statements, explaining reasons for deliberate behavioral intentions to avoid exposure to "sad" and/or "too political" news. Other explanations include perceived irrelevance of the majority of news to a person's life and interests and "not making a difference" in his/her life. Finally, some respondents admit to not having developed a "habit of checking the news", being at the stage in their lives when they are more interested in socializing with friends and enjoying their free time. For them, news is "not entertaining" and those friends who post "serious information" on their Facebook feeds are "annoying". Another coping strategy, associated with consumer news processing constraints, is *filtering the information based on relevance*. The majority of respondents adopting this strategy are not deliberately seeking out news on certain topics, but selectively attending to headlines "pushed" onto them by various media. They are (rather passively) exposed to TV at home, radio in the car, word-of-mouth at work, social media postings by friends, and online news aggregators' and email portals' headlines. Usually, they expend no effort and do not expect any cost to be associated with acquiring news (in fact, they admit to abandoning various content websites as soon as they introduce access fees). This strategy involves pursuing in more depth topics or events deemed relevant (e.g. by clicking on links or searching for them online) after being serendipitously exposed to them. Respondents also filter channels and sources based on *privacy concerns*, choosing not to click on news-related links in social media spaces to avoid exposing their interests and views to broad audiences.

Utilizing technology-enabled *source and content personalization* is another strategy employed by news consumers to cope with information overload while screening news channels, sources and content. Deliberate news seekers in our sample want to be "in the know" of the events developing in the world, evaluate different opinions, and make informed decisions. These motivations shape their behaviors of actively seeking out specific sources and personalities, from which they receive regular news updates (personalized "push" strategy). Almost universally, this attitude inspires subscribing to several newsfeeds from national and international organizations via mobile apps, following prominent politicians and experts via social media, sharing and participating in discussions regarding political events and news issues in blogs. Their news consumption is more goal-directed and less serendipitous.

Selecting a more active *"pull" approach* to news consumption characterizes those who prefer to control their exposure to news information and not to be indoctrinated by politically biased mainstream news. They may not necessarily be interested in being instantly aware of breaking news and developments. Usually, they utilize online search for the keywords of interest and consult several sources to form unbiased opinion of the situation. This strategy for news stimuli screening often leads to more attention being paid to the materials selected, and may facilitate informed decision-making and more systematic knowledge formation.

Personalized consumption of "push" news information also relies on social media sites and their mobile apps for major news information, taking advantage of the *social curation* and bottom-up news co-creation phenomena. Those who assertively advocate the role of social media as the major news channel cite Twitter's paramount role in delivering breaking news, and the fast and targeted way of news delivery via social media. Other advantages mentioned include possibilities of customizing and personalizing newsfeeds, along with the relevance of the posted news, which are "filtered" by friends with similar interests.

Relative lack of strategies among the obtained responses dealing with information complexity-handling (Grise, 2000) can be attributed to the specifics of news information that is delivered in short, comprehensible chunks and becomes obsolete before it can be organized for in-depth systematic processing. Still, certain organizing strategies are employed by consumers and include determining the order of priority of topics (and sources) in personalized apps and RSS feeds, as well as on free email portals (such as Yahoo or MSN) and *categorizing and sorting* news (and sources) into different folders and bookmarks. Finally, virtually every respondent utilizes accelerated information processing techniques by scanning headlines (or flipping channels) and selecting and prioritizing ("pulling") the topics and sources to attend to, based on interest, relevance, and convenience (Pennington & Tuttle, 2007).

Processing and Interpreting News Information

For effective incorporation of the obtained news information into their cognitive frameworks, news consumers compare the new information to their pre-existing mental schemas, shared meanings and social norms before adopting and assimilating it as part of their knowledge reserve. An important issue identified in this process is *evaluating news trustworthiness and reliability*. Virtually every respondent, regardless of political views, interests, and motivations towards news consumption, or personal characteristics, considers reliability (and trustworthiness) of the news an important issue. To ensure the credibility of the news information received, news seekers carefully filter their sources based on reputation (brand), and intentionally include international independent news providers (such as BBC and Aljazeera) in the pool. Due to the freedom of information on the Internet, and especially the potential of anonymous content creation in social media, reliability and trust were mentioned as particularly critical for these channels. Many respondents avoid clicking on links within their Facebook wall, for example, due to low trust in social media sources, and instead prefer to type key phrases into search engine fields in a new browser tab. *Resisting political bias, seeking independence from institutional media*, and *acknowledging the subjective nature of socially curated and co-created news* represent additional strategies for reducing information overload and making sense of information during its processing and interpreting. One manifestation of these strategies is the verification process via online searches (e.g., on Google) for the news items that attracted the news consumer's attention. Acquiring different perspectives on news events not only facilitates verification of the sources and content, but also exposes individuals to multiple points of view, contributing to the enrichment of pre-existing mental associations. Thus, although the topics one is exposed to may indeed be limited due to purposeful (or organic, for social networks) filtering during the screening stage, attempts to ensure reliability and truthfulness of information can provide certain exposure to a diversity of opinions by its active verification in other channels during the processing and interpreting stage.

An important element of the news interpretation aspect of sense-making is news and opinion sharing and discussing, as well as grounding one's resultant knowledge in socially negotiated structure of meaning. The strategies of *securing social support* and *seeking social legitimacy* of one's views assist with information overload by helping to categorize the amorphous stream of news based on curated content offered by social media participants and shared and co-produced opinions and comments on the issues. Another information overload coping strategy, *seeking timely information*, helps to focus on breaking news and developments and involves using mobile apps, including feeds from social media.

Role of Social Media

Our analysis did not reveal any differences in news consumption behaviors based on the available demographic or socio-economic characteristics of the respondents. While the majority of respondents did not identify social media as their main news source, widely varied opinions about its role in news consumption were expressed by almost all study participants. A broad base of diverse respondents commented on the role of social media in news consumption, ranging from negligible to very important, and underscoring its potential effect both on increase and reduction of information overload. Specifically, respondents noted that social media perpetrate information overload in the following ways:

- Increasing the sheer amount of the news information: "As of late, there has been a lot of political news being shared on Facebook. The main issue that I have with that is the range of information given. Everything from far left to far right, a lot of misinformation and a lot of conspiracies." (Female, 41, newspaper advertising)

- Making it impossible to avoid exposure to news: "Even if I try to avoid getting news, people post about them anyway, making it almost impossible to avoid" (Female, 28, financial advisor)
- Causing concerns about news reliability: "… there can be problems with Facebook trends, as rumors can pile up just as fast as breaking news. A few weeks ago, a couple of my friends posted a status about the presumed death of Bill Nye (the science guy). Astonished, I searched Google for the news article, only to find that Twitter had started this false rumor" (Male, 24, sales rep)
- Causing concerns about news objectivity: "I do not see how Facebook is being considered a news source. It seems like a hive for gossip" (Female, 65, nurse)
- Offering irrelevant content: "Social media does have great sources of information, but often is random and irrelevant to what I want to read about" (Male, 21, undergraduate student)

At the same time, social media could mitigate information overload and assist in sense-making in the following ways:

- Present an initially reduced volume of information: "Twitter allows me to read a short excerpt of what the news stories are to get a general idea and if I am more interested, they give links to click into for more information" (Female, 21, student)
- Filtering information based on its relevance: "Looking at Facebook helps by showing me what others feel is relevant. I hear a lot more from Facebook than any other media. There are stories that my friends post that I probably wouldn't have read on my own … It is an effortless way for me to find out what is going on and it is almost always information that I actually want to hear about because my friends have similar tastes to mine" (Female, 23, service professional)
- Customizing and narrowing down source and content of information: "I think that is ultimately the appeal of social media for news: it will 'ping' you when news happens as opposed to you going out to look for it. In today's society the convenience of getting a 'ping' when big news happens is something that could be very attractive given our busy pace of life." (Male, 28, sales professional)
- Providing socially curated information: "In all honesty, the place I hear about most of my news is on Facebook … For example, the way I first found out about the Batman shooting was through Facebook the morning after it happened … Whenever I see something newsworthy written on Facebook, I am always curious if it is in fact true, so I usually go to CNN.com or another news webpage to double-check the story." (Male, 22, student, part-time employed)

- Strengthening source reliability: "There are certainly many flaws in technology and people have to be very cautious with reading false information. However, if you are following a 'verified' account on Twitter, it is expected to be a real account which tweets quality information." (Female, 22, student)
- Ensuring news timeliness: "I feel that social media sources help with having access to the news quicker and with having more information in which to make a decision about the news easier." (Male, 33, small business owner)
- Offering social legitimacy and support: "On the news feed Facebook will post a catchy headline that at times does catch my attention … A neat thing is that on that article page there will be images of your "friends" and if you scroll over their picture it will show you the articles that they read. Therefore I will continuously click on interesting articles that I would like to read." (Female, 28, city government employee)
- Expanding cognitive diversity: "I feel Facebook is important compared to other forms of media because so many people use it. It gives an insight to many different cohorts and allows people to see what their friends think". (Female, 39, professor)

While enthusiasts of using social media for news consumption emphasize their role in reducing information overload by providing social filtering, timeliness, and better situating the news within the preexisting cognitive schemas, opponents underscore overwhelming information breadth, lack of depth and focus, privacy concerns, and subjectivity. Although news seekers utilize Twitter updates as one of their news sources, they limit the updates they get to certain news providers (mainly prominent reporters and organizations), and get them regularly: they do not rely on incidental and serendipitous "stumbling upon" information as it is usually presented in other social media. All respondents believe that Facebook functionality predisposes it to be more of a discussion and opinion forum than an objective news reporting vehicle. Therefore, its use combines news consumption with social networking to arrive at a "social news consumption" experience where people can see what their friends read, talk about, and are interested in (i.e. their newsfeed is mediated by friends' actions in relation to the news). Respondents also emphasize social media's broader scope and opportunity to access "fringe", and not only mainstream, news and details. In terms of reconciling the incoming news information with the pre-existing civic knowledge framework and the socially accepted views, social media play an important role in legitimizing new content via links posted by friends with similar views and tastes. Thus, in addition to granting legitimacy through social approval, filtering and curation, other advantages of using social media for news include convenience and timeliness, as well as diversity and breadth of the news information available.

In terms of the role of social filtering in creating an information bubble, the opposite views expressed by our respondents suggest that the type of social ties dominant in one's social network may provide different experiences. Those with smaller networks, dominated by strong family and close friends' ties may experience the news "information bubble", where they are exposed to very similar news from the same narrow list of sources. Alternatively, those social media participants who have broad networks of friends characterized by weak ties and representing diverse and divergent views and beliefs, benefit from being exposed to new and unexpected news insights and sources.

Conclusion, Contributions to Theory and Future Research

Surrounded by 24/7 news feeds, individuals appear remarkably uninformed about current events (Denning, 2006), primarily because they cannot make sense of the news-related information they receive. Research (e.g. Klausegger et al., 2007) has shown that the natural limit to mental processing in the short-term memory is between five and nine "chunks" of information before information overload sets in. When the total amount of information exceeds this saturation point, the individual engages in "muddling" through irrelevant, marginally useful, or contradictory information and can no longer engage in sense-making processes to derive meaning (Denning & Raj, 2011). When information is present, people strive to organize it and set it in order (Thorson et al., 1985; Zillmann & Bryant, 1985). Our study uses the information overload and sense-making lenses to understand how individuals go beyond just imbibing news *information*, to understanding the contextual implications and informing their *knowledge* or view of the world. We can reach several conclusions from this study.

First, we show that while information is abundant, converting it to knowledge requires the consumer to be able to engage in sense-making by dealing with information overload. This leads the user to make choices with respect to how much information they are willing to process and what strategies they use to make sense of it. The rise of the Internet, particularly social media, has fostered complex patterns of information creation, distribution, and consumption. Our study integrated the conceptual frameworks of information overload and sense-making to reveal *how* individuals consume news, driven by the need to address information overload and engage in sense-making.

Second, we clarify the role of social media in online news consumption. Experts and researchers disagree on the effectiveness of social media in informing the individual about civic society, some pointing to its constructive role in enhancing civic knowledge and enabling citizen journalism (Green et al., 2011; Weisberg, 2011), and others to its constraining role in socially filtering news information (Pariser, 2011). We demonstrate that social media plays a *nuanced* role in online news consumption and identifies both its benefits and its "dark side". In particular, we clarify two aspects of the role of social media. One, we highlight the *positive* aspect of social media-enabled news consumption by ensuring socially negotiated sense-making. We note that when the individual draws upon his or her social network for online news consumption, he or she is able to expand a structure of meaning through the socialization process that provides a framework for sense-making about civic life. Two, we reveal a *non-beneficial* aspect of social media-enabled news consumption, namely, the potential for a "filter bubble". We note that when individuals rely on their strong-tie social networks for news, the information tends to be filtered through the attitudinal preferences of this network and may not provide an encompassing, balanced or diverse knowledge about civic society. Therefore, while social curation can be an effective strategy for handling information overload and providing socially supported cognitive frameworks, it may not necessarily facilitate the cognitive diversity aspect of sense-making. Our results suggest that the strength of ties within informational social networks may moderate the role of social curation in civic (and potentially other domains of) knowledge formation, implying a potentially fruitful research direction of the role of tie strengths in socially mediated information processing and knowledge formation.

Implications for Social Media, News Producers and Consumers

Our findings suggest that contemporary news consumers utilize new media tools to cope with information overload in their process of making sense of the ever-increasing content from the growing number of sources in order to form their civic and political knowledge and opinions. These coping strategies may negatively affect news providers by filtering them out of the consideration set of information sources. In order to avoid being marginalized by news consumers seeking to reduce their information load, news providers should consider offering both complexity-reducing and load-adjustment tools (Grise & Gallup, 1999) on their websites. For instance, they should enhance capabilities for categorizing, sorting, and searching information, as well as offer content personalization by collecting customer preferences and creating interest-based stimuli that would draw their customers' attention. Further, news consumers employ source personalization strategy to ensure their exposure to trusted and verified news providers. This implies that developing brand value by offering high quality journalistic offerings will provide a competitive advantage to news organizations and may potentially strengthen subscription-based revenue, as consumers would be willing to pay for premium-quality trusted content in the ever-growing stream of unverified news information.

By offering contextual and in-depth coverage of the news items, news organizations will be able to facilitate the formation of stronger associations between new news events and pre-existing cognitive frameworks, thus aiding in sensemaking. News organizations should also take advantage of features such as social tagging and linking among information sources such as blogs to provide greater opportunity for social curation. By introducing discussion forums on their websites, news providers will create a basis for construction of social meaning, thus facilitating news information legitimacy and civic knowledge formation. It is also recommended that news organizations actively participate in social media by establishing their own accounts to offer their readers more diverse exposure to various sources offering relevant information, and to minimize possible "filter bubbles". While a number of news websites provide opportunities for social networking through links with Twitter and Facebook, relatively few websites encourage or alert the user to increase the topical conceptual diversity of their news consumption. Most of the linking strategies adopted by content websites provide links to *similar* topics. Our findings suggest that new consumers should be encouraged to explore cognitively *diverse* topics for better sense making of news and hence a more informed view of civic society.

The majority of news consumers in our study represented passive attitudes towards news consumption, as evidenced by a stronger presence of load adjustment (rather than complexity handling) information overload handling strategies such as news avoidance. Their assumption of news ubiquity and reluctance to expend resources to obtain news may present a potential problem for news providers who are relying on subscriptions and "freemium" models. Given that advertising revenues are being diverted towards more targeted media channels, such broadcast-reliant news organizations as network TV, local radio stations, and newspapers (including their online versions) may have to limit their content to topics of more narrow focus that may interest incidental news consumers. However, pursuing this niche strategy may further contribute to the "filter bubble" phenomenon and negatively affect civic participation in communities, necessitating the creation of publicly funded news organization.

References

Ackoff, R. L. (1967). Management misinformation systems. *Management Science*, 14(4), B–147.

Aldoory, L. & Van Dyke, M. A. (2006). The roles of perceived 'shared' involvement and information overload in understanding how audiences make meaning of news about bioterrorism. *Journalism & Mass Communication Quarterly*, 83(2), 346–361.

Beaudoin, C. E. (2008). Explaining the relationship between internet use and interpersonal trust: Taking into account motivation and information overload, *Journal of Computer-Mediated Communication*, 13, 550–568.

Berger, P. L. & Luckmann, T. (1966). *The Social Construction of Reality: A Treatise in the Sociology of Knowledge*. New York: Doubleday.

Bogner, W. C. & Barr, P. S. (2000). Making sense in hypercompetitive environments: A cognitive explanation for the persistence of high velocity competition. *Organization Science*, 11(2), 212–226.

Bruns, A. (2008). The active audience: Transforming journalism from gatekeeping to gatewatching. In C. Paterson & D. Domingo (Eds.), *Making Online News: The Ethnography of New Media Production* (pp. 171–184). New York, NY: Peter Lang.

Bruns, A. & Highfield, T. (2012). Blogs, Twitter, and breaking news: The produsage of citizen journalism. *Produsing Theory in a Digital World: The Intersection of Audiences and Production in Contemporary Theory*, 80, 15–32.

Carver, L. & Turoff, M. (2007). Human-Computer interaction: The human and computer as a team in emergency management information systems. *Communications of the ACM*, 50(3), 33–38.

Chung, C. J., Nam, Y. & Stefanone, M. A. (2012). Exploring online news credibility: The relative influence of traditional and technological factors. *Journal of Computer-Mediated Communication*, 17(2), 171–186.

Daft, R.R. & Weick, K., (1984). Toward a model of organizations as interpretive systems, *Academy of Management Review*, 9, 284–295.

Davenport, T. H. & Beck, J. C. (2000). Getting the attention you need, *Harvard Business Review*, September-October, 119–126.

Denning, P. J. & Raj, R. (2011). Managing time, Part 2. *Communications of the ACM*, 54(9): 31.

Denning, S. (2006) Effective storytelling: strategic business narrative techniques. *Strategy & Leadership*, 34(1), 42–48.

Eppler, M. J. & Mengis, J. (2004). The concept of information overload: A review of literature from organization science, accounting, marketing, MIS, and related disciplines. *The Information Society*, 20(5), 325–344.

Eveland, Jr, W. P. & Dunwoody, S. (2002). An investigation of elaboration and selective scanning as mediators of learning from the Web versus print. *Journal of Broadcasting & Electronic Media*, 46(1), 34–53.

Fiol, C. M. (1994). Consensus, diversity, and learning in organizations. *Organization Science*, 5(3), 403–420.

Fiske, S. & Taylor, S. (1991). *Social Cognition*. New York: McGraw-Hill.

Galambos, J. A., Black, J. B. & Abelson, R. P. (1986). *Knowledge Structures*. Hillsdale, NJ: L. Erlbaum Associates Inc..

Galbraith, J. R. (1974). Organization design: An information processing view. *Interfaces*, 4(3), 28–36.

Gans, H.J. (1980). *Deciding What's News: A Study of CBS Evening News, NBC Nightly News, Newsweek, and Time*. New York, NY: Vintage.

Greene, D., Reid, F., Sheridan, G. & Cunningham, P. (2011). Supporting the curation of twitter user lists. *arXiv preprint arXiv:1110.1349*. Available at http://arxiv.org/abs/1110.1349

Grisé, M. L. & Gallupe, R. B. (1999). Information overload: Addressing the productivity paradox in face-to-face electronic meetings. *Journal of Management Information Systems*, 16(3), 157–185.

Harrison, T. P. & Rosenthal, R.E. (1988). An implicit/explicit approach to multiobjective optimization with an application to forecast management planning. *Decision Sciences*, 19(1), 190–210.

Hiltz, S. R. M. & Turoff, M (1978). *The Network Nation: Human Communication Via Computer*. London: Addison Wesley.

Ho, J. & Tang, K. (2001). Towards an optimal resolution to information overload: An infomediary approach. In S. Ellis, T. Rodden, and I. Zigurs (eds.), Proceedings of the 2001 International CM SIGGROUP Conference on Supporting Group Work. Boulder, CO: ACM Press, pp. 91–96

Holton, A. E. & Chyi, H. I. (2012). News and the overloaded consumer: Factors influencing information overload among news consumers. *Cyberpsychology, Behavior, and Social Networking*, 15(11), 619–624.

Jones, Q., Ravid, G. & Rafaeli, S. (2004). Information overload and the message dynamics of online interaction spaces: A theoretical model and empirical exploration. *Information Systems Research*, 15(2), 194–210.

Kassarjian, H. H. (1977). Content analysis in consumer research. *Journal of Consumer Research*, 4(1), 8–18.

Kelly, G. G. & Bostrom, R. P. (1995, April). Facilitating the socio-emotional dimension in group support systems environments. In Proceedings of the 1995 ACM SIGCPR conference on Supporting teams, groups, and learning inside and outside the IS function reinventing IS, 10–23.

Kiesler, S. & Sproull, L. (1982). Managerial response to changing environments: Perspectives on problem sensing from social cognition. *Administrative Science Quarterly*, 27(4), 548–570.

Klausegger, C., Sinkovics, R. R. & Zou, H. J. (2007). Information overload: A cross national investigation of influence factors and effects, *Marketing Intelligence and Planning*, 25(7), 691–718

Kolbe, R. H. & Burnett, M. S. (1991). Content-Analysis research: An examination of applications with directives for improving research reliability and objectivity. *Journal of Consumer Research*, 18, 243–250.

LeCompte, M. D. & Schensul, J. J. (1999). *Analyzing and Interpreting Ethnographic Data*. AltaMira Press.

Lee, H. H., & Jin Ma, Y. (2012). Consumer perceptions of online consumer product and service reviews: Focusing on information processing confidence and susceptibility to peer influence. *Journal of Research in Interactive Marketing*, 6(2), 110–132.

Lee, I. H. (1998). Market crashes and informational avalanches. *The Review of Economic Studies*, 65(4), 741–759.

Lee, B. K., & Lee, W. N. (2004). The effect of information overload on consumer choice quality in an on-line environment. *Psychology & Marketing*, 21(3), 159–183.

Lehtonen, J. (1988). The information society and the new competence. *American Behavioral Scientist*, 32(2), 104–111.

Liang, T. P., Lai, H. J. & Ku, Y. C. (2007). Personalized content recommendation and user satisfaction: Theoretical synthesis and empirical findings. *Journal of Management Information Systems*, 23(3), 45–70.

Malhotra, N. K., Jain, A. K. & Lagakos, S. W. (1982). The information overload controversy: An alternative viewpoint. *The Journal of Marketing*, 46(2), 27–37.

Marcusohn, L. M. (1995). The information explosion in organizations. *Swedish Library Research* 3, 25–41.

McCracken, G. (1988). *The Long Interview* (Vol. 13). Thousand Oaks: Sage Publications, Inc.

Miles, M. B. & Huberman, A. M. (1994). *Qualitative Data Analysis: An Expanded Sourcebook*. Thousand Oaks: Sage Publications, Inc.

Miller, G. (1956). The magical number seven, plus or minus two: Some limits on our capacity for processing information. *The Psychological Review*, 63, 81–97.

MSI (2014), MSI call for research proposals on social interactions and social media marketing. Marketing Science Institute. Retrieved July 16, 2017, from http://www.msi.org/uploads/files/2013-11-07_MSI_Social_Media_Competition.pdf

Nielsen (2012), *State of the Media: The Social Media Report*. Retrieved from http://www.nielsen.com/us/en/insights/reports-downloads/2012/state-of-the-media-the-social-media-report-2012.html

Nonaka, I. (1994). A dynamic theory of organizational knowledge creation. *Organization Science*, 5(1), 14–37.

O'Brien, H. L. (2011). Exploring user engagement in online news interactions. *Proceedings of the American Society for Information Science and Technology*, 48(1), 1–10.

Oppenheim, C. (1997). Managers' use and handling of information. *International Journal of Information Management*, 17(4), 239–248.

O'Reilly, C. A. (1980). Individuals and information overload in organizations: is more necessarily better? *Academy of Management Journal*, 23(4), 684–696.

Pariser, E. (2011). *The Filter Bubble: What the Internet is Hiding from You*. Penguin Press HC.

Pennington, R. & Tuttle, B. (2007). The effects of information overload on software project risk assessment*. *Decision Sciences*, 38(3), 489–526.

Perrault W. & Leigh, LE. (1989). Reliability of nominal data based on qualitative judgments. *Journal of Marketing Research*, 26(2), 135–148.

Pew Research Center (2010). *Millennials: A Portrait of Generation Next* – Feb 24. Retrieved from http://www.pewsocialtrends.org/files/2010/10/millennials-confident-connected-open-tochange.pdf

Pew Research Center (2012). *The State of the News Media 2012: An Annual Report on American Journalism*. Retrieved from http://stateofthemedia.org/files/2012/08/2012_sotm_annual_report.pdf

Pollar, O. (2003). *Surviving Information Overload: How to Find, Filter, and Focus on What's Important*. USA: Crisp Learning.

Rogers, E. M., R. Agarwala-Rogers. (1975). Organizational communication. G. L. Hanneman, W. J. McEwen, eds. Communication Behaviour. Addison Wesley, Reading, MA, 218–236.

Schick, A. G., Gordon, L. A. & Haka, S. (1990). Information overload: A temporal approach. *Accounting, Organizations and Society*, 15(3), 199–220.

Schultz, U. & Vandenbosch, B. (1998). Information overload in a groupware environment: Now you see it, now you don't. *Journal of Organizational Computing and Electronic Commerce*, 8(2), 127–148.

Schütz, A. (1945). On multiple realities. *Philosophy and Phenomenological Research*, 5, 533–576.

Schütz, A. (1970). *Alfred Schutz on Phenomenology and Social Relations*. Chicago, IL: University of Chicago Press.

Shenk, D. (1997). *Data Smog: Surviving the Information Glut*. San Francisco, CA: HarperEdge.

Stanley, A. J. & Clipsham, P. S. (1997). Information overload – myth or reality? *IEE Colloquium on IT Strategies for Information Overload*, London.

Strauss, A. & Corbin, J. (1998). *Basics of Qualitative Research*. Thousand Oaks, CA: Sage Publications.

Tewksbury, D., Weaver, A. J. & Maddex, B. D. (2001). Accidentally informed: Incidental news exposure on the World Wide Web. *Journalism & Mass Communication Quarterly*, 78(3), 533–554.

Thorson, E., Reeves, B. & Schleuder, J. (1985). Message complexity and attention to television. *Communication Research*, 12(4), 427–454.

van de Ven, W. P. & van Vliet, R. J. (1995). Consumer information surplus and adverse selection in competitive health insurance markets: An empirical study. *Journal of Health Economics*, 14(2), 149–169.

Waller, M. J., Huber, G. P. & Glick, W. H. (1995). Functional background as a determinant of executives' selective perception. *Academy of Management Journal*, 38(4), 943–974.

Walsham, G. (2006). Doing interpretive research, *European Journal of Information Systems*, 15, 320–330.

Weick, K. E. (1995). *Sensemaking in Organizations*. Thousand Oaks, CA: Sage Publications.

Weick, K. E., Sutcliffe, K. M. & Obstfeld, D. (2005). Organizing and the process of sense-making. *Organization Science*, 16(4), 409–421.

Weisberg, J. (2011, June 10). Bubble trouble: Is web personalization turning us into solipsistic twits? Retrieved from http://www.slate.com/articles/news_and_politics/the_big_idea/2011/06/bubble_trouble.html

Wilhelm, K. (2000). Ground zero for a data explosion. *Far Eastern Economic Review*, 163, 40–42.

Zillmann, D. & Bryant, J. (1985). *Selective Exposure to Communication*. Hillsdale, NJ: Lawrence Erlbaum.

PART V

New Opportunities and Challenges for Social Media

The concluding section of this book has some dark side elements, but also some positive or beneficial elements as well. First, consider the case of wearables, or things like the Apple Watch or the Fitbit devices that consumers wear for a number of rational reasons. These are great and beneficial, and likely a reason that sales are surging and that the popularity of wearables is becoming mainstream. For instance, we can see how many steps we made today, what our calendar is tomorrow, and get alerts when it is time to go to work. But, what do we think about the fact that some wearables connect to social media? We can check Facebook on our Apple Watch—as if we are not connected enough. Some consumers are literally addicted to social media and having a social media capacity on the wrist can be not so good for certain vulnerable or social media addicted consumers. It could be a generational thing, where some members of the up and coming generation who are digital natives feel compelled to check their social media regularly like working professionals check their e-mail regularly. What about the privacy issues with wearables? That is precisely the question tapped into in Chapter 10, "The New Wearable Mobile Economy and Privacy".

Subsequently, in Chapter 11, the notion of how higher education is using social media is explored. There again, are many beneficial and creative and effective, rational synergies between social media and colleges or universities. vast literature review about how social media is used in colleges and universities—by students and professors alike. To this end, we ask: What are the challenges to using social media tools in a higher education classroom setting as perceived by students? We first outline research examining social media in higher education through a comprehensive literature review and provide summary tables as reference guides. Next, we detail our exploratory research examining students' perceptions of using social media in the classroom. Lastly, we illustrate our findings and pose implications for educators on how to overcome some dark side issues or unintended consequences for mixing social media with higher education.

The section, and the book concludes with a look at mommy blogs; again— not purely a dark side aspect to online consumer behavior. Mommy blogs can be a bright side topic as we will reveal in Chapter 12 that mommy blogs bring a community hope and, at times, joy. It is crucial to understand the psychology of mothers in the workforce—as reflected by their comments in online communities. Often, these online communities are informally termed "mommy blogs". While not all who use mommy blogs are in the workforce, many are (including the four authors here)—and these women face particular challenges and at times seek refuge or advice online. The objective of this netnography is to gather insights regarding perspectives of working mothers as seen by their posts to online communities or "mommy blogs". The sense of community that mommy blogs bring people is a bright side topic to overcome some commonly espoused stressors. The contribution is to help understand how women use mommy blogs as an online community that can offer a place to vent and support. Theoretical contributions are in the areas of role conflict and the "second shift" (i.e., working 9am–5pm at work and then 5pm–9am at home). Reasons for the need for this research include vast social and economic justifications. Women represent a market larger than India and China combined, and yet many companies are not understanding nor serving women (Silverstein & Sayre, 2009), so this is a step in doing so.

10

CONSUMER PRIVACY AND THE NEW MOBILE COMMERCE

Alexandra M. Doorey, Gary B. Wilcox, and Matthew S. Eastin

Since the birth of the information age, the sharing, collection, and use of personal data has grown exponentially, with an ever-increasing amount of personal data collected from a number of new and evolving sources. For marketers, the value of this data lies in the ability to better understand consumers' wants, needs and behavioral histories, enabling a more focused understanding of audiences, segmentation opportunities, and even individual consumers.

Implementations of these insights acquired from data-driven marketing practices are utilized to engage consumers and form stronger relationships that serve the needs of both marketers as well as consumers. Mobile and wearable devices are further enhancing the consumers' "digital presence" by allowing them to interact with and leverage emerging technologies in new and novel ways. As consumers become increasingly connected, these technologies are becoming more capable of delivering targeted, relevant communications through geo-location, behavior monitoring and emerging health information. With improving sophistication, sensors found in wearable and mobile technologies even have the ability to provide a better understanding of people's feelings and emotions.

As the amount of data multiplies, digital marketers have the capability to examine their audiences in more detail, providing them with hyper-targeted, personalized messages and services. Business models are quickly adapting to encompass these new efficiencies, with behavioral marketing and predictive analytics reaching new levels of sophistication. This strategic shift toward personalization allows marketers to customize content and delivery for specific consumers and ultimately achieve greater efficiencies (Adomavicius & Tuzhilin, 2005, p. 83). In exchange for personalized services and information access, consumers are often willing to disclose their private information (Tezinde et al., 2002; Chellappa & Sin, 2005; Awad & Krishnan, 2006; Xu et al., 2011).

Carefully constructed profiles based on individual needs and preferences allow marketers to communicate with consumers with highly relevant messages often at the precise point of purchase. The number of criteria used to build and describe individual profiles has expanded with the rich contextualization and behavioral information mobile technologies are capable of tracking, enhancing convenience, and overall experience for consumers.

Mobile technology, and the big data revolution it is helping to drive, has brought about a need for a new way of thinking as well as new methods of managing data. The elements of the current privacy framework are in need of re-examination to reflect existing technological and organizational realities. This includes pervasive data collection and the consumers who are not equipped to meaningfully review and negotiate the terms of updated privacy policies. The manner in which businesses as well as government regulators in the United States treat the ownership, collection, and use of consumers' data is of increasing interest to society and points to a re-examination of policy and self-regulatory guidelines.

Consumer groups and privacy advocates have demanded mechanisms that can adequately manage the access, movement and dissemination of personal information, particularly data streams accessed from personal devices such as smartphones, tablets and wearables. However, the industry has largely failed to regulate itself by consistently implementing privacy controls in broad strokes, overlooking the intricacies of consumer needs and information sensitivities. Some of this has been naiveté, while some has been the deliberate and explicit stretching of the boundaries of individual expectations and the implicit social contracts with consumers (Dutta & Bilbao-Osorio, 2014). Marketers and organizations that recognize privacy issues, anticipate market demands, and work to understand and alleviate consumer privacy concerns by setting new standards for data capture, use and individual protections will not only protect their reputations and the value of their business models, but gain a competitive advantage by distinguishing them as advocates and innovators of new community standards that honor the aspects of personal privacy rights.

Organization of the Chapter

This chapter examines the changing nature of consumer data and information acquisition as it intersects with consumer privacy and security. The following sections provide an up-to-date perspective of emerging technology and privacy issues within social media, wearable and mobile devices. First, a discussion of the use of big data to facilitate personalized marketing will be followed by a mobile usage and marketing technologies update. The next section will discuss the integrated future of mobile technology, wearables and personalized health data. Following that discussion, privacy and security issues raised by technology use will be explored. The chapter concludes with recommendations for future regulation relating to consumer privacy and security.

Digital Behavioral Marketing

The technique driving personalized marketing and individualized ad experiences has been identified as "behavioral marketing" and used to uniquely engage each consumer through the recording and analysis of their characteristics, behaviors and preferences to direct targeted offers based on use patterns. The collection and aggregation of personal information to target consumers with messages has existed throughout the digital age, but marketers previously relied primarily on third-party data to inform marketing strategies. Companies only recently began to capture and understand the value of dynamic, first-party data that can be observed or inferred passively in real time (O'Hara, 2015).

Assembling individualized consumer profiles built from data-driven insights allows marketers to target messages to consumers on a one-to-one level, reaching individuals efficiently and effectively while improving customer satisfaction and driving customer loyalty. Today, advancing digital technologies are able to collect, aggregate, and synthesize real-time behavior and location information with past behaviors (both online and offline) and integrate additional knowledge about cohorts of consumers with similar profiles. The combination of new user-generated data streams derived from sophisticated information tracking and processing capabilities enables marketers to explore and interpret data to find their benefit (Dutta & Bilbao-Osorio, 2014).

The technologies necessary to leverage actionable insights from data have previously lacked the refinement and reliability to deliver truly relevant messages to consumers. Analytics engines are becoming increasingly capable of storing and evaluating a consumer's data path from location, relationships, schedule, alerts, purchase behaviors, and interests in real time, and combining this information with past behaviors and social media profiles to assemble highly personal insights about consumers and offer targeted individualized messages (Harland, 2015; Morgan et al., 2015).

Marketing interest in behavioral targeting has surged in recent years with intuitive technologies and machine learning capabilities creating intricate, exhaustive individual marketing dossiers through the practice of onboarding—the fusion of data collected from diverse sources with specific identifying information (Revella, 2015). In a 2014 report, the FTC revealed that Acxiom, one of the largest data brokers, had more than 3,000 data points on every adult in the U.S. (FTC, 2014b).

As affirmed by MIT Technology Review Editor in Chief Jason Pontin,

> The next frontier of big data will be the individual. From healthcare, to different ways to make data more accessible, data is becoming highly personalized and new services are rolling into the market. But at the same time, new questions are raised as we consider what implications might be for security as well as privacy (Sweeney, 2013).

The true power for marketers in the "big data" revolution, therefore, is not data about depicting the environment, but individual models of consumers' personal "little data" universes. The implications for advertisers and businesses are immense, as software continues to hasten the evolution and inflation of the "application economy". The market's momentum to innovate, appeal to consumer interests and upend current business models will require that the industry views privacy and security as a competitive differentiator and apparatus of trust for individuals and organizations (Espinel, 2015, p. 33).

Mobile Technology and Marketing

The ubiquity and proliferation of mobile devices and technologies allows marketers to observe, understand, and reach consumers more readily and rapidly than ever before with hyper-targeted, personalized messages. Mobile marketing and mobile commerce have evolved almost as quickly as the technologies that make them possible. The explosive growth in smartphone and smart device ownership over the past several years has fueled a shifting focus to mobile in the digital marketspace. Today, 68% of consumers in the United States own a smartphone, almost double the 35% who owned these devices in 2011 (Anderson, 2015). Further, a recent study revealed that smartphones are owned by 78% of online adults, nearing the saturation point, with nearly universal penetration expected to occur by 2020 (Hulkower, 2015a).

In addition to being the most commonly owned device among American adults, time spent with mobile devices has grown at a surprising rate. Consumers continue to spend more time and attention with mobile technology, transitioning online activities in almost every category from both desktops and laptops to smartphones. Time spent with mobile devices approached triple-digit growth in 2011 and 2012, occurring almost simultaneously with the proliferation of smartphone availability. Mobile device use and interaction continues to rise, outpacing and overtaking virtually every other medium in importance. In fact, mobile is the only device category projected to increase in time spent and engagement over the next two years, while every other media channel is expected to decline, including TV, radio, desktop, and print (eMarketer, 2015).

Much of this growth is attributable to the rise and success of smartphone apps. Categories with high app usage have experienced a pronounced behavioral shift to mobile, and those with stronger app engagement have been the most effective in piloting the transition to mobile (Harland, October 2015; Anderson, 2015). According to the 2015 U.S. Mobile App Report released by comScore, total digital media usage has increased 49%, with mobile application usage having increased 90% and contributing to 77% of the total growth in digital media consumption (Lella et al., 2015).

Smartphone apps already account for the vast majority of time users engage with mobile devices, and mobile apps are quickly approaching one-half of consumers' total digital media time. Strong growth has been observed across every market segment, with the average mobile user spending 26 hours per month on social apps (Lella et al., 2015). Personal mobile technologies and the applications, connectivity, and ubiquity they provide have become an everyday essential for almost every consumer.

Mobile advertising has been defined as "any paid message communication by mobile media with the intent to influence the attitude, intentions, and behavior of those addressed by the commercial messages" (Mir, 2011, p. 3). Industry data reveals that expenditures on mobile advertising by marketers have increased rapidly in recent years and are predicted to continue to increase. Mobile advertising revenues continue to gain a greater share of total marketing expenditure, beginning to close the gap between mobile media usage and spending. According to the 2015 Internet Advertising Bureau (IAB) Internet Advertising Revenue Report, mobile advertising represented 30% of the overall ad revenues reported in the first six months of 2015. This figure represents a sizeable increase from the 23% of total revenues reported in the first half of 2014, and doubling from the 15% in the same time period of 2013.

Similar to consumer usage patterns with mobile devices and smartphone applications, mobile apps contribute to two thirds of overall digital media engagement (Lella et al., 2015), eroding the share of ad revenues of other formats (Internet Advertising Bureau, 2015). In the second quarter of 2015 alone, mobile advertising revenues reached $4.4 billion, contributing to 31% of total dollars spent and increasing 56% from the $2.8 billion reported in the second quarter of 2014, further demonstrating the trend towards mobile.

In addition to the amount of time consumers spend with mobile devices, offering greater opportunities for brands to reach individuals with marketing messages, mobile ads have proven to be more successful than advertising on other formats. The comScore 2015 Mobile App Report measured the effectiveness of mobile advertisements against desktop across four key brand metrics—aided awareness, favorability, likelihood to recommend, and purchase intent—and found that ads served to mobile devices caused point lifts that were two to three times higher than ads delivered on desktop.

Further, the comScore report found that mobile performed strongest in "bottom-funnel" brand metrics, including likelihood to recommend (4.3 on mobile versus 1.4 on desktop) and purchase intent (4.3 on mobile versus 1.3 on desktop), which are most valuable to brands and marketers (Lella et al., 2015). The ability to offer advertisements and special offers to consumers in real-time and based on location information allows for such messages to be received with closer proximity to point of purchase, making these messages more relevant. Furthermore, less ad clutter on mobile platforms may also contribute to mobile advertising effectiveness.

The blurring of physical and digital worlds will continue to offer marketers the opportunity to create digital experiences for consumers in years to come. With the smartphone and tablet markets each expected to grow by at least half a percentage point per month over the next two years, mobile Internet use and mobile shopping will continue to increase. Reported mobile ad sales and mobile shopping point to the dramatic growth in mobile commerce, with mobile ad sales increasing 76% in 2014 and 41% in 2015. Similarly, mobile shopping sales grew 57% in 2014 and 32% in 2015 (Hulkower, 2015a).

Mintel research projects strong growth in mobile commerce, with mobile shopping sales expected to rise from $76.8 billion in 2015 to $175 billion in 2019, and mobile advertising sales estimated to increase from $17.6 billion to $37 billion over the same time. Brands recognize the potential of this emerging marketspace, with 98% of marketers affirming they believe offline and online marketing is merging, and ranking digital commerce as the top area of investment for marketing technologies in the future. As a result, marketing budgets are growing to address opportunities in technology innovation, and senior management at agencies and organizations expect that marketing's responsibility will increase, with digital commerce and innovation in marketing being the top areas of growth (Gartner, 2015).

The Future of Mobile Commerce

Mobile technology with targeted, specific, and timely access to consumers will be a fundamental component in the integration of information into the big data universe. As this becomes an increasing reality for the United States and beyond, data collected from mobile technology will become a central focus of government agencies, business models, industry-wide innovations and privacy policy. As a result, it is imperative to address questions of information privacy and protection for individuals' personal data in these varying contexts, with specific focus on consumers' information sensitivities to types of data captured as well as their privacy preferences.

A variety of legal, technical and self-regulatory policies have emerged in response to heightened concerns about the collection and processing of personal data and the sending of unsolicited marketing communications to mobile users (Milberg et al., 1995; Cranor, 2005; Solova, 2006; FTC, 2010; Dutta & Bilbao-Osorio, 2014). However, the effectiveness of such policies in ensuring adequate protection to mobile users, while encouraging a free market economy and growth of the m-marketing industry, has not been established. Furthermore, the current state of mobile online behavior tracking and data collection has not been adequately examined in detail at either the industry or consumer level. As both federal and industry self-regulation have fallen behind the pace of mobile device proliferation, there exists the potential for exploitation of consumer information and consumer privacy.

The recent interest in wearable technology using mobile health and fitness tracking technology will bring brands previously unimaginable opportunities to establish themselves competitively and communicate with consumers. The eco-system of connected devices integrates traditional, mobile and Internet of Things (IoT) devices, creating value through increased density of interactions between people, businesses, and smart devices. This digital network enables delivery of experiences that are integrated and holistic, dissolving the distance between people and devices. To unlock this potential, brands and advertisers must inno-vate meaningful applications of users' active and passive data streams to create a more immersive user experience while respecting the privacy of consumers' personal information.

The new health ecosystem, including mobile health tracking technology, stands at a crossroads today. Health and biometric data can be used in several key applications to bring consumer benefits and enhance user experience. At the same time, with the mobile and wearable market largely unregulated, the capture and redistribution of highly personal health information may heighten consum-ers' information sensitivities and data privacy concerns. As consumers increas-ingly incorporate digital technologies into their lives, the information accrued not only offers users a variety of conveniences and benefits, but also introduces opportunities to gain access to their personal data for marketing purposes. Moreover, the quantity and breadth of personal information being collected is surprising.

According to the 2014 Global Information Technology Report, over two and a half quintillion bytes of data are created each day, and more than 90% of the world's total stored data was created in the previous two years alone (IBM, 2013). The accelerated growth of "big data" is partially attributed to the prolif-eration of information-sensing technologies (including mobile phones and quantified self-devices), radio-frequency identification (RFID) readers, surveil-lance cameras, microphones, and wireless sensor networks (IBM, 2013; Eastin et al., 2016).

Further, mobile technology and the targeted, specific, and constant access to consumers that it permits will be a central contributor to the big data universe. And, while total traffic over IP networks is projected to triple from 2012 to 2017, mobile traffic data is forecasted to grow *thirteen-fold*, representing a more signifi-cant share of all data generated and transmitted (Cisco, 2014). As a result, data collected from personal mobile devices will be a central focus of marketers, busi-nesses, and regulators as they seek out effective tactics for their communication campaigns.

McKinsey defines big data as "datasets so large that typical database software tools are unable to capture, store, manage, and analyze them" (Manyika et al., 2011, p. 1). Expanding digitization and the commoditization of data has shifted the center of gravity for marketers and businesses at an increasingly rapid rate. New devices and advancing analytic capabilities are connecting data that is taking a number of industries into new territories of business opportunity, and simulta-neously bringing recently realized weaknesses and threats to personal security and privacy. Digital business models have the potential to utilize considerable amounts of data accumulated from connected devices to understand customers, personalize services and improve user experiences in real-time. Millions of events stream from smart mobile devices every second, making it possible to obtain detailed, accurate data on individuals in real-time and facilitating instant interactions and information exchange.

Marketers now have the ability to aggregate multiple information sources to build personal profiles about consumers, which can be used to narrowly target profitable audience segments with personalized marketing communications (Vesanen, 2007). The alleged value of data-driven marketing for consumers is that they receive highly relevant, personalized messages based on their individual behaviors, interests and preferences, often at the precise point of need.

However, a recent study found that many individuals are concerned about the amount of personal data being collected (particularly within sensitive contexts), via search engines, websites, mobile devices, and data aggregators, with 68% reporting an unfavorable view of this practice because of privacy concerns (Purcell et al., 2012). Moreover, 91% of Americans feel they have lost control over their personal information online and express a consistent lack of confidence about the privacy of their data (Rainie & Duggan, 2016). This reaction is well supported by industry research showing that consumers are increasingly turning to technologies that allow them to elude tracking, encrypt communications, block online ads, and register on do-not-track lists (Lerman, 2014).

Information privacy and the protection of personal data have long been viewed as fundamental human rights (Schwartz & Solove, 2011). Human recognition (or "personally-identifiable information") currently delineates the legal threshold condition for the loss of anonymity or privacy. However, the rapidly evolving nature of digital communication suggests a need to rethink this definition for the modern age. A person's digital identity encompasses a wide range of traceable offline characteristics (e.g., age, income, education, residence, etc.) in addition to an array of online profiles, pin numbers, access codes, behaviors and mobile location records—all of which establish concrete links between social and technological concepts of identity (Wessels, 2012).

Today's digital consumer is no longer entirely anonymous since essentially every form of communication and behavior produces data that can be captured, aggregated, and analyzed (Zwick & Dholakia, 2004; Buckingham, 2008; Wessels, 2012; Eastin et al., 2016). Information collected for one purpose can be readily retrieved for another, and the possible association between aggregated data about a consumer makes nearly every point of accessible data personally identifiable. In its 2010 report, the Federal Trade Commission acknowledged and addressed the "diminishing distinction between personally identifiable information … and supposedly anonymous or de-identified information" (p. 93).

While the definition of personalized advertising continues to evolve with the tools and technologies that make it possible, most contemporary scholars agree the practice involves proactively tailoring marketing messages and delivery platforms to reach individual consumers based upon their preferences and personal information while maintaining the principles of mass message marketing (Chellappa & Sin, 2005; Dolnicar & Jordaan, 2007). A key differentiator between modern message personalization and what was possible just a few years ago is the development of hyper-targeted message delivery based on connecting and analyzing real-time location with consumers' online and offline behavior to glean cross-channel insights about individual customers (Teradata, 2015).

Where companies engaged in mass marketing in the past, targeting audiences based on demographic information of readers, viewers and listeners of traditional print and broadcast media, advertisers today employ increasingly sophisticated technologies that track individual consumers' characteristics, preferences and behaviors in real-time to construct individual-specific profiles and deliver highly customized, targeted messages (Schwartz & Solove, 2011). Successful personalized advertising therefore hinges upon marketers' ability to acquire and process consumer information and personal data, as well as consumers' willingness to share information and to accept and use personalization services (Chellappa & Sin, 2005).

The industry is developing into a "science-based, data-driven business" with the increasing ability to reach consumers in highly targeted and effective ways. This emerging digitally targeted world offers extraordinary opportunities for advertisers and organizations to deliver the right message to the right consumer at the right time and immediately analyze messaging effectiveness (Dutta & Bilbao-Osorio, 2014). Marketers with the greatest ability to collect and process the most comprehensive constellations of consumer data will lead the market by having the most complete and precise understanding of their audiences (Dutta & Bilbao-Osorio, 2014). This shift from audience segmentation to real-time one-to-one personalization has only tapped the surface of the profound marketing opportunities and possibilities that big data promises.

Although consumer awareness of the personalized advertising ecosystem remains relatively low, data-driven marketing is a massive and quickly expanding business. In a 2010 study, Krux Digital, Inc. estimated the value of the 'gray market' harvesting and reuse of consumers' online behavioral data business to be $850 million per year (Krux Digital, 2010). As companies continued to place greater emphasis on the tracking and collection of consumer behavioral information, the business has grown exponentially.

The 2015 IAB Internet Advertising Revenue Report reveals that targeted digital advertising revenues in the United States hit a historic high of $27.5 billion in the first half of 2015. This figure represents a 19% increase over the $23.1 billion in ad revenues over the same time period in 2014, and continues an upward trend of double-digit growth recorded nearly every year since the IAB began tracking online advertising spending in 2002. Adding to the already noteworthy growth in the half-year, the second quarter growth in 2015 rose 23% from the same period in 2014, the highest quarter on record.

As reflected by this growth, marketers have taken considerable strides in generating business benefit from their data-driven marketing in recent years. And, while strong gains are expected in the near future, marketers will need to overcome barriers involving efficiency, measurement, and targeting to harvest benefits and competitive advantage from consumer data (Teradata, 2015). However, consumer concern for privacy and data security emerges in the forefront of this developing marketing paradigm, threatening not only the process but also mass collection and use of consumer data.

Wearables and the New Health Economy

Even though double-digit growth for smartphones has ended, smartphone and mobile Internet users will continue to increase. In 2016, the total number of mobile phone users is expected to increase 1.6% from 2015 to 262.2 million, and mobile Internet users are projected to reach 210.5 million in 2016, an 8.6% increase from 2015. With the growth rate slowing, new devices such as wearables are generating more interest (Kaul & Wheelock, 2015).

Computing has seen a transition from PC and laptop to mobile devices, including the smartphone and tablet, causing the industry to shift to a point where consumer interaction with computers and the Internet is moving closer to the body and becoming significantly more personal (Kaul & Wheelock, 2015). That is, most innovation in the last year has taken place around smart machines and wearables, and the rapid growth of sensors, both physical and virtual, will provide devices with more perception and context of the physical world, enabling them to work more autonomously to support and harvest consumer insights. Wearable computing is proliferating and will undoubtedly revolutionize the future of human interaction with technology.

The wearables market encompasses a wide range of devices, applications and use cases. Wearable devices include a combination of device types, which are worn or attached to the body to serve a specific function or provide a utility (Barnes, 2014; Hulkower, 2015b; eMarketer, 2015). These devices allow consumers to actively track their health and fitness behaviors while passively monitoring their vitals and physical biometric information, providing users a much deeper understanding of their bodies and immediate environment as well as richer information to better manage their health. These advantages are generating growing interest among consumers, making the wearables market the fastest-growing tech sector (Salesforce, 2015). However, wearable devices are still in the early stages of the technology and product adoption lifecycle, with only 20% of American adults indicating that they currently own a wearable device and 10% using it daily (Barnes, 2014).

New, more sophisticated and integrated technologies and the improved quality and accessibility to personal health information are expected to drive future adoption and sales. For example, the Apple Watch represented one mass-market consumer wearable in 2015, and has helped spawn large-scale interest and momentum in the industry (Kaul & Wheelock, 2015). Though the wearable user base is yet to reach the critical mass necessary, the massive amounts of new data being generated are likely to increase as the market continues to mature.

With a large total addressable market, manufacturers are quickly developing new products that are more attractive to consumers and thus escalating their demand. Mintel research estimates that sales of smartwatches rose from $351 million in 2014 to $1.8 billion in 2015, with fitness trackers expected to reach $4 billion in manufacturing sales in 2015 (Hulkower, 2015b). A 2015 report from the International Data Corporation (IDC) Worldwide Quarterly Wearable Device Tracker forecasts that 72.1 million wearable devices will be shipped in 2015, representing a 173.3% increase from the 26.4 million shipped in 2014 (IDC, 2015).

Moving forward based on higher volume of sales and products continually being designed with new features, shipment volumes are expected to reach 155.7 million units shipped in 2019, experiencing a compound annual growth rate (CAGR) of 42.6% over the five-year forecast period (IDC, 2015). Smart wearables such as smart watches, which are capable of running third-party apps, are expected to lead the device category in 2016 after seeing a 683% year-over-year growth between 2014 and 2015.

The nearly universal adoption of smartphones is an important factor in many smart wearable and fitness tech products because most pair with mobile applications and require smartphone connectivity for optimal functionality. Most wearable devices are accompanied by mobile apps because the user interface and analytical insights require integration with another technology, such as a smartphone. Users' interactions with their data occur mostly on a smartphone through a compatible mobile app, and in most cases the user interface of the wearable is principally the mobile app, making the app essential and possibly more significant than the wearable itself (Tractica, 2015).

This two-way device integration where data from the smart watch or smart wearable is simultaneously transmitted and analyzed on the smartphone creates enhanced and more adaptive user experiences, and will continue to grow in importance for brands (Nudd, 2015). Over the next two years, growth is expected to triple in areas including creating immersive customer experiences, accessing customer data and location-sensing technology to create a more connected customer experience (Salesforce, 2015). While the value of the collection and analysis of personal data is immense, privacy and security issues over access and use are still a major concern for consumers. Users of mobile health applications and fitness trackers are confronted with particularly salient privacy challenges, which have yet to be addressed in government or industry. Specifically, mobile health technologies collect far more sensitive information about the individual than other online and mobile applications, as many health tracking devices collect data continuously over prolonged periods of time (Avancha et al., 2012).

Such devices also allow for a broader range of health-related information to be collected, from passively produced biometric information to self-reported features of the users' lifestyles, activities, behaviors, and often moods. Despite cultural and social norms that command greater privacy over health and medical data (as well as financial, familial, and relationship information) than any other type of information, Americans' behaviors are inconsistent with those beliefs. This apparent dichotomy between privacy attitudes and privacy behaviors is receiving mounting attention from social media (Barnes, 2006), online commerce (Awad & Krishnan, 2006), and smartphones (Sutanto et al., 2013). This phenomenon has been termed broadly as the "privacy paradox" or "personalization-privacy paradox" when data privacy considerations are in the context of consumer targeting for personalized marketing.

Consumers' adoption and use of mobile health apps and fitness trackers demonstrates the evolving nature of today's health ecosystem and app economy, where individuals are increasingly willing to track their behavior when doing so is convenient and provides useful insights into their health. Recent research found that 52% of consumers use at least one mobile health app, with the average user tracking their health and fitness behaviors on at least two apps (Healthline, 2015). As smartphone apps and mobile healthcare platforms become more sophisticated, providing useful insights that are interoperable, engaging, and outcomes-driven, users will habitually integrate health-monitoring technologies into their daily lives.

Smartphone Integration

Product designers are increasingly driving the adoption of technologies that interpret different sensing inputs, facilitate faster connectivity between devices and mobile payments, detect location, and enable context awareness. The way individuals interact with devices has changed considerably. Many factors such as screen sizes, interaction styles, platforms, and architectures are changing and becoming available, and advances in technologies are accelerating in areas such as sensors, displays, wireless and more. Wearable devices that stream data about consumers and their environment in real-time and sensors in smartphone applications that detect location and movement are contributing substantially to the big data universe.

Personal health data is being generated more frequently than ever before, with consumers passively tracking data points about themselves on smartphones and wearable devices, including vitals such as heart rate and blood pressure, glucose and hydration levels detected from sweat, pedometer and accelerometer information, sleep metrics, stress levels, and weight scales. Most of these tools also enable users to record and analyze their behaviors, including physical activity and exercise, diet and nutrition, medications and prescriptions taken, and clinical data (FTC, 2014; Kaul & Wheelock, 2015).

Deep learning analytics and sophisticated algorithms are increasingly capable of harnessing, analyzing, and synthesizing data from smart apps and smart devices and individuals' digital trails, enabling intelligence, awareness, and enormous personalization opportunities for marketers (Barnes, 2015; Gartner, 2015). However, even brands that have adopted wearable technology into their marketing strategies indicated that they are not yet ready to gain actionable insights from wearable data, with only 8% of adopters reporting readiness to use wearable-generated customer data for personalized messaging and services (Salesforce, 2015). But many businesses are actively working to innovate and improve capabilities for understanding and utilizing wearable and mobile data to connect with customers in new ways with immersive experiences and targeted offers.

The data-driven "new health economy" is appearing, driven by the adoption of wearable and mobile health trackers. A 2014 Healthcare Research Industry report suggests growing consumer interest in receiving health information from new health-sensing technologies, with nearly half of consumers indicating they are likely to purchase a fitness tracker in the next year (Barnes, 2014). Of those individuals interested in purchasing a health or fitness tracker, over one-third plan to buy a smart watch and 30% intend to purchase fitness apps over the same one-year period (CTA, 2015). The total addressable market for wearables and fitness trackers make up the majority of online adults, with 70% of online adults showing one or more interests that could be satisfied with a wearable technology product (Hulkower, 2015a).

Consumer Privacy and Security

Marketers and organizations collecting personal and behavioral information about consumers online frequently argue that consumers are willing to share personal data despite privacy risks in exchange for the value offered by personalized offers and services (Culnan, 1993; Culnan & Armstrong, 1999; Milne, 2000; Tezinde et al., 2002; Chellappa & Sin, 2005). But as digital life becomes inseparably linked with an individual's physical life, and their digital presence holds interactions across a multitude of online platforms, many more intimate insights can be gained about consumers. Previous research has focused primarily on consumers' perceived risks and privacy concerns about personal data at the individual level, but privacy threats are amplified substantially for data at the aggregate level. As Dutta and Bilbao-Osorio (2014, p. 64) conclude:

> Learning a great deal about a person by combining factors that may seem harmless at the discrete level but, when taken together, may give away

information that the person would not want generally known … Each discrete piece of information is not meaningful, but in the aggregate can make someone a potential victim.

Health data is widely regarded as one of the most confidential and sensitive types of personal information, and has traditionally been protected with much more stringent regulatory regimes and controls. However, as noted earlier, health and fitness applications collect and transmit sometimes sensitive personal information about users' health details to third parties. A recent FTC investigation of 12 widely used mobile health apps found that the apps tested transmitted information to no fewer than 76 third parties.

The information shared included: device model or language setting; consumer-specific identifiers including user name, email address, and a string of identifiers; unique device IDs, MAC address or IMEI; unique third-party specific identifiers; and personal consumer information including exercise routine, symptom searches, dietary habits, zip code geo-location and gender (FTC, 2014). The FTC also identified third-party ad servicing that received information from four separate health apps including the same unique identifiers that were transmitted to the third parties from various apps on the mobile device.

Data aggregators are increasingly capable of tracking users across devices and interactions, associating information collected from other services, such as customer loyalty cards, frequent flier cards and credit card purchases. An additional threat to the privacy of information collected and stored on smartphone apps is the fact that mobile device platforms rely heavily on cloud computing, and consequently private health data from these apps is being constantly stored by this network of remote servers.

Disagreement exists between groups of researchers and practitioners regarding how to view and address consumer privacy concerns in the face of data-driven marketing, especially where health data is involved. On one hand, marketers assume that consumers are becoming accustomed to being tracked and that living a public life is the new default for Internet-connected users (Sayre & Horne, 2000; Mitchell et al., 2014; Rainie & Anderson, 2014; Madden & Rainie, 2015). They argue that people's norms are changing with technologies, and consumers will become increasingly accepting of the sharing and collecting of data as a part of life. Most individuals will accept the special offers and personalization features in return for the information they give up, and those who object may become resigned to this new reality and eventually stop fighting. As Wright notes in response to a Pew Research study about the future of privacy:

> A new way of looking at privacy may be established. The Internet will know you—your family, your doctor, your bank, where you get coffee in the morning, everything substantial and seemingly trivial about your

life and what you do—and that will erase your privacy but will also protect you. This is a frightening concept, but is already well down the road. Norms are already changing due, in part, to the ubiquity of social media use. What [previous generations] considered strictly private is completely shareable for the next generation ... In the future, I expect that no one will be able to control one's image online enough to be spotless, and the sting of revealing too much will lessen. (Rainie & Anderson, 2014, p. 74)

On the other hand, researchers and industry practitioners believe consumer suspicion about connected technology could stymie innovation and curtail use and adoption if marketers do not adequately address privacy concerns (Mottl, 2015). They argue that by attending to current users' concerns about device security and data privacy while, more importantly, educating and informing potential users about how their personal information is being used, consumers will feel greater assurance that their data is well protected, as well as feel greater control over their own information.

Current research on consumer attitudes, opinions, and behaviors regarding the privacy of their personal data from wearable technologies and mobile health applications has consistently established that consumers are concerned about the breadth and quality of personal information being collected about them (Ackerman, 2013; Kavassalis et al., 2003; Lee & Benbasat, 2003; Watson et al., 2002). A recent study examining consumers' sentiments about data collected for marketing purposes, reported that 91% of individuals do not want marketers selling their information, even if they are compensated. In addition, two-thirds feel that it should be illegal for companies to collect or use such data without getting prior consent.

This response is well supported by industry research showing consumers are increasingly adopting technologies that allow them to elude tracking, block online and mobile ads (PageFair, 2015), and register on do-not-track lists (Davis, 215). Cranor (2005) identified three central areas of consumers' information privacy concerns, including: the type of data collected, how data will be used, and whether or not the data will be shared. In addition, financial and medical data are of the greatest concern for individuals, as well as the use of their data for marketing lists and consumer profiles.

Research also demonstrates, however, that consumers generally lack awareness and knowledge about what personal data is being collected and by whom, as well as how it is being shared and used (Brinson & Eastin, 2016; Turow et al., 2005). Large percentages of American consumers hold inaccurate assumptions about the collection and use of their personal information and "overestimate the extent to which the government protects them from certain forms of data collection" (Turow et al., 2015, p. 16).

Users are often unaware that data from mobile apps and online activities transfer to a substantial number of servers, including advertising and analytics networks. Thus, research on privacy concerns may not reflect a true assessment of individuals' attitudes and perceptions about data-based marketing practices across the ecosystem of their devices. On mobile devices and in mobile computing contexts, users exercise less caution than in other computing environments despite the more personal and pervasive information generated from these technologies (Mitchell et al., 2014). Consumers' behavior on mobile devices, especially when compared to other computing environments, underscores apparent misperceptions about the privacy and security of personal data.

Reported privacy and security issues tend to take the form of broad concerns, with little known about their intricacies or origins. For example, research has found that 41% of consumers have concerns about security and privacy violations by wellness and fitness apps, though only 35% indicated that they worry that their personal health information will not remain confidential if online (Parks Associates, 2015). Limited research has been conducted about the types of personal information of greatest concern to mobile health and fitness device users, with current studies focusing on which companies or third parties consumers worry most about sharing their health data.

Conclusions and Recommendations

Marketers have embraced the use of behavioral marketing across digital platforms to serve personalized messages to consumers. Online behavioral tracking and social listening remain the industry standard for compiling relevant information about consumers for ad personalization, but with mobile device adoption and developments in new technologies marketers have realized the necessity of assuming a mobile-first approach to consumer interactions.

The industry is in constant change, and the use of consumer-generated mobile data is still in its early stages. As customers become more comfortable sharing this information, the market will see more experimental and innovative use cases. Marketers predict that more precise emotional targeting and message personalization gleaned from data-driven insights will be commonplace in the next five to ten years. This includes capturing data from novel sources such as wearables, mobile health and fitness application, in-store facial recognition software, and more advanced mobile sensing capabilities combined with information captured from current behavioral marketing techniques.

From an industry perspective, access, understanding, and use of health and biometric data offer intriguing opportunities to add value to consumers through personalized services such as reaching consumers at the right place and right time with relevant and acutely personalized messages. The value to consumers includes enhanced buying experiences and services that cater to their interests. However, the way in which marketers, industry practitioners and policymakers address the ownership, collection, and use of personal data should be of increasing importance to consumers.

Marketers and organizations in the industry that are best prepared to capture, understand, and use the influx of consumer-generated mobile data will enjoy a competitive advantage so long as users accept the increased personalization and do not view the use of their data as an invasion of privacy. However, instead of relying on legal guidelines for fair information practices and consumer data protection set by governmental regulators, it is critical for the industry to adopt meaningful self-regulatory guidelines based on thorough understanding of future benefits and drawbacks, why they matter, and how they will shape individuals, the industry, and society. It is here that consumer understanding and trust will emerge as key concepts in the growth and acceptance of big data collection practices and hyper-personalized messaging.

Future Research Agenda

The intricacies of such complex and personal issues require further exploration into factors influencing perceptions of privacy for data collection via mobile and wearable technology. Analysis of the root causes of privacy factors that rank highly for consumers requires continued review. To develop comprehensive, flexible policies and self-regulatory mechanisms that reduce privacy concerns while facilitating the growth of mobile and digital marketing, a clearer understanding of consumers' perceived risks involved with data disclosure is necessary, particularly when considering information about commerce and health related activities.

For marketers and industry practitioners to advance and even continue data-driven marketing practices, considerations of data collection contexts and information sensitivities must be understood and addressed. Identifying the changing conditions where consumers welcome ad personalization and data-driven messaging strategies requires ongoing, continual research as new technologies emerge, devices become more connected, and privacy perceptions evolve. Such a research agenda would allow for researchers to develop policy recommendations for industry to consider, before stringent government regulations potentially restrict growth.

References

2010 Krux Cross-Industry Study Summary Findings, Presented to the Media Law Resource Center Web Conference (Feb. 9, 2011).

Ackerman, L. (2013). *Mobile Health and Fitness Applications and Information Privacy*. San Diego, CA: Privacy Rights Clearinghouse.

Adomavicius, G. & Tuzhilin, A. (2005). Personalization technologies: a process-oriented perspective. *Communications of the ACM*, 48(10), 83–90.

Anderson, M. (2015, October 29). Technology Device Ownership: 2015. Pew Internet & American Life Project. Retrieved from http://www.pewinternet.org/files/2015/10/PI_2015-10-29_device-ownership_FINAL.pdf

Avancha, S., Baxi, A. & Kotz, D. (2012). Privacy in mobile technology for personal healthcare. *ACM Computing Surveys (CSUR)*, 45(1), 3.

Awad, N. F. & Krishnan, M. S. (2006). The personalization privacy paradox: an empirical evaluation of information transparency and the willingness to be profiled online for personalization. *MIS Quarterly*, 30(1), 13–28.

Barnes, K. (2014), Health wearables: Early days, PricewaterhouseCoopers (PwC) Health Research Institute and Consumer Intelligence Series, 2–11.

Barnes, S. B. (2006). A privacy paradox: Social networking in the United States. *First Monday*, 11(9) http://journals.uic.edu/ojs/index.php/fm/article/view/1394/1312.

Boyles, J. L., Smith, A. & Madden, M. (2012, September 5). Privacy and Data Management on Mobile Devices, Pew Internet & American Life Project. Retrieved from http://www.pewinternet.org/2012/09/05/privacy-and-data-management-on-mobile-devices/

Brinson, N. H., & Eastin, M. S. (2016). Juxtaposing the persuasion knowledge model and privacy paradox: An experimental look at advertising personalization, public policy and public understanding. *Cyberpsychology: Journal of Psychosocial Research on Cyberspace*, 10(1).

Buckingham, D. (Ed.). (2008). *Youth, Identity, and Digital Media* (pp. 119-142). Cambridge, MA: MIT Press.

Chellappa, R. K. & Sin, R. G. (2005). Personalization versus privacy: An empirical examination of the online consumer's dilemma. *Information Technology and Management*, 6(2-3), 181–202.

Cisco. (2014). VNI global IP traffic forecast, 2013–2018. Retrieved from http://www.cisco.com/c/en/us/solutions/service-provider/visual-networking-index-vni/index.html

Consumer Technology Association. (2015). Consumers Journey to Purchase: Health and Fitness. Retrieved July 16, 2017, from http://www.cta.tech/Research.aspx

Cox, J. T. & Cline, K. M. (2012). Parsing the demographic: The challenge of balancing online behavioral advertising and consumer privacy considerations. *Journal of Internet Law*, March, 3–12.

Cranor, L. F. 2005. Privacy policies and privacy preferences. In Security and Usability: Designing Secure Systems that People Can Use, L. F. Cranor and S. Garfinkel, Eds. O'Reilly Media, Chapter 22, 447–469. Online at http://oreilly.com/catalog/9780596008277/.

Culnan, M. (1993). How did they get my name? An exploratory investigation of consumer attitudes toward secondary information use. *MIS Quarterly*, 17(3), 341–363.

Culnan, M. & Armstrong, P. (1999). Information privacy concerns, procedural fairness, and impersonal trust: an empirical investigation. *Organizational Science*, 10(1), 104–115.

Davis, W. (2015, October 7). Lawmakers call for stronger do-not-track standards. Mediapost Policy Blog. Retrieved from http://www.mediapost.com/ publications/article/259971/lawmakers-call-for-stronger-do-not-track- standards.html.

Dolnicar, S. & Jordaan, Y. (2007). A market-oriented approach to responsibly managing information privacy concerns in direct marketing. *Journal of Advertising*, 26(2), 123–149.

Dutta, S. & Bilbao-Osorio, B. (2014), The Global Information Technology Report 2014 – Rewards and Risks of Big Data, INSEAD and World Economic Forum, 35–93.

Eastin, M. S., Brinson, N. H., Doorey, A. & Wilcox, G. (2016). Living in a big data world: Predicting mobile commerce activity through privacy concerns. *Computers in Human Behavior*, 58, 214–220.

eMarketer (2015, October). *Cross-Device Marketing Roundup*. Retrieved from https://www.emarketer.com/public_media/docs/eMarketer_Cross_Device_Marketing_Roundup.pdf

Espinel, V. (2015, September 1). Deep Shift: Technology Tipping Points and Societal Impact. Retrieved from http://www3.weforum.org/docs/WEF_GAC15_Technological_Tipping_Points_report_2015.pdf

Federal Trade Commission. (2010). Protecting Consumer Privacy in an Era of Rapid Change: A Proposed Framework for Businesses and Policymakers. December 2010, 72-119.

Federal Trade Commission. (2014a). Spring Privacy Series: Consumer Generated and Controlled Health Data. Retrieved from https://www.ftc.gov/system/files/documents/public_events/195411/2014_05_07_consumer-generated-controlled-health-data-final-transcript.pdf

Federal Trade Commission. (2014b). Data Brokers: A Call for Transparency and Accountability. Retrieved from https://www.ftc.gov/system/files/documents/reports/data-brokers-call-transparency-accountability-report-federal-trade-commission-may-2014/140527databrokerreport.pdf

Genovese, Y., Sorofman, J., Virzi, A., (2015, October 20). *CMO Spend Survey 2015-2016: Digital Marketing Comes of Age*. Retrieved from Gartner database.

Harland, B. (2015, May). *Internet Ads: Search, Display and Video – US*. Retrieved from Mintel Oxygen database.

Harland, B. (2015, October). *Mobile Apps – US*. Retrieved from Mintel Oxygen database.

Healthline (2015, July 28). The New Healthcare Ecosystem: Emerging Digital Health Trends. Retrieved from http://www.healthline.com/health/healthline-survey-personal-health-data

Hulkower, B. (2015a, July). *Mobile Advertising and Shopping – US*. Retrieved from Mintel Oxygen database.

Hulkower, B. (2015b, December). *Wearable Technology – US*. Retrieved from Mintel Oxygen database.

IBM (2013). *Big Data*. Retrieved July 16, 2017, from http://ibm.com/big-data/us/en/.

International Data Corporation (2015, June 18). Worldwide Wearables Market Forecast to Grow 173.3% in 2015 with 72.1 Million Units to be Shipped, According to IDC. Retrieved from https://www.idc.com/getdoc.jsp?containerId=prUS25696715

Internet Advertising Bureau (2015). *Internet Advertising Revenue Report*. Retrieved from http://www.iab.com/wp-content/uploads/2015/10/IAB_Internet_Advertising_Revenue_Report_HY_2015.pdf

Kaul, A. & Wheelock, C. (2015). Wearables: 10 Trends to Watch, Tractica LLC., 3-11. Retrieved from https://www.tractica.com/wp-content/uploads/2015/08/WP-WD10T-15-Tractica.pdf

Kavassalis, P., Spyropoulou, N., Drossos, D., Mitrokostas, E., Gikas, G. & Hatzistamatiou, A. (2003). Mobile permission marketing: Framing the market inquiry. *International Journal of Electronic Commerce*, 8(1), 55–79.

Lee, Y. E. & Benbasat, I. (2003). Interface design for mobile commerce. *Communications of the ACM*, 46(12), 48–52.

Lella, A., Lipsman, A. & Martin, B. (2015, September 22). The 2015 U.S. Mobile App Report. Retrieved from http://www.comscore.com/Insights/Presentations-and-Whitepapers/2015/The-2015-US-Mobile-App-Report

Lerman, K. (2014). Beyond the bull's-eye: Building meaningful relationships in the age of big data. Retrieved from: https://www.communispace.com/uploadedfiles/researchinsights/best_practices/bestpractices_beyondthebullseye_ buildingrelationshipsintheageofbigdata.pdf.

Madden, M. & Rainie, L. (2015, May 20). Americans' Attitudes About Privacy, Security and Surveillance. Pew Internet & American Life Project. Retrieved from http://www.pewinternet.org/files/2015/05/Privacy-and-Security-Attitudes-5.19.15_FINAL.pdf

Manyika, J., Chui, M., Brown, B., Bughin, J., Dobbs, R., Roxburgh, C., & Hung Byers, A. (May, 2011). Big Data: The Next Frontier for Innovation, Competition and Productivity. McKinsey Global Institute Report. Retrieved from http://www.mckinsey.com/insights/business_technology/big_data_the_next_frontier_for_innovation.

Milberg, S. J., Burke, S. J., Smith, H. J. & Kallman, E. A. (1995). Values, personal information privacy, and regulatory approaches. *Communications of the ACM*, 38(12), 65–74.

Milne, G. R. (2000). Privacy and ethical issues in database/interactive marketing and public policy: A research framework and overview of the special issue. *Journal of Public Policy & Marketing*, 19(1), 1-6.

Mir, I. (2011). Consumer attitude towards m-advertising acceptance: a cross-sectional study. *Journal of Internet Banking & Commerce*, 16(1), 1–22.

Mitchell, M., Wang, A. I. A. & Reiher, P. (2014). Mobile Usage Patterns and Privacy Implications. Retrieved from http://www.cs.fsu.edu/~awang/papers/permoby2015.pdf

Morgan, R. M., Parish, J. T., & Deitz, G. (2015). *Handbook on Research in Relationship Marketing*. Cheltenham: Elgar.

Mottl, J. (2015, August 11). Consumers remain wary over safety of health wearables, wellness apps. Retrieved from http://www.fiercemobilehealthcare.com/story/consumers-remain-wary-over-safety-health-wearables-wellness-apps/2015-08-11

Norberg, P. A., Horne, D. R., & Horne, D. A. (2007). The privacy paradox: Personal information disclosure intentions versus behaviors. *Journal of Consumer Affairs*, 41(1), 100–126.

Nudd, T. (2015, January 2). How Brands Can Use Biometric Data in Ways That Go Far Beyond Fitness. Retrieved from http://www.adweek.com/news/advertising-branding/how-brands-can-use-biometric-data-ways-go-far-beyond-fitness-165108

O'Hara, C. (2015, May 26). Report: Brand Marketers Are Warming To Programmatic. *Krux Digital*. Retrieved from http://www.krux.com/blog/data-driven-marketing/report-brand-marketers-are-warming-to-programmatic/

O'Connor, F. (2015, July 23). HP study finds smartwatches could do more to keep user data safe. *PC World*. Retrieved from http://www.pcworld.com/article/2952352/security/hp-study-finds-smartwatches-could-do-more-to-keep-user-data-safe.html

PageFair. (2015). The 2015 Ad blocking report. Retrieved from https://blog.pagefair.com/2015/ad-blocking-report/

Parks Associates (2015, August 4). One-quarter of consumers have privacy concerns about using connected health devices. Retrieved from http://www.parksassociates.com/blog/article/pr-aug2015-health-privacy

Petronio, S. (2002). *Boundaries of Privacy*. Albany, NY: State University of New York Press.

Purcell, K., Brenner, J., & Rainie, L. (2012). Search engine use 2012. Pew Internet & American Life Project. Retrieved from http://pewinternet.org/Reports/2012/Search-Engine-Use-2012.aspx

Rainie, L., & Anderson, J. (2014, December 18). Digital Life in 2025: The Future of Privacy. Pew Internet & American Life Project. Retrieved from http://www.pewinternet.org/files/2014/12/PI_FutureofPrivacy_121814_pdf1.pdf

Rainie, L., & Duggan, M. (2016, January 14). Privacy and Information Sharing. Pew Internet & American Life Project. Retrieved from http://www.pewinternet.org/files/2016/01/PI_2016.01.14_Privacy-and-Info-Sharing_FINAL.pdf

Revella, A. (2015). *Buyer Personas: How to Gain Insight into your Customer's Expectations, Align your Marketing Strategies, and Win More Business*. John Wiley & Sons.

Salesforce Research. (2015). State of Wearables Report: Putting Wearables to Work, Insights on Wearable Technology in Business. Retrieved from https://secure.sfdcstatic.com/assets/pdf/misc/StateOfWearablesReport.pdf

Sayre, S. & Horne, D. (2000). Trading secrets for savings: how concerned are consumers about club cards as a privacy threat? *Advances in Consumer Research*, 27(1).

Schwartz, P. M. & Solove, D. J. (2011). PII problem: Privacy and a new concept of personally identifiable information. *NYUL Rev.*, *86*, 1814.

Solove, D. J. (2006). A taxonomy of privacy. *University of Pennsylvania Law Review*, 477–564.

Stutzman, F., Vitak, J., Ellison, N. B., Gray, R. & Lampe, C. (2012, June). Privacy in Interaction: Exploring Disclosure and Social Capital in Facebook. In *ICWSM*.

Sutanto, J., Palme, E., Tan, C. H., & Phang, C. W. (2013). Addressing the personalization-privacy paradox: an empirical assessment from a field experiment on smartphone users. *Mis Quarterly*, 37(4), 1141–1164.

Sweeney, D. W. M. (2013, October 16). EmTech MIT 2013 Media Roundup. Retrieved from http://www.technologyreview.com/view/520376/emtech-mit-2013-media-roundup/

Teradata. (2015). *Global Data-Driven Marketing Survey: Progressing Toward True Individualization*. Retrieved from http://applications.teradata.com/DDM-Survey/welcome/.ashx

Tezinde, T., Smith, B. & Murphy, J. (2002). Getting permission: Exploring factors affecting permission marketing. *Journal of Interactive Marketing*, 16(4), 28–36.

Tractica LLC. (2015). *Emerging Interface Technologies for Mobile Devices*. Retrieved from https://www.tractica.com/research/emerging-interface-technologies-for-mobile-devices/

Turow, J., Feldman, L. & Meltzer, K. (2005). Open to Exploitation: America's Shoppers Online and Offline. University of Pennsylvania.

Turow, J., Hennessy, M. & Draper, N. (2015). The tradeoff fallacy: How marketers are misrepresenting American consumers and opening them up to exploitation. The Annenberg School for Communication, University of Pennsylvania. Retrieved from https://www.asc.upenn.edu/sites/default/files/TradeoffFallacy_1.pdf

Vesanen, J. (2007). What is personalization? A conceptual framework. *European Journal of Marketing*, 41 (2007), 409–418.

Watson, R. T., Pitt, L. F., Berthon, P. & Zinkhan, G. M. (2002). U-commerce: Expanding the universe of marketing. *Journal of the Academy of Marketing Science*, 30(4), 333–347.

Wessels, B. (2012). Identification and the practices of identity and privacy in everyday digital communication. *New Media & Society*, 1461444812450679.

Xu, H., Luo, X. R., Carroll, J. M. & Rosson, M. B. (2011). The personalization privacy paradox: An exploratory study of decision making process for location-aware marketing. *Decision Support Systems*, 51(1), 42–52.

Zwick, D., & Dholakia, N. (2004). Whose identity is it anyway? Consumer representation in the age of database marketing. *Journal of Macromarketing*, 24(1), 31–43.

11

EXPLORING THE CHALLENGES OF SOCIAL MEDIA USE IN HIGHER EDUCATION

Linda Tuncay Zayer, Stacy Neier Beran, and Purificación Alcaide-Pulido

Recent scholarship has examined the potential of using social media in higher education through the lens of different disciplines, classroom environments, tools, and assessing a diverse range of educational outcomes. While much of the scholarly work in this area focuses upon the advantages and successes of using social media tools, this chapter seeks to uncover the potential challenges and downsides. To this end, we ask: what are the challenges to using social media tools in a higher education classroom setting as perceived by students? We first outline research examining social media in higher education through a comprehensive literature review and provide summary tables as reference guides. Next, we detail our exploratory research examining students' perceptions of using social media in the classroom. Lastly, we illustrate our findings and pose implications for educators.

Literature Review

The use of social media in higher education has generated much interest by academics eager to explore the possibilities that these new tools may hold for learning. While social media tools offer a multitude of ways to transfer knowledge, such tools also support collaboration and interactivity between educators and students. Research into the diverse in-class experiences of faculty and students reveals varying levels of acceptance of social media in higher education settings. Some educators have been cautious about adopting the tools for classroom use, seeking theoretical or pragmatic reasons for implementation. Therefore, these educators remain in a temporary, evaluative stage as they navigate traditional course activities and social media applications (Tess, 2013). Recognizing that little research exists to document the educational benefits associated with the use of social networking sites (SNSs), for example, some educational researchers investigate specific classroom projects to measure gains resulting from utilizing social media in curriculum (e.g., Brady et al., 2010, use of social network site Ning). Such inquiry may be an initial step in uncovering how the use of social media influences important educational outcomes including reasoning, analysis, and student engagement. On the other hand, students' perceptions and motivations driving social media use are also important to investigate because they may reveal the receptivity of students to using such tools for academic purposes (see Neier & Zayer, 2015). Thus, much is left to be discovered on the uses, benefits and challenges to using social media in higher education. In the following sections, we outline major research conducted on social media in higher education as well as studies examining the use of specific social media tools.

Web 2.0 and Social Media in Higher Education

The use of Web 2.0 and social media has become popular within higher education; however, definitions and uses can vary in academic settings (Davis et al., 2012). Social media has become a practical part of daily activity for most college students (Liu, 2010; Pawelzik, 2011) who both formally and informally use social media with academics (Dabbagh & Kitsantas, 2012). At times, traditional course communications have adapted due to social media trends, resulting in changing classroom management (Rojas & Albuquerque, 2015). The openness of Web 2.0 revolutionized higher education by allowing students' roles to become participatory with easily created content. Further, students may shift away from previous passive roles and the traditional authoritatively driven delivery of course content may be modified (Rodriguez, 2011; Selwyn, 2012). However, students who embrace Web 2.0 technologies with great enthusiasm potentially create an educational divide between their practices and instructors who are overwhelmed by dynamic technology changes (Liu, 2010). Moreover, Paul et al. (2012) also point to the negative relationship between academic performance and time spent on SNSs by students, providing a counter argument for the use of social media. Thus, educators need be thoughtful and objective with regard to the use of social media (Selwyn, 2012).

Many educators believe social media tools offer new educational access for students (Poellhuber et al., 2011). Selwyn (2010) holds that the use of social media may be motivated by three interrelated factors: 1) the highly connected student; 2) the evolving nature of students' consumption and construction of knowledge; and 3) the emergence of "user-driven" education. However, as educators seek to take advantage of the perspectives, access, and interactions of social media in their pedagogic practice (Hemmi et al., 2009; Madge et al., 2009; Selwyn, 2012), many find themselves expected to catch up with applications as well as negotiate users' expectations for quick feedback (Ebner et al., 2010; López & García, 2012; Selwyn, 2012).

In sum, educators face both opportunities and challenges as they attempt to navigate the use of social media in higher education. Research investigating the benefits and obstacles associated with the use of Web 2.0 and social media tools in the classroom are further summarized in Table 11.1. We now turn to discussions of how particular social media tools have been used in higher education settings.

Facebook

Recognizing "user-driven" education pervades current higher education settings (Selwyn, 2010), identification of specific social media tools students use and how these tools may be integrated in teaching and learning activities is necessary (Liu, 2010). For example, Facebook, started by Mark Zuckerberg in 2004, initially provided access only to students in higher education, leading users to perceive the site as a private community (Roblyer et al., 2010). boyd and Ellison (2007) affirm, "As Facebook began supporting other schools, those users were also required to have university email addresses associated with those institutions, a requirement that kept the site relatively closed and contributed to users' perceptions of the site as an intimate, private community" (p. 218). Facebook eventually permitted anyone interested to participate in the activities students experienced, regardless of academic affiliation (Davis et al., 2012). Facebook's user base is diverse and inclusive, representing various education levels and communities. (Roblyer et al., 2010).

While Facebook has garnered greater acceptance in classrooms, research still demonstrates potential obstacles and concerns with its use in higher education for pedagogical purposes. For example, Irwin et al. (2012) find that while 78% of students expected benefits to using Facebook in a course, in post-course surveys, only half indicated it aided their learning. In an earlier study, Mazer et al. (2007) also outline the advantages and disadvantages to using Facebook. The authors state:

> Students may perceive a teacher's use of Facebook as an attempt to foster positive relationships with his or her students, which may have positive effects on important student outcomes ... [However], teachers may violate student expectations of proper behaviors and run the risk of harming their credibility if they utilize Facebook. Despite this potential consequence, teachers may enhance their credibility among students by signifying an understanding of contemporary student culture. (2007, pp. 3–4)

In a similar vein, Taylor et al. (2012) recognize Facebook to be potentially problematic in the classroom due to students' attempts to compartmentalize professional and personal identities as well as concerns about potential employer and faculty reactions to information posted on the SNS. Please refer to Table 11.2 for more detail on how scholars have investigated the use of Facebook in higher education classrooms.

TABLE 11.1 Studies about the Use of Web 2.0 in Higher Education Classroom

Author/s	Objective	Sample	Main results
Ajjan & Hartshorne (2008)	Investigated faculty adoption and perceptions of Web 2.0 applications.	136 faculty members, varying in age and rank at a large university in southeastern U.S.	Faculty indicated that blogs were among the most beneficial social media tools to adopt for pedagogical purposes. Specifically, faculty reported awareness about the role of blogs to increase collaboration within the classroom community and advance learning outcomes including student writing. Nonetheless, faculty resisted integration of social media in their courses. Most faculty either did not use or would not use social media even though they recognized benefits.
Sendall, Ceccucci, & Peslak (2008)	Examined the implementation of Web 2.0 tools in classroom, including blogs, wikis, Second Life, and social networking.	29 students from two northeastern U.S. universities. (At the first university, 21 students in an e-Business class; at the second university, 8 students in the introductory information systems course.)	After implementation in the course, students' knowledge of how to use social media tools increased. Gains in knowledge were correlated with comfort in using the tools. Moreover, social media tools were perceived to also have a role in the careers students envisioned after their coursework.
Trinder, Guiller, Margaryan, Littlejohn, & Nicol (2008)	Examined how informal learning of students in higher education occurs through students' use of technologies in their academic roles and their lives outside higher education.	Multimethod study: 160 engineering and social work students at two Scottish universities; 8 individual interviews with students and 8 interviews with staff members as follow-up.	Findings indicated use of a range of tools—from cell phones, cameras, and gaming consoles to emails and messenger. The authors hold that using these tools in higher education may support strategies for educators to associate benefits between formal and informal learning.

Study	Purpose	Sample	Findings
Hemmi, Bayne, & Land (2009)	Case studies explored how higher education has implemented social media technologies within pedagogy.	Three groups of students in three degree programs at two Scottish universities.	Authors discuss the challenges of academia with new media. Faculty and students were observed as practicing "rein in" (pg. 29) behaviors given the relative newness of tools like blogs and wikis.
Brady, Holcomb, & Smith (2010)	Determined student's perceptions of Ning as an education-focused social networking site for e-learning benefits.	Sample of 20 graduate students in an asynchronous distance education course; two hybrid synchronous courses at North Carolina State University (17 and 15 students respectively).	Findings reveal general support for the use of social network sites in distance education. Students believed Ning allowed for collaboration with peers and "82% agreed that it aids communication outside of the classroom" (Brady et al., p.155).
Jones, Blackey, Fitzgibbon, & Chew (2010)	Explored students' experiences with use of using social software, reasons for use, and how accepted the tools were for learning purposes.	Students from four anonymous universities: 76 responses collected from a questionnaire, and 14 in-person student interviews.	Although 70% of students reported accessing a social media account, the accounts were used for personal activities. Data suggested students' desire for separation between academics and their personal lives. Moreover, students reported concerns with information overload, restrictions on time, and how capable faculty were in social media environments.
Moran, Seaman, & Tinti-Kane, H. (2011)★	Explored the use of social media sites by faculty members.	Faculty from all disciplines within higher education. A total of 1,920 faculty members completed an online study.	While a majority of faculty has incorporated social media into their classrooms, concerns about privacy and the quality of student work held faculty back from consistent use in their

(Continued)

TABLE 11.1 Studies about the Use of Web 2.0 in Higher Education Classroom (Continued)

Author/s	Objective	Sample	Main results
*Report from Pearson Education.			courses. When social media was used, however, collaboration was prioritized as a benefit, and tools including video, podcasts, and wikis added the most value to the classroom experience.
Poellhuber, Anderson, & Roy (2011)	Within a distance learning setting, authors investigated social media and collaboration tools.	Researchers from four large Canadian education institutions worked together in order to conduct a survey of over 3,000 students.	Findings distinguished that students' desire to use social media exceeded how much experience they have had with tools. Also, significant differences between men and women emerged in the data. In particular, men reported their usage of social media to be more positive than women.
Kilian, Hennigs, & Langner (2012)	Examined traditional and new media usage among Millennials.	A total of 813 respondents participated in an online survey made available through a variety of channels including email lists and forums.	Results indicated that social media usage varied by subgroups of Millennials the authors identified (Restrained Millennials, Entertainment-Seeking Millennials, and Highly Connected Millennials). The authors also demonstrated the continued importance of traditional forms of media as well as illustrated differing motives for use across social media tools.

Paul, Baker, & Cochran (2012)	Developed a general framework in order to define the direct and indirect key drivers of academic performance. Examined various factors related to student achievement including time spent on social network sites.	340 business students at a large state university in the U.S.	Findings indicated a negative relationship between time spent on social networks and academic performance.
Neier & Zayer (2015)	Examined students' perceptions about the use of social media in higher education.	Multimethod study: two rounds of survey data of 138, 135 undergraduate students at private university in U.S.; qualitative interviews.	Results indicated students were open to using social media in the classroom, particularly driven by interactive and information motives, and expressed positive views of faculty and universities using social media.
Gengeswari & Sharmeela-Banu (2016)	Examined social media's usage intention by the international students.	Semi-structured interviews with 4 informants from public higher education institutions; each interview lasted 45 minutes.	Results revealed students' preferences for how social media is used. Students report that information shared by their university provided a level of quality they expected. Students also shared information among other students and educators, so social media showed potential to shape experiences in "the life of a student" when learning was facilitated through technology.

TABLE 11.2 Studies on the Use of Facebook in Higher Education Classroom

Author/s	Objective	Sample	Main results
Madge (2009)	Explored the use of Facebook for pedagogical purposes.	213 undergraduate British students from University of Leicester Teaching Enhancement Forum (TEF).	Demonstrated that students did not strongly perceive the use of Facebook as a formal teaching tool, but rather as an important network for informal learning purposes.
Ophus & Abbitt (2009)	Explored the importance of Facebook as a communication vehicle between students and educators.	110 students from a biology course at a Midwestern university in the U.S.	Results indicated that a large majority of respondents (95.5%) used Facebook either daily or several times each day, and 77% used Facebook with their classmates for communication. Although open-ended items discovered that participants favored the use of Facebook as a tool in their higher education courses, 85.5% also stated that they had never used Facebook to communicate with faculty.
Schroeder & Greenbowe (2009)	Examined the effects of Facebook as a course communication tool versus a Learning Management System (LMS).	128 undergraduate students at Iowa State University in the U.S.	Authors found nearly 60% of students did not join the course Facebook group; however students did actively post on the site (400% greater) as compared to the Learning Management System.
Kirschner & Karpinski (2010)	Investigated the relationship between Facebook use and academic performance.	102 undergraduate and 117 graduate students at a large, public, Midwestern university in the U.S.	Authors reported that a majority of students (66%) used Facebook at least once daily. Moreover, nearly 74% reported that usage of Facebook had no impact on academic performance. However, when probed with qualitative questions, 35 students referenced Facebook as a distraction and influence on time management skills.

McCarthy (2010)	Explored the use of Facebook as a host site for a blended learning environment.	120 architecture students (including 27 international students) in their first-year elective course at University of Adelaide in Australia. A comparative study between 2008 and 2009.	Findings demonstrated the benefits of Facebook use on peer interaction and course engagement.
Roblyer, McDaniel, Webb, Herman, & Witty (2010)	Examined the use of Facebook for personal and educational reasons, comparing the use of students and faculty.	62 faculty and 120 students at a mid-sized southern university in the U.S.	Educators and students differed in terms of how they currently use Facebook. Both educators and students expressed uncertainty with Facebook's role in education, and neither group was "particularly warm" (p. 138) to utilizing it for educational purposes.
Kabilan, Ahmad, & Abidin (2010)	Examined students' perceptions of Facebook as an online space for learning the English language.	300 undergraduate students completed a survey at the University Sains Malaysia.	Results demonstrated that close to 80% of students believed that Facebook could be an effective environment for communication and reading skills in English while over 70% agreed it could be used to practice writing. In addition, 70% of the respondents thought Facebook could enhance their confidence to read, write, and communicate in English. Additionally, more than 70% of students agreed that their participation in Facebook instilled a more positive attitude with regards to learning ESL.

(*Continued*)

TABLE 11.2 Studies on the Use of Facebook in Higher Education Classroom (Continued)

Author/s	Objective	Sample	Main results
Wang, Woo, Quek, Yang, & Liu (2011)	Investigated the use of Facebook in a classroom setting in lieu of and as an addition to a traditional Learning Management System (LMS).	Two groups (16 school teachers and employers; and 15 undergraduate students) registered at a teacher education institute in Singapore.	Participants were satisfied with Facebook as a Learning Management System for the class; however it presented certain practical constraints and posed some privacy concerns.
Irwin, Ball, Desbrow, & Leveritt (2012)	Examined the use of Facebook pages based on student perceptions and the integration of these pages into several university courses in order to assess its efficacy as a course learning tool.	210 total students within two undergraduate courses and 32 postgraduate students. All students were enrolled at Griffith University in Australia.	Findings illustrate students were receptive to using Facebook for educational purposes, thus, offering an opportunity for educators. Benefits to students included notifications of course-related information, as well as an increased participation and interaction in discussions.
Junco (2012)	Investigated frequency and type of Facebook use in relation to student engagement.	2,368 students from a northeast college in the U.S. participated in an online survey.	Results found that the use of Facebook as well as non-communicative activities (e.g., games, browsing friends) on Facebook negatively impact student engagement. Frequency of using Facebook chat negatively influenced time spent preparing for class. Results were mixed with regard to Facebook and time spent in co-curricular activities.

Twitter

Twitter is a social media site which allows users to "tweet" short content and links to a broad set of users. Ebner et al. (2010) classify Twitter as a microblog and provide the following definition: "A microblog can be seen as a weblog that is restricted to 140 characters per post but is enhanced with social networking facilities" (p. 93). Twitter emphasizes communication exchange. For example, Twitter links to the user profiles of other social media interfaces (Davis et al., 2012). While much less research has been conducted on the use of Twitter in the classroom, early research indicates benefits ranging from enhanced language skills among students learning English (Borau et al., 2009) to increased engagement and higher semester GPAs (Junco et al., 2011). And while Lowe and Laffrey (2011) reveal students' perceptions of using Twitter tend to be positive, barriers still exist in incorporating this tool into the classroom. Please see Table 11.3, which includes a summary of educators' experiences with Twitter in the classroom.

Additional Social Media Tools

Other social media tools, including blogs and media sharing sites, have been adopted by educators for classroom use as well. Wiki pages allow entire classroom communities to edit existing content and directly publish new content online, including text, images, and hyperlinks. As students benefit from developing unique content through wikis, they also benefit from the community-driven nature of this social space (Wheeler et al., 2008). Table 11.4 summarizes how educators have incorporated blogs and wikis in higher education. In general, existing studies indicate that blogs and wikis can be useful tools in forming social connections.

Scholarship has also investigated the use of YouTube videos to engage students with new and diverse topics. For example, the use of videos in the classroom can be useful for class discussions, where students apply class knowledge and understand new topics beyond the classroom (Tan & Pearce, 2012) as well as garnering increased behavioral, cognitive, and emotional engagement from students (Roodt & Peier, 2013) and enhanced motivation and communications (Payne et al., 2011). Table 11.5 further summarizes research exploring YouTube's role in the classroom.

In summary, while much of the current research reports favorable outcomes, some studies point to drawbacks on the educational use of social media in classroom and student achievement (e.g., Tess, 2013). Students show adaptability in using social media to support learning; however, there are many unanswered questions as to how educators can develop pedagogical strategies that incorporate such tools. Further, little research captures the range of challenges that educators may face as they utilize these tools in the classroom.

TABLE 11.3 Studies on the Use of Twitter in Higher Education Classrooms

Author/s	Objective	Sample	Main results
Borau, Ullrich, Feng, & Shen (2009)	Described the use of Twitter to build communication and cultural competence in a blended English language class.	96 English students at the Distant College of Shanghai Jiao Tong University.	Results indicated the suitability of the site in language learning; students felt a sense of community using Twitter and a greater sense of cultural awareness and competence from interacting with native English speakers.
Lowe & Laffey (2011)	Evaluated the use of Twitter for learning goals in marketing courses.	123 students of a marketing course where instructor asked them to follow the tweets of the course; 80 students followed.	Findings revealed limited interaction among students. In addition to lacking anonymity, course size, and the relative novelty of Twitter may have limited students' use of the tool. However, students' perceptions of Twitter were overall positive.
Junco, Heiberger, & Loken (2011)	Explored the use of Twitter in the classroom in order to analyze the relationships related to student engagement, collaboration, and learning outcomes.	132 students in seven sections of a pre-professional health seminar course were randomly assigned to a semester-long experimental study.	Researchers found greater engagement as well as higher semester grade point averages among students.

TABLE 11.4 Studies on the Use of Blogs and Wikis in Higher Education Classrooms

Author/s	Objective	Sample	Main results
Wheeler, Yeomans, & Wheeler (2008)	Research investigated learning through user-generated content by students with regard to wikis.	35 education students in four groups at the authors' parent institutions.	Students at first felt uncertain about the requirements of using wikis and accordingly expressed confusion. Despite a relatively high learning curve, students slowly contributed to the collaborative space provided by the wiki. Other concerns that emerged included ownership of original content. Students were protective of the content they contributed, so activities such as editing or deleting may require monitoring by faculty.
Deed & Edwards (2011)	Examined strategies among students for active learning related to the use of blogs.	Survey of 400 education students at Liverpool Hope University.	Students completed tasks within an unrestricted blog and completed an online survey about their experiences. Although students reported consistent Internet access, the content posted to the blogs suggested that blogs supported lower levels of thinking and thus represented novice levels of cognitive development.
Deng & Yuen (2011)	Examined to what extent blogs could support the potential for reflective dialogue among students and teachers.	37 student teachers in two sections (15 students from the first group—Class A— and 22 from the second—Class B) completed questionnaires about their experiences with the use of a weblog during their practicum in Hong Kong.	Blogs supported students' willingness to self-reflect and document what they had encountered. Moreover, outcomes included willingness to post pictures, thus suggesting blogs hold potential to share emotions that might otherwise be kept private by the student.

(Continued)

TABLE 11.4 Studies on the Use of Blogs and Wikis in Higher Education Classrooms (Continued)

Author/s	Objective	Sample	Main results
Huang, Huang, & Yu (2011)	Researched the impact of blogs and related technologies for learning. Specifically, the study focused on the results of inserting RSS feeds, keyword searches, and tags on weblogs.	Two groups of engineering science students (57 experimental and 58 control) at a large university in Taiwan. The course was a three-hour weekly class.	Findings revealed differences between the perceptions of students who engaged in a learning activity in a blog-assisted group versus a face to face group. That is, students expressed their views more freely via blogs.
Top (2012)	Examined educators' perceptions about collaborative learning and sense of community.	50 pre-service teachers (25 and 25) enrolled in two undergraduate Information and Communication Technology (ICT) courses at a Turkish university.	Results demonstrated that the pre-service teachers had significant positive feelings related to their perceived and collaborative learning. In addition, pre-service teachers mostly agreed that blogs aided in sharing their experiences and knowledge. However, perceived learning was more strongly influenced when the whole class, instead of smaller groups, critiqued collaborations.

TABLE 11.5 Studies on the Use of YouTube in Higher Education Classrooms

Author/s	Objective	Sample	Main results
Burke, Snyder, & Rager (2009)	Determined professors' utilization of YouTube in their classes, identifying obstacles and limitations.	Data consisted of a convenience sample of 24 health-education faculty members.	Nearly 42% of faculty reported using YouTube in their courses, and although faculty recognized the effectiveness of YouTube, they continue to use other online resources. Even though more than half of the faculty did not use YouTube in their classrooms, they expressed willingness to integrate YouTube.
Payne, Campbell, Bal, & Piercy (2011)	Evaluated the effectiveness of an experiential learning project related to social media marketing. The study aimed to explore students' perceptions and challenges with YouTube, as well as the relevancy of YouTube use in the classroom.	48 students within a MBA marketing foundations course completed an anonymous survey about a four-month experiential project.	Survey results indicated increased student engagement as measured by how often students checked the status of the videos they posted. Additionally, students expressed willingness to reflect on content posted by their peers and the meaning of the content in a viral marketing setting. However, frustration about how much time the project required was also detected.

(Continued)

TABLE 11.5 Studies on the Use of YouTube in Higher Education Classrooms (Continued)

Author/s	Objective	Sample	Main results
Tan & Pearce (2011)	Explored the integration of YouTube into curriculum by creating a playlist and making it available to all enrolled students; sought to describe students' learning in and out of the classroom when they interacted with the online videos.	24 students in total in a series of three focus groups in an introduction to sociology course.	Students identified their preferences to discuss perspectives of the videos they watched in class as a group, in order to recognize multiple opinions about the topics. This preference also supported students' desire for an explanation of the video to confirm relevant fit with the course topics. Finally, students valued the collection of videos screened by educators. Knowing the educators approved of the video led students to trust the content.
Roodt & Peier (2013)	Described the effect YouTube has on Net Generation students and their classroom engagement; revealed how YouTube was used and how students perceived its use.	241 students across two samples (156 and 85 respectively) of 2nd year undergraduate courses at the University of Cape Town completed an online survey.	64% of students reported being at least frequently engaged when YouTube was integrated into their classes. More than 70% indicated their attention increased when YouTube was used. Although 65% indicated they would recommend other classes integrate YouTube, students were cautious to associate YouTube use with their success in class or consistent class attendance.

Method

Our central research question asks: What are the challenges to using social media tools in a higher education classroom setting as perceived by students? To uncover obstacles and potential disadvantages to using social media, we engaged in an exploratory qualitative study conducting semi-structured, in-depth interviews (McCracken, 1988) with undergraduate marketing students at a private university in the United States. Thirteen men and women were interviewed by a graduate student trained in qualitative methods on their general perceptions of using social media in the classroom, the ways in which they have engaged with social media tools, and the benefits and challenges of using social media for educational purposes. While the data was examined holistically indicating students' responses as mainly positive, the researchers particularly focused on student narratives that detailed potential challenges or frustrations with using social media in the classroom in order to better inform educators of possible pitfalls. The in-depth interviews lasted approximately one hour each and resulted in over 100 pages of transcribed text. Two researchers coded the data, converged on themes, identifying three core themes, which we discuss below.

Findings

Students expressed three key notions on the potential drawbacks for utilizing social media tools in a classroom environment and for educational purposes. We label these challenges, as conceptualized by the students, as: 1) maintaining personal boundaries and limits; 2) establishing legitimacy; and 3) managing relevance.

Personal Boundaries and Limits

When probed as to their experiences with using social media and what potential social media tools may have for the classroom, some students expressed reservations about maintaining boundaries or limits between personal lives and interactions with professors and classmates. One student, David, frankly comments on his outlook on using Twitter, "... the downside [is] like having that constant connection to them. It can kind of get annoying for some students, like I don't want to see my teacher's tweets." However, David does not perceive it to be "a big problem" as he explains, "... that could easily be fixed because you can just turn it off or unfollow them."

Another student, Susan, has deeper concerns. She explains that due to the lack of control of pictures and other material posted online, some content may cause embarrassment or awkwardness between a student and professor if they are connected via social media. She states, "... sometimes it could be an invasion of privacy ... like anyone can take a picture of you anywhere and post it anywhere ... [if] the teacher follows the students ... [it would] be like [the] police in a sense, like be able to monitor the content…." Susan believes it could jeopardize the "integrity" of the educational setting. Other students expressed hesitation about specific social networking sites such as Facebook, Instagram as well as Pinterest. Jessica feels Facebook is "a whole other beast," and cannot see a use for the tool due to its personal nature. She states, "If somebody can find a way to use Facebook in the classroom that's effective and educational, that's great. I don't know how it would be done just because my understanding and perception of Facebook is so different and personal." Another student, Mandy seems to hold a similar sentiment: "I don't really see Facebook for an educational purpose. I think it's more of a social, let's connect, let's stay in touch kind of network." She further explains that she does not see a fit between the visual-based social bookmarking site, Pinterest, either: "I'm an avid user of Pinterest. I love Pinterest. I think it's great but I don't think it's really for educational purposes. I think that's more like personal, in your spare time type of thing, clothes, fashion, food, destinations."

Thus, we find in students' narratives of the use of social media for educational purposes, they do see potential disadvantages to being socially connected with their instructors. At times, the blurring of their personal lives with their roles as students causes discomfort. Indeed, this finding is commensurate with past scholarship in regard to Facebook which finds that students do not perceive the social networking site as a teaching tool (see Davies et al., 2009, study of British students) and have a desire to compartmentalize personal and professional lives (Taylor et al. 2012).

Legitimacy

While some students discussed personal limits with regard to social media use in the classroom, other students questioned the legitimacy of using social media tools altogether. Darren, for example, laments the fact that not all information posted on social media is vetted and therefore, the use of social media should be tempered. He states: "… it's all depending on how you are using social media, so you know if somebody is just posting irrelevant information through sites that aren't established-students will be doing that…."

Another student, Jake, expresses strong concerns about the biased nature and opinion-based information on social media, calling social media a "necessary evil" and taking away the "legitimacy" of a classroom environment. He explains: "Downsides to using social media can definitely unintentionally infringe viewpoints on people just because no one is free of biases and if used too much or inappropriately it can take away from the educational matters which are at the core of the class." Jake expands on his ideas, distinguishing its value for business versus for education. "I'm actually not a big fan of social media but I understand its importance and I agree it's very important. Social media, I think, makes everyone a little bit more of a slave to the media and I am already not crazy about the media in general just because it imposes a lot of beliefs and stuff on people that aren't necessarily good but that's me. I'm a little more different than most. But social media though is a very, very useful way to stay in contact, do business. It's kind of like a necessary evil in my opinion and that's what I would categorize it."

Another student, Karen, also discusses the wide range of opinions expressed on social media—Facebook in particular—but expresses ambivalence on the negative nature of this variance. She states: "… a lot of unnecessary opinions that are on there. They could be opinions from uneducated people but I think you could see that from a positive perspective as well by gaining the knowledge of opinions that coincide with your own opinions and being able to see opinions that don't agree with your own is kind of beneficial as well. However, opinions create conflict … ."

In summary, while students did see value in the use of social media in the classroom, some students' feelings were tempered by questions of the legitimacy of the content online and they highlighted the biased, opinion-based material prevalent in social media content. That is, the classroom is seen as a sacred space for learning and while social media provides a wide range of content, the material must come from credible and trustworthy sources.

Relevance and with Purpose

While some students found the use of social media content problematic due to a lack of perceived legitimacy of the content, others' expressed the importance of relevant content and appropriateness of the social media tool used. Students wanted to ensure that social media use was purposive and provided value to the learning process. Mark states that the use of social media depends on how it is used in the course. He states: "If that professor can adequately implement that, then kudos to that professor." He further explains that there needs to be consistent engagement, " … not just once a month or the professor just doesn't say ok tweet about this or look on Facebook about this or connect with me on LinkedIn. If it's frequent and engaging usage of social media then I define it as being adequate."

One student, Andrew, had a professor who used social media for class; however he did not always find it valuable. He explains while he appreciated the connectivity and ease of use of Twitter, "sometimes content wasn't really relevant to what you're doing, it didn't really … sometimes the interest wasn't sparked through the postings." Both Mark and Andrew highlight that the decision to use social media must have a pedagogical reason and provide value to class learning.

Other students balked at the sheer amount of data on social media that lacks relevancy. For example, Jake, discusses the positive aspects of social media in the classroom, but feels frustrated over "there were always a lot of useless data to mine through." In a similar vein, when asked if there is a role for the use of social media in education, another student, Karen, explains, "Yes and no. No in that there are a lot of irrelevant things that are on social media and yes in that I like the updates that [her university] personally sends me whether it's 'Hey we have

class today' or 'Look at this cool article' or 'This guest speaker is coming ... '."
In fact, poignantly, she expresses a "constant battle of love-hate" with social
media in general.

Jessica also expresses both positive and negative views on the use of social
media but is concerned about using social media while the class is in session. She
states, "I feel like right now there is a mixed view. Social media can be used in
the classroom if it is used effectively, positively, etc. but kids that are on social
media when the instructor is not using it is viewed as negative or distracting. I
want to see social media used in the classroom so that it becomes something that's
enhancing instead of distracting." Another student, Kate, explains that while she
has used Twitter for in-class activities before, she would sometimes fall behind on
what was happening because "I was so busy live tweeting." She also laments on
the use of social media on laptops and mobile devices while in class because it
opens up the possibility of distractions, which are not conducive to classroom
objectives. Kate states, " ... you always have those people who are on Twitter
and not tweeting to the class, or that are on Facebook but not actively participating, people like that ... can be a definite downfall ...".

To summarize, students show an appreciation for the vast amount of content
on social media but also want to ensure the content offered in the classroom and
the tools used are purposive and engaging, and commensurate with educational
goals. Some students remained concerned about the possibility of social media
use serving as a distraction to learning objectives and classroom settings.

Implications for Educators

Our exploratory research highlights the ambivalent nature of using social media
in the classroom as expressed by students. While past research has demonstrated
that students remain cautiously optimistic about using social media tools in the
classroom and find it particularly rewarding when it is interactive and informative
(Neier & Zayer, 2015), we highlight some of the potential obstacles and challenges educators may face as they seek to use social media in an educational context. That is, we outline three possible challenges of using social media in the
classroom as conceptualized by students: setting personal boundaries, maintaining
legitimacy, and ensuring relevance. As a whole, we observe that some of the same
criticisms and concerns of Web 2.0 and social media in general (e.g., consumers'
concerns about privacy, see Peltier et al., 2009) also coincide with how students
perceive its use in the classroom. Moreover, while students expressed many positive sentiments about the use of social media in the classroom, they remain
focused on the notion that the material should be relevant, engaging, and used
with purpose. That is, professors should remain vigilant about using tools that
enhance their classroom goals and learning objectives.

As the proliferation of social media tools continues through for example,
applications such as Instagram, Slack, Snapchat, LinkedIn for Higher Education,

and others, educators who seek to take advantage of new technologies and tools will need to grapple with not only how to use these tools, but also to assess appropriateness for higher education learning. This may be increasingly difficult as there is no one-size-fits-all approach, as some students explained that much is also dependent on the class and the professor. While our exploratory research does not capture all of the potential downfalls for using social media in the classroom, it does offer educators some of the most prominent challenges as perceived by our group of informants, and thus, provides some general guidelines for instructors who want to use such tools. One of the limitations of our study was that it was a relatively homogenous group of students attending a private university in a traditional classroom setting. This research does not address the range of challenges and pitfalls that may emerge from other types of students, classroom environments, and course levels (e.g. distance learners, students enrolled in classes with a large number of students, graduate students). In conclusion, while students express openness to using social media in the classroom, educators must be cautious in implementing social media tools and content to avoid some of the common pitfalls we detail in this research.

References

Ajjan, H. & Hartshorne, R. (2008). Investigating faculty decisions to adopt Web 2.0 technologies: Theory and empirical tests. *The Internet and Higher Education*, 11(2), 71–80.

Alcaide-Pulido, P., Gutiérrez-Villar, B. & Carbonero-Ruz, M. (2015, July). Differences between pre-university men and women in the perception about private university. In EDULEARN15 Conference (pp. 5514–5520), Barcelona, Spain. Retrieved from https://www.researchgate.net/publication/280043212_Differences_between_pre-university_men_and_women_in_the_perception_about_private_university

Borau, K., Ullrich, C., Feng, J. & Shen, R. (2009). Proceedings from Microblogging for language learning: Using Twitter to train communicative and cultural competence. In *International Conference on Web-based Learning* (pp. 78–87). Springer Berlin Heidelberg.

boyd, d.m. & Eillison, N.B. (2007). Social Network Sites: Definition, History, and Scholarship. *Journal of Computer-Mediated Communication*, 13(1), 210-230.

Brady, K. P., Holcomb, L. B. & Smith, B. V. (2010). The use of alternative social networking sites in higher educational settings: A case study of the e-learning benefits of Ning in education. *Journal of Interactive Online Learning*, 9(2), 151–170.

Burke, S. C., Snyder, S. & Rager, R. C. (2009). An assessment of faculty usage of YouTube as a teaching resource. *Internet Journal of Allied Health Sciences and Practice*, 7(1), 8.

Dabbagh, N. & Kitsantas, A. (2012). Personal Learning Environments, social media, and self-regulated learning: A natural formula for connecting formal and informal learning. *The Internet and Higher Education*, 15(1), 3–8.

Davis III, C. H., Deil-Amen, R., Rios-Aguilar, C. & Canche, M. S. G. (2012). Social Media in Higher Education: A literature review and research directions. Unpublished Manuscript, University of Pennsylvania, Pennsylvania, United States.

Davies, P., Mangan, J., & Hughes, A. (2009). Participation, financial support and the marginal student. *Higher Education*, 58(2), 193-204.

Deed, C. & Edwards, A. (2011). Unrestricted student blogging: Implications for active learning in a virtual text-based environment. *Active Learning in Higher Education*, 12(1), 11–21.

Deng, L. & Yuen, A. H. (2011). Towards a framework for educational affordances of blogs. *Computers & Education*, 56(2), 441–451.

Ebner, M., Lienhardt, C., Rohs, M. & Meyer, I. (2010). Microblogs in Higher Education: A chance to facilitate informal and process-oriented learning? *Computers & Education*, 55(1), 92–100.

Ellison, N. B. (2007). Social network sites: Definition, history, and scholarship. *Journal of Computer Mediated Communication*. 13(1), 210–230.

Franklin, T. & Van Harmelen, M. (2007). Web 2.0 for content for learning and teaching in higher education. Unpublished manuscript, University of Manchester, Manchester, United Kingdom.

Galinienë, B., Marèinskas, A., Miðkinis, A. & Drûteikienë, G. (2009). The impact of study quality on the image of a higher education institution. *Informacijos Mokslai*, 48, 68–81.

Gengeswari, K. & Sharmeela-Banu, S. A. (2016). Revealing the underlying insights on the use of social media by foreign students—a qualitative approach. *Journal of Business Theory and Practice*, 4(1), 139.

Greenhow, C. & Burton, L. (2011). Help from my "friends": social capital in the social network sites of low-income students. *Journal of Educational Computing Research*, 45(2), 223–245.

Hemmi, A., & Bayne, S. & Land, R. (2009). The appropriation and repurposing of social technologies in higher education. *Journal of Computer Assisted Learning*, 25, 19–30.

Hemsley-Brown, J. & Oplatka, I. (2006). Universities in a competitive global marketplace: A systematic review of the literature on higher education marketing. *International Journal of Public Sector Management*, 19(4), 316–338.

Huang, T. C., Huang, Y. M. & Yu, F. Y. (2011). Cooperative weblog learning in higher education: Its facilitating effects on social interaction, time lag, and cognitive load. *Educational Technology & Society*, 14(1), 95–106.

Hung, H. & Yuen, S. (2010). Educational use of social networking technology in high education. *Teaching in Higher Education*, 15(6), 703–714.

Irwin, C., Ball, L., Desbrow, B. & Leveritt, M. (2012). Students' perceptions of using Facebook as an interactive learning resource at university. *Australasian Journal of Educational Technology*, 28(7), 1221–1232.

Islam, A.N. (2013). Investigating e-learning system usage outcomes in the university context. *Computers & Education*, 69, 387–399.

Jones, N., Blackey, H., Fitzgibbon, K. & Chew, E. (2010). Get out of MySpace! *Computers & Education*, 54(3), 776–782.

Junco, R. (2012). The relationship between frequency of Facebook use, participation in Facebook activities, and student engagement. *Computers & Education*, 58(1),162–171.

Junco, R., Heiberger, G. & Loken, E. (2011). The effect of Twitter on college student engagement and grades. *Journal of Computer Assisted Learning*, 27(2), 119–132.

Kabilan, M. K., Ahmad, N. & Abidin, M. J. Z. (2010). Facebook: An online environment for learning of English in institutions of higher education? *The Internet and Higher Education*, 13(4), 179–187.

Kaplan, A. M. & Haenlein, M. (2010). Users of the world, unite! The challenges and opportunities of Social Media. *Business Horizons*, 53(1), 59–68.

Kilian, T., Hennigs, N. & Langner, S. (2012). Do Millennials read books or blogs? Introducing a media usage typology of the internet generation. *Journal of Consumer Marketing*, 29(2), 114–124.

King, S., Greidanus, E., Carbonaro, M., Drummond, J. & Patterson, S. (2009). Merging social networking environments and formal learning environments to support and facilitate interprofessional instruction. *Medical Education Online*, 14(1), 5.

Kirschner, P. A. & Karpinski, A. C. (2010). Facebook® and academic performance. *Computers in Human Behavior*, 26(6), 1237–1245.

López, M. T., & Sixto García, J. (2012). Las redes sociales como entorno docente: análisis del uso de Facebook en la docencia universitaria. Pixel-Bit. *Revista de Medios y Educación*, 2012,(41): 77-92.

Lowe, B. & Laffey, D. (2011). Is Twitter for the birds? Using Twitter to enhance student learning in a marketing course. *Journal of Marketing Education*, 33(2), 183–192.

Liu, Y. (2010). Social media tools as a learning resource. *Journal of Educational Technology Development and Exchange*, 3(1), 101–114.

Madge, C., Meek, J., Wellens, J. & Hooley, T. (2009). Facebook, social integration and informal learning at university: It is more for socialising and talking to friends about work than for actually doing work. *Learning, Media and Technology*, 34(2), 141–155.

Mazer, J. P., Murphy, R. E. & Simonds, C. S. (2007). I'll see you on "Facebook": The effects of computer-mediated teacher self-disclosure on student motivation, affective learning, and classroom climate. *Communication Education*, 56(1), 1–17.

McCarthy, J. (2010). Blended learning environments: Using social networking sites to enhance the first year experience. *Australasian Journal of Educational Technology*, 26(6), 729–740.

McCracken, G. (1988). *The Long Interview*. Newbury Park, CA: Sage Publications.

McFedries, P. (2007). Technically speaking: All a-twitter. *IEEE spectrum*, 44(10), 84.

Moran, M., Seaman, J. & Tinti-Kane, H. (2011). Teaching, learning, and sharing: How today's higher education faculty use social media. Babson Survey Research Group.

Neier, S. & Zayer, L.T. (2015). Students' perceptions and experiences of social media in higher education. *Journal of Marketing Education*, 37(3), 133–143.

Ophus, J. D. & Abbitt, J. T. (2009). Exploring the potential perceptions of social networking systems in university courses. *Journal of Online Learning and Teaching*, 5(4), 639–648.

Paul, J. A., Baker, H. M. & Cochran, J. D. (2012). Effect of online social networking on student academic performance. *Computers in Human Behavior*, 28(6), 2117–2127.

Păunescu, C., Shahrazad, H., Cantaragiu, R., Găucă, O., & Pascu, A. (2014). Towards an economics higher education based on learning experiences. *Quality in Higher Education*, 1(1).

Pawelzik, W. (2011). An analysis of the differences between student age and social networking utilization within a school of business. *American Journal of Business Education*, 4(9), 37.

Payne, N. J., Campbell, C., Bal, A. S. & Piercy, N. (2011). Placing a hand in the fire assessing the impact of a YouTube experiential learning project on viral marketing knowledge acquisition. *Journal of Marketing Education*, 33(2), 204–216.

Peltier, J. Milne, G. & Phelps J. (2009). Information Privacy Research: Framework for Integrating Multiple Publics, Information Channels, and Responses. *Journal of Interactive Marketing*, 23(2), 191-205.

Poellhuber, B., Anderson, T. & Roy, N. (2011). Distance students' readiness for social media and collaboration. *The International Review of Research in Open and Distributed Learning*, 12(6), 102–125.

Roblyer, M. D., McDaniel, M., Webb, M., Herman, J. & Witty, J. V. (2010). Findings on Facebook in higher education: A comparison of college faculty and student uses and perceptions of social networking sites. *The Internet and higher education*, 13(3), 134–140.

Rodriguez, J. E. (2011). Social media use in higher education: Key areas to consider for educators. *Journal of Online Learning and Teaching*, 7(4), 539–550.

Rojas, T. A., & Alburqueque, C. C. (2015). La gestión de la reputación digital en las universidades: Twitter como herramienta de la comunicación reputacional en las universidades peruanas. *Revista de Comunicación*, 14(27).

Roodt, S. & Peier, D. (2013). Using YouTube© in the classroom for the net generation of students. *Issues in Informing Science and Information Technology*, 10, 473–487.

Sadaf, A., Newby, T. J. & Ertmer, P. A. (2012). Exploring pre-service teachers' beliefs about using Web 2.0 technologies in K-12 classroom. *Computers & Education*, 59(3), 937–945.

Schroeder, J. & Greenbowe, T. (2009). The chemistry of Facebook: Using social networking to create an online community for the organic chemistry laboratory. Innovate: *Journal of Online Education*, 5(4) http://nsuworks.nova.edu/innovate/vol5/iss4/3

Selwyn, N. (2010). Looking beyond learning: Notes towards the critical study of educational technology. *Journal of Computer Assisted Learning*, 26(1), 65–73.

Selwyn, N. (2012). Social media in higher education. *The Europa World of Learning*, 1. Retrieved from http://sites.jmu.edu/flippEDout/files/2013/04/sample-essayselwyn.pdf

Sendall, P., Ceccucci, W. & Peslak, A. (2008). Web 2.0 matters: An analysis of implementing Web 2.0 in the classroom. *Information Systems Education Journal*, 6(64), 1–17.

Stephenson, J. & Yorke, M. (2013). *Capability and Quality in Higher Education*. London: Routledge.

Tan, E. & Pearce, N. (2011). Open education videos in the classroom: Exploring the opportunities and barriers to the use of YouTube in teaching introductory sociology. *Research in Learning Technology*, 19. Retrieved from http://journals.co-action.net/index.php/rlt/article/view/7783

Taylor, S. A., Mulligan, J. R. & Ishida, C. (2012). Facebook, social networking, and business education. *American Journal of Business Education (Online)*, 5(4), 437–448.

Tess, P. A. (2013). The role of social media in higher education classes (real and virtual): A literature review. *Computers in Human Behavior*, 29(5), A60–A68.

Top, E. (2012). Blogging as a social medium in undergraduate courses: Sense of community best predictor of perceived learning. *The Internet and Higher Education*, 15(1), 24–28.

Trinder, K., Guiller, J., Margaryan, A., Littlejohn, A. & Nicol, D. (2008). Learning from digital natives: bridging formal and informal learning. *Higher Education*, 1, 1–57.

Voorn, R. J. & Kommers, P. A. (2013). Social media and higher education: introversion and collaborative learning from the student's perspective. *International Journal of Social Media and Interactive Learning Environments*, 1(1), 59–73.

Wang, Q., Woo, H. L., Quek, C. L., Yang, Y., & Liu, M. (2011). Using the Facebook group as a learning management system: An exploratory study. *British Journal of Educational Technology*, 43(3), 428–438.

Wheeler, S., & Yeomans, P. & Wheeler, D. (2008). The good, the bad and the wiki: Evaluating student-generated content for collaborative learning. *British Journal of Educational Technology*, 39(6), 987–995.

12

MOMMY BLOGS AND ONLINE COMMUNITIES

Emotions and Cognitions of Working Mothers

Angeline Close Scheinbaum, Anjala S. Krishen,
Axenya Kachen, Amanda Mabry-Flynn,
and Nancy Ridgway

> I get recognition for my accomplishments: I love it when my son says
> thank you for his breakfast or thank you when I find his Batman costume
> but it is also great to get a compliment from a coworker, my boss, or a
> client. (Career mother's post to mommy blog)

Mommy blogs, or blogs or websites that cater to working mothers, are often seen on
social media as a source of important insights into the psychology of the mother who
also works outside of the home. As the above post to a mommy blog by a career
mother illustrates, there is a duality in the life of a career mother that goes from finding
a Batman costume for a child to finishing a project for a client. This is at times an
intense duality, which may be associated with role conflict and unique challenges for a
mother who works outside of the home and then goes home to work the "second
shift" of taking care of children, a home, and the important responsibilities therein.
There is a dark side to life as a working mother, as seen in the online postings, which
will ultimately reveal the sacrifices, emotions, and cognitions of them.

Objective and Intended Contribution

The original focus was on any dark side elements; however the netnographic approach
will reveal that these mommy blogs, as online communities, are a positive force as
they provide community-based support and resources to help. The bright side nature
that emerged from social online groups that are not social media, but has some
common characteristics of social media provides some welcome contrast to some dark
side topics earlier in the book. The objective of this netnography is to gather insights
regarding perspectives of working mothers as seen by their posts to online communities or "mommy blogs". The intended contribution is to help understand working

women (as people and as a segment of the marketplace) and how women use mommy blogs as an online community that can offer a place to vent and support for the difficult and unique challenges that women who work outside of the home face. Conceptual contributions are in the areas of role conflict and the second shift. Reasons for the need for this research include vast social and economic justifications for understanding the psychology and behaviors of mothers who are also in the workforce.

Social and Economic Justifications

Women, as a market, are larger than both India and China combined, and yet many companies do not understand or serve women (Silverstein & Sayre, 2009). This point is especially true for working women. Approximately 57% of American women worked outside of the home in 2015; 24 million of these women were mothers to at least one child under the age of 18 years (U.S. Bureau of Labor Statistics, 2015, 2016). As more women work outside of the home, it is crucial to understand their psychology—as reflected by their comments in online communities. Oftentimes, these online communities for mothers are informally termed "mommy blogs". While not all mothers, or parents who read and or post on mommy blogs work outside of the home, many do— and these women face some particular challenges and at times seek refuge or a safe space online to communicate with other women who work outside the home as well.

Roadmap of the Chapter

This chapter is organized as follows. Next, is a condensed literature review that includes two main areas in this literature—role conflict and the second shift. Then there is a summary of the theoretical lens of feminism that informs and guides the research. The literature review is followed by an overview of the methods, which is a netnography or a study of an online community (mommy blogs). The methods and data analysis overview is then followed by the findings—the emerging concepts and nine lower-order themes. The authors identified three meta-themes, and, as such, the results are organized by these three meta-themes. The authors conclude the chapter with a discussion of the findings, limitations, and avenues for future research.

Theoretical Lens and Literature Review

Literature Review

Motherhood penalty and fatherhood bonus. Expectations of the impact of having children and a career tend to be different in men's and women's careers. For men, having children is often called the "Fatherhood Bonus" (Budig & Hodges, 2014). Men's earnings were found to increase more than 6% when they had children. Women, on the other hand, suffer from what is known as the "Motherhood Penalty" (Budig & Hodges, 2014), and suffer decreased earnings of 4% for each child they have. This result has been repeated in other studies (Correll, 2007). In a study of Harvard Business School graduates, men and women want the same things in terms of careers and parenthood (Ely, Stone and Ammerman 2014). Both sexes mentioned job titles, job levels, and professional achievements at roughly the same rates (p. 102). Each equally thought that their careers would be important. However, men expected women to take on the majority of child rearing. Many women with children left jobs because they failed to reach managerial positions, but did not quit working, instead moving onto other jobs. Those women who worked part time to spend more time with their children often found their careers unfulfilling and unchallenging. They believed they had been "Mommy Tracked" by their company. Companies do their part to contribute to this disconnect between women's high career aspirations when graduating from college and their actual career experiences (Adame, Capilure and Miquel 2016). Most companies do not have a work–life balance commitment. Reasons for this include no Human Resources department and the lack of mothers working in managerial roles.

Second shift. The expectation that women shoulder the bulk of childrearing responsibilities is borne out by research finding that women in dual-career homes tend to devote about twice as much time to parenting activities than their male spouses (Bianchi et al., 2006; Kotila et al., 2013). The tendency for women to assume the role as the primary caretaker of children, as well as other household tasks, was characterized as "the second shift" by sociologist Arlie Hochschild (1989) in her groundbreaking book of the same name. Hochschild's research sought to uncover how the modern American family was adapting to the rapidly increasing presence of women and mothers in the workforce. Diary data indicated that after working a full-time job outside the home, most working mothers then engaged in many hours of unpaid work upon returning home (Hochschild & Machung, 1989).

Companies that recognize the stress many working mothers face as they attempt to manage a career and domestic obligations simultaneously, and successfully implement practices that contribute to work–life balance often see positive outcomes. Policies such as flexible work schedules, maternity and paternity leave, and on-site childcare contribute to a supportive work environment. Further, research indicates such policies contribute to effective employee recruitment and retention, as well as increased business productivity (Bloom & Van Reenen, 2006).

Although fathers now spend more time on childrearing and housework than ever before, mothers continue to face societal pressure to maintain the role of primary caretaker (Parker & Wang, 2013). Forty-two percent of American adults report believing that a mother working part time is ideal for children and an additional one-third feel that having a mother that does not work outside the home is ideal for young children (Parker & Wang, 2013). Thus, mothers' working a full-time job outside the home is not viewed as "ideal" by many and may lead to feelings of guilt for working mothers.

Theoretical Lens

This investigation attempts to better understand the role that social media plays in the lives of working mothers and the various influences on their consumer behaviors. This is a topic that has yet to be empirically explored in any great depth. Given the exploratory nature of the study, feminist theory was used as a broad framework to help add context and meaning to the findings.

The idea that women who work outside the home face unique challenges compared to their male counterparts is frequently the subject of feminist theorizing. The concept of equality between the sexes is often cited in this context: from early movements to allow women into various professions to contemporary conceptions of breaking the glass ceiling and receiving equal pay for equal work (Evans, 1994; Hughes, 2002). Workplace gender equality has often been based on minimizing differences between the sexes by ensuring that women are "equal" to men. As such it has been critiqued for denying women the space to express the unique challenges they often face that are different from men because this illuminates, rather than reduces, gendered differences (Smithson & Stokoe, 2005).

However, the reality for many working mothers is that while they may wish to share child-rearing and other domestic responsibilities equally with a partner (who may share this desire as well), they are still likely to spend significantly more time on child-rearing than fathers (Kotila et al., 2013). Further, working mothers may be confronted with socially awkward situations not faced by working fathers such as accidentally leaking breast milk and the need to pump when away from infants.

A feminist theory framework provides a critical lens through which the challenges faced by working mothers can be questioned and explored. Eichler (1980) suggests that, "at its best, feminist writing fulfills three functions: it is critical of existent social structures and ways to perceive them, it serves as a corrective mechanism by providing an alternative viewpoint and data to substantiate it, and it starts to lay the groundwork for a transformation of social science and society" (p. 9).

Method

Netnography

Overview. Netnography is a method used to examine behavior and cultures and social groups as seen in digital (online) environments (Kozinets, 2002). A benefit of the netnographic method is that it entails the observation of visual and textual artifacts and, as such, data collection and analysis come more efficiently than traditional fieldwork (Kozinets, 2002). A netnographic approach allows researchers to observe the population of interest (here, working mothers) in an uninhibited, naturally occurring manner with seeing their visible online behavior (Kozinets, 2002). As such, netnographic methods are less intrusive to consumers and less costly to researchers than traditional ethnography (Kozinets, 2002).

Procedure and analysis. As is evident from multiple interdisciplinary sets of literature, the insights of working mothers are difficult to categorize and explore and online communities of "mommy blogs" and social media provide a rich environment to capture them. The ideas and exchanges of working mothers are layered in complex conceptual categories and thus require sophisticated analysis to understand. Hence, we embarked on a two-phase netnographic analysis of working mother blogs. During the first phase, two trained graduate students who were unaware of the purpose of the research gathered social media comments from working mother blogs. The following steps were provided to the data collectors: (1) search for something related to the topic of working mothers in a forum or consumer group; (2) gather a set of URLs which contain such conversations; and (3) begin construction of a spreadsheet of data containing the forum conversations for each of the forums.

For data analysis, the authors used a lexicographic semantic analysis tool called Leximancer to group the qualitative comments from working mothers (www.leximancer.com). This tool uses a machine learning technique to determine underlying concepts and themes within verbal data (Smith, 2007). Thus, the nine themes that will ultimately result from data analysis are from machine learning; the authors will then collapse these into three bigger picture or "meta-themes" that make sense in context of the aforementioned theoretical lens and literature.

Extant research from various disciplines performs analysis using Leximancer, in particular to gather initial insights for complex topics (e.g., Campbell et al., 2011; Dann, 2010; Krishen et al., 2014). The algorithm for this tool is based on Bayesian theory and augments ideas and concepts which could normally be derived by hand coding techniques of qualitative researchers, in particular because of the complex graphical maps provided (Rooney, 2005). Due to the limited research available with regards to social media and its role with working mothers, this exploratory qualitative tool provides key themes and their relationships to each other as an initial research effort.

Figure 12.1 displays the concepts found in the dataset, and how they connect. For instance, concepts found in the data include words such as: expectations, evenings, questions, afford, routine, transition, favorite, co-workers, shift, income, and harder. Figure 12.2 provides the emergent lower-order themes and their relationship with each other. The left side of this figure provides the key themes, these are: *pump, reasons, gave, thankful, past, priorities, hope, consider,* and *fun.* For Figure 12.2, note that these nine themes are collapsed into three meta-themes: 1) sacrifices by working mothers; 2) cognitions (often self-cognitions) of working mothers; and 3) emotions felt by working mothers.

To make the number of themes more manageable and meaningful on a higher-order basis, the authors will collapse these nine themes into meta-themes, as discussed in the next section (results). Last, Figure 12.3 depicts the concepts and how they fall into the (lower-order) themes.

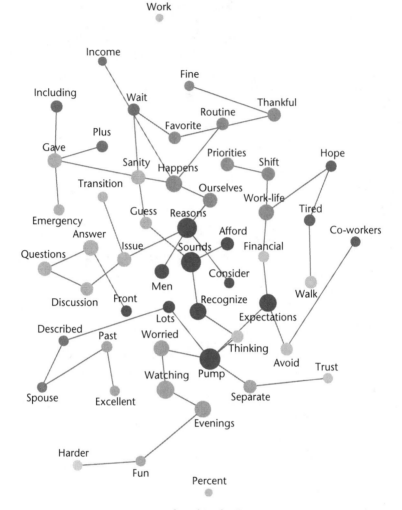

FIGURE 12.1 Concepts Connections found in the Dataset

Results: Emerging Themes

The nine lower-order themes that emerged from the data are collapsed by the authors into three broader meta–themes: **sacrifices** by working mothers, **cognitions** (often self-cognitions) of working mothers, and **emotions** felt by working mothers.

Sacrifices

As seen in the online communities, working mothers make a special set of sacrifices. The three related lower-order themes reflect the working mother's: a) past

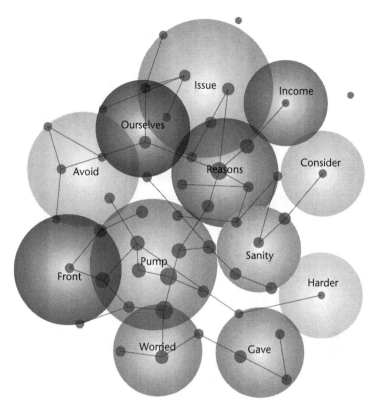

FIGURE 12.2 Emergent Lower-Order Themes

(i.e., life before becoming a mother or more specifically a mother who works outside of the home); b) pumping of breast milk while separated from her baby; and c) what she gave up in order to function as a mother who works outside the home. Next is an overview of each of these.

Past. As seen in the online community, the theme of the "past" relates to the woman's life before motherhood. Specifically to the objective of understanding mothers who work outside the home, this past often relates to the woman's identity as a career woman, an employee, a boss, a leader, or other career-related role. The roles of the past may conflict with current and future roles in the home, and these roles are fluid. This necessitates the parent to be flexible with time and acceptance of a lack of a dependable routine. Change becomes part of the routine. For instance, this woman writes about her sacrifice that she made with respect to her partner's career. She was hit with a stark reality after she returned to work with her second child—that she would be managing a school-age child, a baby, and a career without much help from a partner whose career was skyrocketing:

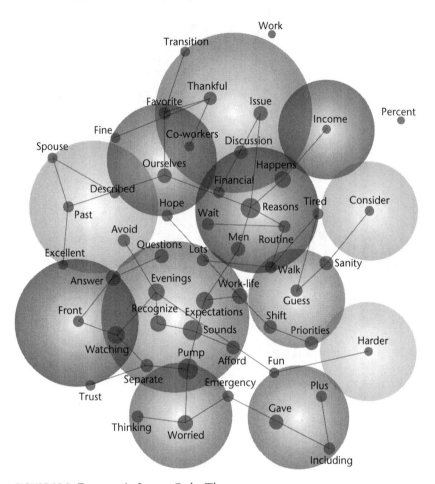

FIGURE 12.3 Concepts in Lower-Order Themes

But soon after returning to work following the birth of my second child, I had to face a stark reality. My husband's career as a partner in the same firm had skyrocketed. His travel rendered me a single mother many nights, which I could manage with one elementary school age child and a career.

Another working mother, who was uncertain as to her decision to be a career mother, found solace in thinking about the quality time she would have with her children if she were to be a stay-at-home mother. She learned that her stay-at-home counterpart may spend more time with their children—but the quality time is just as limited. Being a homemaker is a full-time job in itself, and without help, can make it difficult to find and make quality time with the children. The transformative realization came where she realized the sacrifices that all parents make—regardless of if they have outside employment. Most parents would perhaps agree that they would like to have more quality time with their children. As she explains:

> I had anguished moments when I questioned my decision and read about other moms who had those same doubts. I also saw an article describing how working and stay at home moms often spend similar amounts of quality time with their kids that acted as a counter-balance.

While the prior quote highlighted the realization that all parents sacrifice, the next data point suggests that there is a dark side to some sacrifices that working parents have made for their children in that children could one day feel resentment relating to sacrifices the mother made. For instance, this woman still remembers telling her mother, as a child, that she did not ask her mother to make sacrifices for her. She explains her pushback to her mother years later to the online community:

> Later as a teenager, I pushed back hard against my mother when she called me ungrateful. I vividly recall saying, "I didn't ask to be born. I didn't ask you to make sacrifices for me".

In sum, the past set of quotes illuminated some of the sacrifices that women discuss in the online communities. Most overlap with contexts of career and time. The next sacrifice relates to both career and time—as well as sacrifices made from the female body for a health and bonding benefit for the baby.

Pumping. Pumping (the behavior of pumping breast milk for the baby while at work) is overwhelmingly discussed in the online community. This behavior was discussed so much, that it became it's own theme. The women posted about their pumping challenges—and not one post was about the physical challenges. Instead, the challenges were about the privacy they need to do it at work, their routines and figuring out the correct timing of pumping, and employers' expectations about employees who breast feed. As one woman explains, she used half of her lunch break to pump—even though she could have had separate pumping breaks.

> I'd pump once in the morning, I'd use half my lunch break and pump once in the afternoon. The lunch break pump was something I chose to be courteous as I felt they were generous, telling me that I could pump as much as I needed.

Employers' expectations about pumping mothers and their breaks are not always generous. One woman, who is the only pumping mother at her work, posted online about how she does not get any breaks in the work day because her employer expects her to use her lunch break to pump. The irony of this is that pumping/breastfeeding mothers need to take in extra calories and hydration in order to produce milk, so a breastfeeding mother's lunch break should be taken seriously. As one woman explains:

> Two weeks ago, they changed their mind and said that they expected me to use my lunch break, and they also amalgamated my breaks and pumping breaks, so I no longer have 15 minute rest breaks. I'm the only pumping mother at work now.

Another mother mentions how fortunate she was to find childcare that enables her to not have to pump. Having access to the baby is a wonderful fortune that most women do not have so frequently during the work day—especially in the beginning when pumping every few hours is taxing to the body. It adds some exhaustion to an otherwise sleep-deprived state.

> Fortunately, I found a wonderful woman to watch my kids so at least I didn't have to worry about that, but it forces you to go back before you're completely healed, before your breast milk has a chance to regulate and before you're emotionally ready to leave your child. Not to mention the fact that you're still feeding every 3–4 hours at that point so you're getting little sleep and pumping often.

Another woman comments on the sacrifices she chose in breastfeeding and how hard it is to make changes in the baby's feeding routine when maternity leave ends. As she explains,

> It's just terrible to leave them like that. I was still building the breastfeeding relationship when my leave ended and was worrying about milk supply and if I would continue to produce enough for him while pumping at work.

A final sub-theme that emerged from the data is how the working mothers gave.

Gave. Working women have sacrificed a lot, and they have given a lot. Many of the online posts directly or indirectly illuminate what was given. Some are sacrifices but here, the attention is more on what they gave and what their partner gave as well. For instance, while other women discussed how they sacrificed in going back to work after motherhood, this woman notes what her fortunate situation of having a partner who works from home has given her. It has given her peace of mind, which is invaluable.

> Lucky for us, my husband worked from home, and managed to juggle his job with caring for our baby girl while I worked. Our childcare situation gave me great peace of mind, and allowed me to focus on my job.

The sacrifices illuminated in the quotes are not without cognitions—or the thoughts related to the reasons behind their life-choices/role as a working parent and priorities as a whole.

Cognitions

In addition to the unique sacrifices by mothers who work outside of the home seen in the data, these women have cognitions—often self cognitions related to their dual roles. At times, these dual roles are in conflict. The three themes relating to the meta-theme of cognitions include: reasons, priorities, and considerations.

Reasons. It is clear from the data that mothers who work outside the home consistently have thoughts/cognitions about the reasons justifying their behaviors related to being a mother who works outside the home. Many of the posts represent cognitions as they give reasons for their related decisions and behaviors. For example, one woman felt compelled to give a reason (convenience) for why she chose a daycare that is close to her home and not because of other reasons (such as it is the top-rated, etc.). It seems she is even putting herself down a bit by calling herself "that mom". As she explains,

> And I'm that mom who sends him on my rare days off so I'd rather not drive out towards work. There are other convenient reasons I chose close to home.

Another representative quote that shows how these women feel compelled to give reasons is due to finances. Some of the posts imply some sense of guilt about being a career mother, and that the reason why they work is to help provide financially. As one woman explains, she does not like having to hear that it was her choice. As she articulates her anger:

> But what rankles more is the line about "You chose to be there," which implies that these choices are made by individual women in a societal vacuum. A lot of working parents, both men and women, would love to spend more time at home, but they can't because their families need the money (and of course, not every parent has a partner).

Priorities. The working parents think a lot about their priorities in life as evidenced by their online posts to the online communities. Priorities are what people choose to make a priority in their life, and they are driven by values among other things. Priorities may be driven by societal values as well—such as independence, health, materialism, or youth. As one parent shares online, sometimes work commitments are and must be a priority. However, the broader priority or terminal value she has is in her work–life balance. She notes to be successful in this terminal value of balance, that putting work as a top priority that comes first can happen some (i.e., not all) of the time. This distinction is important as she notes:

> I work full time in the UK. If you're going to have work life balance, work priorities/commitments can only come first some of the time.

These otherwise enduring values change, and experienced working mothers share their experiences and what they have learned with respect to establishing and managing priorities in life. One woman posts a quote that is meaningful to her that she learned from a career coach that relates to the shift in priorities and values:

According to Karen Steele, career coach and creator of The Passion Shift,

> When you become a mom, you experience a shift in your priorities and values. Many women don't want to go back to the high-powered, high-stress job they had before kids.

While many women may welcome the change, for others, maintaining and nurturing a career is empowering and part of the self-schema or identity. As seen, most posts relating to priorities are at the level of the self, in other words, the mother's priorities in life as they relate to parenting and a career. One post however, sticks out because she refers to the work–life balance priority at a macro-level. Her point is that systemically the culture, society, and politicians have both a role and a responsibility to citizens for their work–life balance. This applies to all working people, not just parents. As she questions:

> … we should stop apologizing and start talking about [our] sorry cultural, societal and political choices that leave us in this position, is absolutely right. Why can't our politics and our entrepreneurial culture find a vocabulary to debate the need and scope for care and reciprocity? Why can't we nourish those relationships that will allow us all of us to grow?

Just as parents bring up priorities they think about, other thoughts are about things they are considering with respect to their lifestyle and choices as a working parent.

Considerations. The women tend to think about considerations they have; these considerations are often details and situations that are important to the families and their unique circumstances. One of the bright sides to these online communities is that the parents come together to help another think through the considerations shared. This is part of a sharing economy seen in online communities (Belk, 2014). For instance, one post probes the mother considering a nanny versus daycare to think about overnight work. Even if overnight travel or work is rare, when it does happen, it can be a very hard barrier for working parents if trustworthy overnight childcare is not available. She also asks about in-town commutes, as sometimes the logistical considerations help make the decisions easier. She asks:

> Other factors to consider; do either of you travel for work, even 1–2 times a year? Do you work in opposite ends of town?

Economic considerations and logistical considerations are commonly discussed in such online communities. Another woman considers the notion of her teenage children working during the holiday breaks. While some could condemn this choice as it makes the little time the parent has with the children even more scarce, she felt the need to point out the sad situation and her family's economic need. As she explains her economic consideration to the group:

> They are now doing this while off from school. It has been a great income opportunity for us since their father just disappeared few years ago.

As another example of the importance of working parent's economic considerations, this mother shares the importance of investing in things that can simplify life especially during the harder stages. She reminds the group the importance of a budget—and really looking at that budget with respect to allocating it for services and products to make things simpler. She offers this advice to the group to consider:

> Smart moms have figured out that if they spend money where it really counts—on things that make their lives simpler—it's a good investment. Sometimes taking a hard look at your budget will reveal some interesting possibilities. For example, if you haven't watched a cable movie in a month, maybe that money would be better allocated elsewhere.

Collectively, the working mother's thoughts and considerations relate with some specific emotions and feelings repeatedly seen in the data.

Emotions and Feelings

The third meta-theme of working mothers' emotions and feelings goes hand-in-hand with their cognitions. As seen in the online community data, the three most prevalent emotions expressed by mothers who work outside the home include: thankfulness, hope, and fun. Each of these emotions are explained next.

Thankfulness. Despite the dark side to being a mother who works outside of the home, there is a positive sentiment of thankfulness. Some women are simply thankful to have a career or a job where they have a place to go for much-needed interaction with adults. It can be very challenging to stay home with young children at times because it can be very lonely. As this mother posts, she is thankful to get to catch up with adults and use her education:

> I get to enjoy adult interaction: While one of my favorite topics has been and always will be my children, it is nice to have a built-in break from this chatter and sometimes talk about customers, reports, current events, and even a nice dose of office gossip. For this, I am thankful.

Another woman posted about how thankful she is of her husband, who stays home with their young children. After expressing her thankfulness, a separate emotion emerges—guilt. While she is overwhelmingly thankful for the opportunity to work at an accounting firm, she admits to feeling consumed with "working mom guilt". That is the type of guilt where the mother feels guilty when spending quality time with the child(ren) because she is not working. At the same time, it is the type of guilt where the mother feels guilty when working because she is not spending quality time with her child(ren). As she feels:

> I've recently been dealing with guilt and I don't really have an answer. My husband stays at home with our ten month old daughter and our five year old son when he isn't in school, and I work at a public accounting firm.

Another woman is thankful for her deep sense of herself that she gets while fulfilling her career role. Her identity is truer when she has an identity as a business woman and as a mother. She feels thankful for the ability to have these separate identities that enrich her self-schema:

> But, I still strive for a deeper sense of self. Working allows me to have an identity that is separate from my life at home. For this, I am thankful.

Hope. As another counter to the often dark side of being a mother who works outside of the home due to its very real challenges, another positive emotion of home emerges from the data. These women seem to use hope to keep them going. Being a woman with a career and children is very demanding. These women work the second shift at home; this second shift (after working a full day) often entails childcare, often times helping get dinner, dishes, laundry, baths, reading stories, teeth brushed, bedtime, packing lunches, backpacks, and cleaning the home. This is very tiring, as one woman posts:

> No wonder so many women I know are so tired! The following tips may not solve every time-management challenge that confronts you, but hopefully they'll help you think about ways to simplify and save time as you manage your own unique schedule and circumstances.

She hopes that the tips that she has learned for simplifying and how to deal with the tireless challenges can help other women, as she shared them on a mommy blog. It is important to note that these women on the mommy blogs seem to turn to hope externally (in that they hope other women can overcome the hurdles) and internally (in that they hope things for themselves in the journey to motherhood for career women). As one career-oriented woman shares on a mommy blog, she is turning to the emotion of home to become pregnant:

> I am not pregnant yet but hoping to be soon. So, I know I'm jumping the gun a bit but I'm a planner by nature.

She notes how she is a planner, and getting pregnant is difficult and at times even impossible to plan. It is a blessing to be able to become pregnant, and mothers should feel blessed and fortunate for the opportunity to provide life. While the struggles of day-to-day responsibilities can feel at times overwhelming, it is important to go back to the positive emotions of thankfulness and hope.

Fun. After thankfulness and hope, fun is the third emotion or feeling emerging from the online communities. The women who work outside of the home have noted that despite the challenges of role conflict and time demands, there is an emotion or feeling of fun with being a parent. At times or certain stages of the child's life, parenting has seemed especially fun. For instance, this mother explains how her son became more fun to be around after he found a sense of community in his school and peers:

> His grades improved, he joined his school's Football Team and his social skills and life improved greatly. He was actually fun to be around at this point. This is much harder than work ever was, but a lot more fun too!! I joke that I need to go back to work for a vacation.

Discussion

Summary of Findings

In conclusion, although these online communities or "Mommy blogs" do reveal some darker side issues such as difficulties and challenges, the overall collaborative and mainly supportive nature of these communities represents a bright side of social media. Recall, the objective of the study was to gather insights regarding perspectives of working mothers from social media platforms via a netnography of "mommy blogs". The intended contribution is to help understand working women (as people and as a segment of the marketplace) and how women use mommy blogs as a safe space. The analysis of the mothers' postings reveal lower-order themes that emerged from the netnographic data: *pump, reasons, gave, thankful, past, priorities, hope, consider,* and *fun.* These nine lower-order themes observed in the data are collapsed into three broader emerging themes: **sacrifices** by working mothers, **cognitions** (often self-cognitions) of working mothers, and **emotions** felt by working mothers.

Limitations and Future Research Opportunities

There are limitations to this research and to the netnographic method to address here. The main limitation is the narrow scope of the population examined— mothers who are balancing children and careers. A next step to address the limitation of scope is to do a similar study but focus on fathers and examine any commonalities in the issues fathers face in balancing careers and fatherhood. Another avenue to address this limitation in a next study is to focus on a sample of same-sex parents who are also balancing careers. Such is an important sample because of the increases in reproductive technologies and adoptions by same-sex couples and these consumers are likely to have some unique challenges and perspectives.

Another limitation is the lack of generalizability from the online communities examined. For one, the dataset analyzed could be more representative if more types of online communities were included. To address this limitation, repeating the study with other online communities on the topic or mommy blogs can help confirm or extend the emergent themes.

The last limitations are common in the netnographic method itself; the authors make an assumption that those who post on mommy blogs/communities for mothers are indeed mothers. The method has a lack of generalizability; when netnography is used along with other methods, triangulation of methods can address issues of generalizability while increasing data richness (Kozinets, 2002). To address this limitation with the method, subsequent studies with complementary methods such as depth interviews or experiments to look for any causality in the themes can strengthen the contribution of this research. The limitations of this exploratory study brings opportunities for research on both bright side and dark side topics in online communities, and how such online communities integrate with social media content. Scholars can re-examine these thematic findings in other types of online consumer behavior settings- such as within Facebook groups or communities.

References

Adame, C., Caplliure, E., & Miquel, M. (2015). Work-life balance and firms: a matter of women? *Journal of Business Research*, 69(4), 1379–1383.

Belk, R. W. (2014). You are what you can access: Sharing and collaborative consumption online. *Journal of Business Research*, 8, 1595–1600.

Bianchi, S. M., Robinson, J. P. & Milkie, M. A. (2006). *Changing Rhythms of American Family life*. New York: Russell Sage Foundation.

Bloom, N. & Van Reenen, J. (2006). Management practices, work—life balance, and productivity: A review of some recent evidence. *Oxford Review of Economic Policy*, 22(4), 457–482.

Budig, M. J. & Hodges, M. J. (2014). Statistical models and empirical evidence for differences in the motherhood penalty across the earnings distribution. *American Sociological Review*, 70, 358–364.

Campbell, C., Pitt, L. F., Parent, M. & Berthon, P. R. (2011). Understanding consumer conversations around ads in a Web 2.0 world. *Journal of Advertising*, 40, 87–102.

Correll, S. J. (2007). Getting a job: Is there a motherhood penalty? *American Journal of Sociology*, 112 (March), 1297–1339.

Dann, S. (2010). Redefining social marketing with contemporary commercial marketing definitions. *Journal of Business Research*, 63, 147–153.

Eichler, M. (1980). *The Double Standard*. New York: Frederick Ungar.

Ely, R. J., Stone, P. & Ammerman, C. 'Rethink what you "know" about high-achieving women.' *Harvard Business Review* 92, no. 12 (2014): 100–109.

Evans, M. (Ed.) (1994). *The Woman Question*. London: Sage Publications.

Hochschild, A. & Machung, A. (1989). *The Second Shift: Working Parents and the Revolution at Home*. New York: Viking.

Hughes, C. (2002). *Key Concepts in Feminist Theory and Research*. London: Sage Publications.

Kotila, L. E., Schoppe Sullivan, S. J. & Kamp Dush, C. M. (2013). Time in parenting activities in dual learner families at the transition to parenthood. *Family Relations*, 62(5), 795–807.

Kozinets, R. V. (2002). The field behind the screen: Using netnography for marketing research in online communities. *Journal of Marketing Research*, 39(1), 61–72.

Krishen, A.S., Agarwal, S. & Kachroo, P. (2016) "Is having accurate knowledge necessary for implementing safe practices?: A consumer folk theories-of-mind perspective on the impact of price", *European Journal of Marketing*, 50(5/6), 1073–1093. Retrieved 15th August 2017 from https://doi.org/10.1108/EJM-01-2015-0027

Parker, K. & Wang, W. (2013). Modern parenthood: Roles of moms and dads converge as they balance work and family. Pew Research Center, Social & Demographic Trends. Retrieved July 16, 2017 from: http://www.pewsocialtrends.org/2013/03/14/modern-parenthood-roles-of-moms-and-dads-converge-as-they-balance-work-and-family/

Rooney, D. (2005). Knowledge, economy, technology and society: The politics of discourse. *Telematics and Informatics*, 22, 405–422.

Silverstein, M. J. & Sayre, K. (2009). The female economy. *Harvard Business Review*, September. 46–53.

Smith, A. (2007). *Leximancer Manual (Version 2.2) [Electronic Version]*: from <http://www.leximancer.com/documents/Leximancer2_Manual.pdf>.

Smithson, J. & Stokoe, E. H. (2005). Discourses of work–life balance: negotiating 'genderblind' terms in organizations. *Gender, Work & Organization*, 12(2), 147–168.

U.S. Bureau of Labor Statistics. (2015). Civilian labor force participation rate by age, gender, race, and ethnicity. Retrieved July 16, 2017 from http://www.bls.gov/emp/ep_table_303.htm

U.S. Bureau of Labor Statistics. (2016). Employment characteristics of families summary. Retrieved July 16, 2017 from http://www.bls.gov/news.release/famee.nr0.htm

INDEX

Manago, A. 51
Mayer, J.D. 112
Mazer, J.P. 203
Meier, Megan 41–2
Mick, D.G. xxi
microblogs 212
Milkman, K.L. 51
Millennials 38–9
Mir, I. 183
Missouri, State of 41
mobile commerce, future prospects for 184–8
mobile technologies 179–85
"mommy blogs" 178, 225–6, 229, 239
Moor, James 23
Moore, Adam 23–4, 28
Moore, Hunter 15–16, 20
Mukherjee, Ashesh *author of Foreword*
multiplayer games 80–6

narcissism xx–xxii
needs, psychological 73–8
Neier Beran, Stacy xiii; *co-author of Chapter 11*
netnography 53, 72, 80, 178, 226–31, 239–40
networking *see* social networking
news avoidance strategy 164, 171
news coverage 8, 147–8, 153–69;
    diversity in sources 153; processing and interpretation of information 165–6; *pull* and *push* approaches to 164–5; social media as a source for 165–9
Nike brand 139
"ninja looting" 82–3, 86

"onboarding" 181
online communities 9, 78, 80, 178, 225–7;
    literature review of 226–7
opinion-based information 218–19
ownership: *legal* and *psychological* 83;
    sense of 71, 73, 76, 80, 84; *see also* psychological ownership

Pariser, E. 151
Paul, J.A. 202
Pearson, C.M. 128
Pentina, Iryna xiii; *co-author of Chapter 9*
Perera, B. Yasanthi xiii–xiv; *co-author of Chapter 8*
personalization of messages and services 179, 186–7, 191, 194–5
"personalization–privacy paradox" 190
Peter, Paula C. xiv; *co-author of Chapter 7*

Pierce, J.L. 72, 76–7
Pinkmeth (website) 16
Pinterest 218
Pitt, Leyland *author of Foreword*
"play nice" policies (PNPs) 85
Pokémon Go (game) 5
Polisano, Elena 132
Pontin, Jason 181
pornography online 61–3; non-consensual *see* "revenge porn"
primary concerns within news coverage 164
privacy 177, 180, 184–6, 190–5; concept and theories of 21–5, 28–31; policies on 79
procrastination, behavioral 39, 89, 110–19; emotional intelligence as moderator of 115–18; relative to excessive online consumption 116–18
"produsage" 147
profiles of consumers 186
pruning of information 149
Przybylski, A.K. 38
psychological ownership 71–86; collective 76–7; contested 79–80; definition of 72; of games 82–3; mechanisms of 74–5; motivations for 73–4; outcomes of 75–6; theory of 71–3, 85–6
public relations 8
Pullig, C. 128
Puma brand 139
"pumping" mothers 233–4

qualitative research 153–4
"Quit Facebook Day" campaign 79

Rademaker, Claudia xiv; *co-author of Chapter 3*
Ravi, Dharun 33
reputation, organizational 127–9
Restricted Access/Limited Control (RACL) theory 23–4
"revenge porn" 13–31, 42; categories of 19–21; definition of 18–21; rise of 15–18
Reynolds, Diamond 4
Ridgway, Nancy xiv–xv; *co-author of Chapter 12*
"roasting" 41
Royne, Marla B. xv; *co-author of Chapter 3*

Sacco, D.T. 43
Salovey, P. 112
Sanchez, Linda 42
Sauven, John 133